D1431038

HD 5708.5 .R42 1986

Redundancy, layoffs, and
plant closures

Fairleigh Dickinson University Library
Teaneck, New Jersey

REDUNDANCY, LAYOFFS AND PLANT CLOSURES:
Their Character, Causes and Consequences

Redundancy, Layoffs and Plant Closures

Their Character, Causes and Consequences

Edited by Raymond M Lee

Fairleigh Dickinson
University Library

Teaneck, New Jersey

CROOM HELM
London • Sydney • Wolfeboro, New Hampshire

© Raymond M Lee 1987

Croom Helm Ltd, Provident House, Burrell Row,
Beckenham, Kent, BR3 1AT

Croom Helm Australia, 44-50 Waterloo Road,
North Ryde, 2113, New South Wales

British Library Cataloguing in Publication Data

Redundancy, layoffs and plant closures: their
    character, causes and consequences.
    1. Employees, Dismissal of
    I. Lee, Raymond M.
    331.13'7   HF5549.5.D55
    ISBN 0-7099-4129-3

Croom Helm, 27 South Main Street,
Wolfeboro, New Hampshire 03894-2069 USA

Library of Congress Cataloging-in-Publication Data
Redundancy, Layoff, and Plant Closures.
    Includes index.
    1. Layoff systems. 2. Plant shutdowns. 3. Employees,
    dismissal of. I. Lee, Raymond M.
    HD5708.5.R42 1986   331.13'7   86-19851
    ISBN 0-7099-4129-3

Printed and bound in Great Britain by
Biddles Ltd, Guildford and King's Lynn

HD
5708.5
.R42
1986

CONTENTS

Contents

ACKNOWLEDGEMENTS

I am grateful to Peter Sowden at Croom Helm for his encouragement and assistance and to Maria Wilch for preparing the manuscript for publication.

I am also grateful to Beryl Mason for secretarial help and Christopher Lee for assistance at a number of crucial points.

NOTES ON CONTRIBUTORS

Mel Bartley is a postgraduate student in the Department of Social Policy at the University of Edinburgh.

Bill Bytheway is Senior Research Fellow in the Department of Sociology and Anthropology at the University College of Swansea. He has previously held posts at the University of Keele and the University of Aberdeen.

Claire Callender is Lecturer in Social Policy at the University of Leeds. She was formerly Tutorial Fellow and subsequently Lecturer in the Department of Social Administration at University College, Cardiff.

Daniel B. Cornfield is Assistant Professor at Vanderbilt University. He received his Ph.D. from the University of Chicago in 1980. His research interests include unionization, union democracy, labour markets, industrial and organizational sociology and economy and society. He was recently awarded a research grant from the Russell Sage Foundation for his current work on the changing social characteristics of elected union leaders.

Cynthia Deitch is Assistant Professor of Sociology and of Women's Studies at the University of Pittsburgh. She received her doctorate in Sociology from the University of Massachussetts.

Robert Erickson teaches sociology and economics at Carlow College in Pittsburgh, Pennsylvania. He received a doctorate in Planning from Cornell University and is a member of the board of the Tri-State Conference on Steel.

Ralph Fevre is New Blood Lecturer in Sociology at the University College of North Wales, Bangor. He was previously Lecturer in Sociology at Portsmouth Polytechnic and has carried out research on the textile industry in West Yorkshire and the steel industry in South Wales.

C.C Harris is Professor of Sociology, University College of Swansea. His published works include The Family and Social Change (with Colin Rosser), The Family, Fundamental Concepts and the Sociological Enterprise and The Family and Industrial Society.

Notes on Contributors

Olivier Kourchid is a full-time researcher in sociology at the Centre National de la Recherche Scientifique and teaches graduate courses on labour movements at the University of Paris. After a number of studies on militancy and consciousness in France and in the USA, he is now involved with the social, economic and political history of coal production.

Raymond M. Lee is Senior Lecturer in Sociology, St. Mary's College, Twickenham. He has carried out research on redundant steelworkers and has also done work on Northern Ireland and in the sociology of religion.

Lydia D. Morris is New Blood Lecturer in Sociology in the Department of Sociology and Social Policy, University of Durham. She has carried out fieldwork in Puerto Rico, Mexico City and South London. She was formerly a research officer in the Department of Sociology and Anthropology at the University College of Swansea and has been a researcher for Lambeth Council.

Iain Noble is a Research Fellow in the Department of Sociological Studies, University of Sheffield. He was previously a graduate student at the University of Essex, Lecturer in Sociology at the University of Reading and Social Survey Officer at OPCS. He was research officer on the After Redundancy Project and is co-author of The Privately Rented Sector.

Carolyn C. Perrucci is Professor of Sociology at Purdue University. Complementing her research on blue-collar unemployment is a long-standing interest in professional career patterns. Recent publications concern gender equity in academia and science-based career patterns.

Robert Perrucci is Professor of Sociology at Purdue University. In addition to research on plant closures, he is currently studying how interorganizational relations shape the structure of community power and human service delivery systems.

Dena B. Targ is Associate Professor of Family Studies in the Department of Child Development and Family Studies, Purdue University. Her research concerns the intersection of social problems and family problems. The impact of plant closings on displaced workers and their families is the most recent focus of her research.

Harry R. Targ is Professor of Political Science, Purdue University. He is currently doing research on plant closings and the interconnections between organized labour and United States foreign policy. He has published in the areas of international relations, foreign policy and the United States political economy.

Chapter One

INTRODUCTION

Raymond M. Lee

With some exceptions Western economies have
witnessed over the past decade a decline in levels
of industrial employment and a rise in the numbers
of those without work (Thirlwall, 1982). Such
decline - frequently described as a process of
'deindustrialization' (see, for example, Blackaby,
1979) - has been most visibly manifested by what is
termed in Britain 'redundancy' and described in the
United States as 'lay-offs' or 'terminations'; the
closure of plants, in other words, and the
contraction of workforces through firms shedding
their labour.[1] The aim of this book is to bring
together some of the results of recent theoretical
and empirical work by sociologists, anthropologists
and social policy analysts on both sides of the
Atlantic who are interested in the causes,
character and consequences of redundancies whether
these result from partial workforce reductions or
from the total closure of a plant.

There are difficulties involved in producing
an overall estimate of the total magnitude of job
loss in either Britain or the United States
although it is possible to discern at least some
broad trends. Using information from US Establishment
and Enterprise Microdata records, Candee Harris
(1984) has explored the impact of plant closings in
large manufacturing firms in the United States.
(Her study therefore ignores both partial redundancies
and closures in establishments having fewer than
100 employees.) According to Harris, closures made
up one quarter of all dissolutions in manufacturing
establishments between 1978 and 1982, although they
accounted for two-thirds of jobs lost - a level,
according to Harris, equivalent to one quarter of
all jobs in large establishments. (A further
notable feature of these data is, as Harris notes,

1

that workforce contractions in large firms tend to come about through the closure of branch plants.) Harris concludes that large firms in the US eliminated 16 million jobs between 1976-82. Putting this another way, since the mid-1970s job losses in the United States have been running at a rate of around 900,000 per year.

It is rather easier to derive estimates of the number of individuals affected by redundancy in Britain since the Department of Employment and the Manpower Services Commission collect figures for notified redundancies, redundancy payments and redundancies 'confirmed to occur'. This last series, collected by the Manpower Services Commission, is probably the most accurate and reliable of the three sets of statistics (Noble, 1981) although it does exclude establishments with less than 10 employees, thus underenumerating redundancies occurring in small firms and those spread through a number of small establishments within a larger firm.

Taking these figures for 'confirmed' redundancies Martin (1984) shows that prior to the recession the incidence of redundancy in Britain displayed no discernible trend. Levels of redundancy rose sharply, however, towards the end of 1979 and peaked dramatically thereafter with around 400,000 confirmed redundancies occurring in both 1980 and 1981. From 1982 onward the figures level out but at a rate substantially higher than that seen in the pre-recession period. In the British case around 30% of redundancies are due to plant closures (Martin, 1982).

In an important sense, of course, these figures tell only the beginnings of a story. As Bluestone (1984) points out job loss is best not seen in aggregate terms but by reference to specific industries or regions. Reacting to critics in the United States who have concluded on the basis of aggregate data on output, investment and employment that deindustrialization is a myth, Bluestone (1984) has argued that the impact of plant closures needs to be understood in relation to the 'absorptive capacity' of labour markets. That is, the extent to which jobs lost in specific industries or regions have been replaced. Bluestone (1984) points out that, controlling for cyclical factors, particular regions in the United States and particular industries - especially production industries - show clear evidence of deindustrialization in the sense in which he uses the term. More generally, Harris (1984) notes that only nine out of ten jobs lost in the United States through plant closings have been replaced. Moreover, since new firm formations usually follow patterns of population migration, new jobs tend not to be generated in regions affected by closure, a process which has helped to develop in her view 'pockets of serious economic distress'.

In a similar way Martin (1982, 1984) has pointed to regional disparities in the incidence of redundancy in Britain. In particular he notes (1982) that four regions - Wales, Scotland, the North and the North West - produced 45% of redundancies in Britain during the peak period for redundancies, from June 1979 to June 1981, while accounting for only 30% of the country's manufacturing labour force. Martin (1984) also shows that while redundancy is only one component of employment decline and in some British regions at least, not necessarily even the most important one,[2] in some other regions, notably Wales, high rates of redundancy have been coupled with low levels of labour turnover generally, a combination of factors which has, as he puts it, 'produced labour market conditions highly inimical to the task of relieving the high rate of redundancy there' (1984, 455). (For detailed studies of specific industries and local labour markets in Britain, see, for example, Massey and Meegan, 1982; Murgatroyd and Urry, 1985; Cooke and Rees, 1984 and Lloyd and Shutt, 1985).

Redundancy, then, has become a relatively widespread social phenomenon in the life of Western industrialized nations. To the extent that the jobs eliminated have been within particular and often hitherto strategic industries or are replaced at sites remote from those where employment had been lost, some kind of fundamental economic restructuring seems to be indicated. Moreover, as communities like Youngstown, Ohio and Consett in North East England, both of which have stood as visible and potent symbols of the blight caused by plant closures show, redundancy can produce serious disruptive consequences at the local level. It is not surprising, therefore, that, as in the depression of the 1930s which saw a burgeoning literature focussed on the effects of job loss, social scientists in the wake of the present recession have again turned their attention to an understanding of redundancy. Much of the work reported in this book attempts to go beyond that earlier literature and the later work of labour economists who have tended to look in the main at the _effects_ of redundancy and tended to conceive of those effects in a primarily individualistic way.

Indeed, as has been argued elsewhere, a good deal of popular and social scientific thinking about redundancy has been premised implicitly on what has been called the 'bathtub model' (Lee, 1985; Lee and Harris, 1985). In its crudest form the model treats a plant and its workforce as being analogous in some way to a bathtub full of water. The plug in the bathtub is pulled, though little thought is given to how or why this might be, and the water, ie. the workers, pours out. Some water is soaked up quickly as those who are better qualified and/or more enterprising get jobs. Those not soaked up settle, unemployed, into stagnant pools with the least qualified lying at the bottom to wait there either to be siphoned back into the system or until someone gets around to improving the drainage, as it were, in the sense of increasing the overall demand for labour.

Stated in this way the 'bathtub model' is an obvious caricature and one which does some injustice to a number of earlier studies (eg. those of Wedderburn, 1964; 1965). However, it is not entirely a bad likeness of the approach from labour economics or of many of the existing policy-oriented studies. The deficiencies of the model are therefore worthy of exploration. First, there is the danger that one is led by the model to see redundancy primarily as a discrete event rather than as a process. One result of this is that questions of how and why the plug is pulled are ignored and little thought is given to what Wood and Cohen (1977-78) have described as the 'social production of redundancy' both in the sense of how decisions to make workers redundant are made and how those decisions are implemented and legitimated. Interestingly the charge of having ignored the social production of redundancy is one which can be levelled less at industrial geographers (see, eg. Massey and Meegan, 1982) who have been interested in the regional consequences of corporate disinvestment decisions than at sociologists. Until comparatively recently sociologists other than Wood (Wood, 1982; Wood and Dey, 1983, but see also Thomas and Madigan, 1974) have also been relatively slow in trying to understand how redundancy is legitimated within plants (although Wood himself in his published writing has tended to under-estimate the difficulties of gaining access to redundancy situations (but see Wood, 1980)).

Secondly, the bathtub model tends to treat those made redundant in a relatively undifferentiated way. As a consequence, the characteristics of the redundant population are seen, for example, as a starting point for analysis rather than as a problem for investigation. In addition, the model tends also to suggest that redundancy engenders only a limited range of outcomes with, typically, only a simple opposition between employment and unemployment being posited. Many pre-recession studies of redundancy undertaken in times of relatively full-employment tend to assume that the period immediately after redundancy is a kind of limbo between one permanent job and another. In times of recession, however, there has perhaps been an opposite tendency to elide the categories 'redundant' and 'unemployed'.

It is important, however, <u>not</u> to assume that redundancy will inevitably lead to any particular position in the labour market, and to recognize, as Wood and Cohen have also argued, that the relationship between redundancy and its aftermath cannot be treated as being unproblematic and may in fact be rather complex. In other words, instead of studying the redundancy and labour market situations of redundant workers separately, attention should be paid rather to their interrelation. For example, a study of a large scale redundancy at a steel plant in South Wales suggested (Lee, 1985) that the way the redundancies were managed tended to produce a population of redundant workers whose social and personal characteristics disadvantaged them in the labour market. At the same time, however, the redundancies affected the operation of the labour market in a way which produced employment instability as an outcome of redundancy by providing a pattern of regular access to irregular employment to some former steelworkers but not to others.

Finally, the social structures, processes and relationships within which redundant workers are embedded and which affect both the redundancy process and labour market behaviour after redundancy tend to be ignored in the bathtub model. Crucially ignored in this regard is the role of power in the redundancy situation, on the one hand, and the relational contexts within which redundant workers operate, on the other. Both of these aspects of redundancy are extremely important. As Bob Fryer has pointed out (1981, 141).

> In any society where a group or individual has the power, both material and cultural, to fracture the relationship of others to the principal means of subsistence, 'redundancy' must remain a potential channel for the realisation of the interests of the powerful.

Arguing that the class context of collective dismissal needs to be recognised, Fryer goes on to suggest that public policy in relation to redundancy in Britain has been based on managerial definitions and has served primarily to secure the acquiescence of labour to the restructuring of capital in post-war British society. Wood and Dey (1983) have challenged this view, arguing that workers do not inevitably define their interests as being opposed to those of their employers and may in fact evaluate redundancy situations on the basis of a rather complex calculus which depends on the range of choices and constraints which confront them. Nevertheless, Wood and Dey recognize that 'the distribution of power embodied in existing social relations' (1983, 106) remains a powerful factor affecting workers' definitions of the situation. Their own work suffers somewhat, however, from the lack of an adequate conceptualization of power. This in turn leads to a failure to recognize fully that power, as Cynthia Hardy (1985, 16-19) has shown, can be used within a redundancy situation not only to defeat conflict but also to prevent it arising in the first place.

At the same time Wood and Dey are surely right to point out that workers' roles outside work can in some way shape their perception of redundancy. The relational context in which redundancy and its aftermath takes place has remained relatively understudied in the literature. Its importance is suggested, though, by the work of Seglow (1970) who has shown in a comparison of two different workshops within a factory facing closure how reactions to redundancy were in part a product of informal social relations within each shop. (See also Thomas and Madigan, 1974). In a slightly different context, but equally usefully, Lydia Morris (1984) has examined the interconnexions between post-redundancy labour market behaviour, patterns of domestic organization and the character of local social networks.

There seem to be two main reasons for the dominance of the bathtub model. Firstly, in Britain at any rate, much of the work on redundancy and plant closures carried out in the 1960s and 1970s was frequently officially funded research informed by policy considerations aimed at making the labour market more efficient in terms of manpower allocation and utilization. Much of this writing tends to take its assumptions from orthodox labour economics and to be concerned with the methods and strategies used by workers to find new jobs. The concern, in other words, is less with redundancy as a social phenomenon and the processes which produce it and by which it is managed, and more with 'job search', that is, the purposive exploration of opportunities on the demand side of the labour market. (For criticism of the literature on job search, see Granovetter, 1981; Lee and Harris, 1985).

A second reason why it has been difficult for researchers to transcend the limits of the bathtub model is, of course, that the model itself reflects implicitly the power dynamics of the redundancy situation. Another way of putting this is to say that often social scientists who study redundancy situations can find themselves in the same position as the workers facing dismissal, that is they must respond - often with little time available - to a situation already set in train. Accordingly, as Gordus et. al. (1981) point out,

> Only in cases where management has pledged cooperation can (redundancy) studies be mounted early; there are only a few cases in the literature and a few situations of this type currently in progress. The utility of even these few cases can be doubted because the type of labour-management climate which permits such incursions is unfortunately not common.

Indeed this last remark is something of an understatement since redundancy by its very nature produces problems of social control for management. Partial redundancy, for example, necessarily implies invidious selection between those workers who are to remain attached to their jobs and those who are to be dismissed. In the case of total closure, management must still ensure production up to the point of closure and must ensure that the disposal of surplus plant, for example, is not disrupted. (A very clear example of this kind of managerial thinking is given by Hardy, 1985). In either event individual resentment must be

contained and the possibility of collective
resistance minimized. It is this presumably which
lies behind the perceived sensitivity of redundancy
situations on the part of managers and the
corresponding difficulty of gaining access for
research purposes (Wood, 1980).

The methodological implications of all this
are, as Gordus et. al. (1981) point out, far from
trivial. In the first place, the redundancy
literature is made up of a set of more or less
discrete case studies which tend by and large to
bear relatively little relationship to one another.
(Even in one of the relatively rare instances (Wood
and Dey, 1983) where a number of case studies have
been brought together, the authors show a curious
reluctance to make systematic comparisons across
cases. But see Hardy, 1985). Secondly, since
studies of redundancy are the product of opportunity
and/or successful access, neither of which are
likely to be randomly distributed, certain kinds of
redundancy situation - presumably those involving
large-scale unionized plants - are, in consequence,
more likely to be studied. In sum, research on
redundancy is both fragmentary and partial.

Gordus et. al.'s review underlines the irony
that even policy orientated studies of the
aftermath of redundancy have been based usually on
what is for evaluation purposes a notoriously
impoverished research design; one in which there
are no pre-redundancy measures and no control group
(Campbell and Stanley, 1957). It is scarcely
surprising, therefore, to find them suggesting a
move towards longitudinal studies of a prospective
kind and with the use of appropriate control groups
as a suitable strategy for remedying the deficiencies
which they identify in the redundancy literature
(Gordus et. al., 1981, 157). Yet, arguably,
redundancy research already relies too heavily on
the survey as a methodological tool to the
exclusion of other alternative or complementary
research strategies. A number of contributors to a
recent symposium by British industrial geographers
(Massey and Meegan, 1985), looking at topics such
as job loss in relation to issues of theory, method
and research, have stressed the utility of
'intensive' as well as 'extensive' research designs
(see especially Massey and Meegan's introduction,
the paper by Sayer and Morgan, and the more
extended discussion in Sayer, 1984). That is,
research based around qualitative techniques in
which 'the primary questions concern how some

causal process works out in a particular case or limited number of cases' (Sayer and Morgan, 1985, 150) as opposed solely to the use of large samples, standardized questionnaires and sophisticated statistical analysis. Although sample surveys are well-suited to charting the subsequent fate of those who have shared a common experience such as redundancy, they can seem inappropriate, given their essentially atomistic character, where one must investigate, for example, the dynamics of the labour market or how the demand for labour is structured. Less atomistic strategies are necessary, too, if one is to explore how redundancy situations work themselves out and how, in particular, the processes which they contain affect the interplay between social positions, social relations and definitions of the situation.

In any event, whatever one's methodological predilections, abandoning the 'bathtub' model entails some kind of commitment to examine the variability of redundancy situations. This, in turn, suggests the efficacy of a comparative approach across plants, organizations, labour markets, industries and countries. The articles collected here take at least a small step in this direction by drawing on the work of both American and European researchers, in some cases drawing on or reviewing research carried out in more than one country, while in others research on a specific industry or a specific topic is addressed by both American and British authors.

Turning to the individual contributions it is perhaps worth recalling Blakely and Shapira's (1984, 99) comment that,

> As a result of industrial restructuring, large numbers of workers will never return to their former jobs. Millions of other workers will find that the jobs they are able to obtain have been quite radically changed, with adverse implications for working conditions, wages, job satisfaction and career mobility. Many people will be unable to find any stable work, at all ...

Although this assessment is descriptively apt it provides little basis for an adequate conceptualization of the impact of redundancy, lay-offs and plant closures. In their respective papers both Harris and Morris seek to relate redundancy to existing theoretical traditions as a means of theorizing these consequences. Harris offers the intriguing thought that the current wave of job loss may in fact presage, in Britain at least, the 'redundancy of redundancies'. This is so, he argues because the economic restructuring currently underway seems to be accompanied by the replacement of workers formerly located within internal labour markets by contract or other kinds of short-term, 'peripheral' labour who will not in the future need to be 'shed' en masse but who can be hired and fired at will. This in turn leads to a situation in which workers, who have been made redundant and whose characteristics are those formerly associated with the 'primary sector', find themselves doing work of a kind they had done previously, but within quite different and markedly inferior market and employment contexts. Harris suggests that a shift of this kind may be indicative of changes taking place in the bases of differentiation within the British working class, and as such merits the attention of stratification theorists. According to Harris, Marx understated the importance of the labour market in relation to class formation and the extent to which social classes may be thought of as what he calls, following T.H. Marshall, 'diffuse identity groups'. From the point of view of class analysis, then, redundancy is an event which links change in the productive process and changes in the labour market to the formation of class fractions which may be characterized in terms of the ways in which workers use class identities as resources in the labour market.

Morris takes a rather different tack. An anthropologist who has carried out research not only in declining areas of Britain but also in Latin America, she is concerned with the impact of redundancy on local social structures. Drawing on research on redundant workers and on shanty town dwellers she asks how far concepts drawn from recent studies of underdeveloped countries provide a valid basis for an understanding of the local-level effects of deindustrialization. She concludes that the comparison between underdevelopment and deindustrialization is less useful than it first appears by drawing attention to the fundamental differences in economic structure which underlie a set of superficial similarities.

A number of contributions examine redundancies and plant closures taking place in the steel industry in Europe and in the United States. Steel is, of course, an industry central to the post-war regeneration of Western nations and is strategically important to the industrial character of modern technological society. It is also an industry which has been hard hit in Western countries by the recession. Thus, between 1979 and 1982 employment in the US steel industry declined from 453,000 to 247,000 (Benyon and Bourgeois, 1984), while European steel producers have also faced major problems. Under the terms of the Treaty of Paris which set up the European Coal and Steel Community (ECSC), 'readaption benefits' are available to steelworkers who lose their jobs in the EEC due to industry restructuring. In the decade between 1975 and 1984 readaption benefits were made available to 222,332 workers throughout the EEC, with 48% of payments over this period being made to the United Kingdom. (These figures are derived from the Annual Reports of the European Commission).

Steel provides a useful context in which to look at policy responses to large scale redundancy. It has been argued (see eg. Hooks, 1984) that policy responses to lay-offs and plant shutdowns in the United States lag somewhat behind those found in European countries. Fevre and Bytheway examine in their respective papers a large scale steel redundancy in Britain and point to some of the unintended consequences of social policies based around the ECSC readaption benefits scheme mentioned earlier. Such policies, it seems, do cushion the impact of redundancy for the individual. In overall terms, however, they also tend to assign particular categories of worker to the margins of the labour market.

Fevre looks at the role of readaption benefits in relation to attempts made by the British Steel Corporation (BSC) to reduce the numbers of its direct employees by putting out to contract many operations formerly carried out by its own workers. Steelworkers who had been made redundant could find work with contracting firms and have their wages 'made-up' to a proportion of their former earnings under the readaption benefits scheme. Fevre does not believe that 'make-up' per se influenced BSC's decision to bring in contractors, but does show in discussing the possibility, that serious questions can be raised about the extent to which redundancies generated cost savings for the enterprise. However, even if the availability of 'make-up' did not in itself influence BSC's decision to bring in contractors, the availability of readaption benefits did have a number of consequences on the local labour market. In particular, those in the local community who worked outside the steel industry suffered the unemployment created by the redundancies, which tended to be displaced onto them, while redundant steelworkers found jobs, including work with the contractors at BSC. However, although redundant workers did at least find work with contractors, in so doing they moved into a disadvantaged position in terms of conditions of service and employment stability relative to their former workmates. Eventually, too, the period during which earnings were made up expired and the real wages of those steelworkers who had gone to work for contractors fell. Fevre goes on to argue that the unintended consequences of an apparently enlightened readaption benefits policy may have been damaging for all of the workers concerned. Fevre's conclusions concerning the cost benefits arising to the firm as a result of the redundancies must in part be tentative because of the difficulties involved in obtaining reliable information. However, as Gordus et. al. (1981, 158) point out, 'Little research has been done to validate the general assumption that [redundancies] do promote economic efficiency', and in this respect Fevre's contribution is a very creditable first step.

In another study of the same redundancy situation Bytheway focusses on older workers; those for whom redundancy often forms the transition into 'early retirement'. According to Bytheway, such workers are a group ignored by industrial sociologists because they have already left the labour market and by gerontologists because they have not yet reached statutory retirement age. He notes that in comparison with other countries policy directed towards older workers in the United Kingdom - such as it is - encourages labour market withdrawal. There were two reasons why this was even more clearly the case for the steelworkers he studied. First of all, while the readaption benefits scheme offered a strong financial incentive to younger workers to find work (almost literally at any price), no such incentive was available to older workers. Secondly, there was informal moral pressure on older employees to make way for younger workers. Bytheway examines the post-redundancy careers of these older workers and points to the complex interrelationship between chronological age, health, motivation and employment opportunity.

Introduction

Bytheway's paper is complemented in a number of respects by Bartley's contribution which looks at the relationship between redundancy and health and by Cornfield's paper which examines the relationship between lay-offs where selection for redundancy is based on seniority and patterns of ethnic group disadvantage. Bartley critically reviews a number of American and European studies on the health effects of redundancy. She notes that there is an attempt in most existing studies to treat redundancy as a physiologically stressful event. She argues that as a result there is a neglect of the mediating role of redundancy and labour market processes. 'Perhaps', she suggests,

> in the same way that studies of the health effects of bereavement are situated within an understanding of the psycho-social aspects of family life, studies of the health effects of redundancy should be situated more firmly within an understanding of the labour process and labour markets ...

Bartley goes on to introduce the concept of 'social overhead costs' as a way of allowing the health consequences of redundancy and their implications for social policy to be more readily understood. Cornfield examines patterns of ethnic inequality in lay-off chances. Using logistic regression analysis to assess the relative impact of a range of variables on the probability of being made redundant, Cornfield shows that minority group members may find themselves in an invidious position. The increasing bureaucratization of American business and the attempt by unions to curtail the power of capital by insisting on the development of universalistic rules and procedures has produced a trend towards seniority-based lay-off agreements. However, such agreements may differentially affect minority group members who tend, because of patterns of past discrimination, to have shorter lengths of service. At the same time, although conclusive evidence is more difficult to obtain, minority group members in non-union firms may find that they are subject to selection for redundancy through the application of particularistic criteria. Cornfield concludes that a major challenge for the civil rights and trade union movements in the United States is to develop approaches which reconcile the conflicting goals and outcomes of seniority-based lay-off agreements

13

and procedures based on affirmative action.
By introducing unionization and bureaucratization as key <u>variables</u> in his analysis, Cornfield provides a useful reminder that one should be careful not to assume that the experiences of workers in the kind of large-scale telecommunication company he studied or in the steel industry should be taken necessarily as typical. In other words, while redundancy procedures are likely to be relatively formalized in the large-scale bureaucratized and unionized plants typical of the steel industry, for example, in other contexts one might expect to see rather more <u>ad hoc</u> and invidious arrangements. In this regard it is important to remember that the recession has affected not just heavy industry but medium and small-size firms as well. Moreover, as already noted, in Europe the range of benefits available to redundant workers is unusually favourable in the case of steel, and large companies are in a better position than small ones to 'top up' statutory levels of redundancy compensation.

Related to patterns of size, bureaucratic organization and unionization is the whole question of occupational segregation. Touched on by Cornfield in relation to ethnic minorities, the topic is also relevant to the two papers, by Callender and by Perrucci <u>et. al</u>., which deal with women and redundancy. The point is made in both papers that female redundancy has been understudied in comparison with that of men. Now, one response to this charge might be that it is precisely the older male-dominated industries which have been hardest hit by redundancy, and that the imbalance in the literature reflects imbalances in the incidence of redundancy itself. However, this does not explain why, for example, the attention given to the steel industry in Britain has not been matched by studies of the almost as badly hit, but female-dominated, textile industry (see Martin, 1982), the sector upon which Callender's paper is based.

Callender provides a case study of a redundancy at a clothing factory with a predominantly female workforce located in the South Wales valleys. In her paper she is concerned to do a number of things. First of all, she describes the complexities of the redundancy process and of the reactions to it. Secondly, she demonstrates how women are disadvantaged in redundancy because the assumptions built into redundancy legislation and

into selection procedures take male rather than
female employment patterns as the norm. Thirdly,
she traces patterns of gender disadvantage in the
micropolitics of the redundancy situation itself.
More specifically, Callender points to how the
management in the factory she studied maximized
uncertainty and encouraged factionalism and the
pursuit of self-interest among the workforce, and
how the male-dominated trade union served the
interests of male workers rather better than those
of female workers. Fourthly, she describes the
emotional reactions produced by redundancy, the
sense of hurt, shock and incomprehension produced
by redundancy in the women she studied. Callender
does, however, go on to challenge the notion that
women workers are prone to acquiescence in
redundancy situations by showing that, even where
collective mobilization is absent, individual
resistance remains possible.

Perrucci et. al. note that studies from the
Great Depression considered only the impact of job
loss on male breadwinners. They suggest that the
exclusion of women from studies of redundancy has
persisted until the present and go on to compare in
a systematic manner the economic, social and
psychological effects of redundancy on male and
female workers laid off from a factory in a small
town in Indiana. They show that the women they
studied made substantial contributions to the
income of their households and suffered, as a
result, the economic distress caused by redundancy
no less than men. Similarly, while men and women
retained a sense of mastery over their lives and
were able to derive support from those around them,
there were social and psychological costs arising
from redundancy which affected women as well as
men.

Just as women have been ignored in much of the
mainstream redundancy literature, relatively little
attention seems to have been paid to the collective
responses of workers to job loss and in particular
to the extent to which redundancy may produce
either political radicalization or apathy. In
Britain at least some of the predictions made about
civil disorders in areas affected by substantial
job losses proved scarcely prescient, although the
frustrations of other disadvantaged groups,
especially inner-city black young people, did make
themselves felt in rioting. Three of the papers in
the present collection, all of which again look at
the steel industry, make good the deficiency just

noted in the literature. Two of the papers, by
Kourchid and by Deitch and Erickson, look at the
actions taken by steelworkers in defence of their
jobs, while Noble's paper examines the relationship
between redundancy and political attitudes.

The first of these three papers is a
contribution by a writer in the French neo-Marxist
tradition, which in recent years has seen an
upsurge of interest in workers' movements and
struggles partly inspired by the work of the French
neo-Marxist urban sociologist, Manuel Castells
(see, for example, Castells, 1977). In his paper
Kourchid looks at the quite different responses to
plant closure to be found among steelworkers in the
Longwy area of Lorraine in France compared to those
of workers at steel plants in Youngstown, Ohio.
Kourchid's paper is divided into three main
sections. First of all, he documents the series of
mergers and closures which hit the steel community
of Youngstown between 1977 and 1980, and the
attempts made by workers, unions and a local
coalition of religious leaders to buy out the
plants involved. He then moves on to explore the
differing contexts within which workers' struggles
developed in both countries. On the one hand, in
the United States, the workings of giant business
conglomerates aided by a state which appeared to be
relatively disinvolved were found ranged against
workers and religious groups who defined their
situation in economic and moral terms. In France,
on the other, a situation could be found where the
state, wider European institutions and, until
nationalization in 1981, private sector steel firms
faced unions and workers who were politically
differentiated both horizontally and vertically.
Finally, Kourchid contrasts the relative lack of
direct action in the Youngstown case (a brief and
isolated occupation of the local headquarters of US
Steel apart) with what he describes as a
'quasi-insurrectional' situation in Lorraine, one
which in his view echoed earlier revolutionary
ferments in France.

In a sense the paper by Deitch and Erickson
brings the story up to date at least as far as
closures in the US steel industry is concerned,
with an account of the ultimately unsuccessful
campaign of workers in the Pittsburgh area to 'save
Dorothy 6' - a blast furnace and associated plant
which came to stand as a symbol of resistance to
corporate disinvestment in steel. The workers
studied by Deitch and Erickson had three goals: to

prevent Dorothy 6 being demolished, to obtain the legal right to acquire the works and to finance its re-operation. Deitch and Erickson draw on the resource mobilization perspective within the social movements literature in order to understand how the movement to save the plant was shaped by the resources and constraints available to redundant workers and their allies. Following Erik Olin Wright, Deitch and Erickson see these resources and constraints as being in themselves shaped by class interest. However, they also want to argue that particular corporate disinvestment strategies and the response of workers to them vary from case to case, particularly so in steel in the United States where, in contrast to Europe, the federal government has had relatively little role to play in restructuring the industry. In line with this argument they show clearly how US Steel's closure of Dorothy 6 and its associated plant arose from a decision to move investment out of steel towards more profitable activities and towards steel finishing at the expense of basic steelmaking; strategies quite different to those adopted by other steel companies.

As part of a research team based at the University of Sheffield, Noble studied the political attitudes of workers made redundant from one of the city's private-sector steel firms widely regarded as having had a deferential workforce. As in other steel redundancies in Britain (Bytheway, this volume; Lee, 1985) labour market withdrawal was a major consequence of redundancy for older workers and Noble makes a useful distinction between non-employment - the transition into economic inactivity - and unemployment as outcomes of the redundancy process. Although for the workers studied by Noble unemployment following redundancy was distressing, the economic insecurity thus engendered seems to have had little radicalizing impact. Noble suggests that this may have been due to three factors; the social atomization produced by redundancy, the rigidification of existing attitudes and the inability of the Labour Party in Britain to take advantage of public concern over unemployment. Ominously, however, what Noble does point to is that those who have experienced redundancy may lay some of the blame for their fate at the door of immigrant workers.

In conclusion, a few themes can be picked from the foregoing which may bear reiteration. One is that we must understand more clearly how corporate disinvestment strategies are developed and put into operation. One further thought is that, since it is management which is difficult to study in redundancy situations, we must become more methodologically adventurous - perhaps, for example, by studying the redundancy process through simulation techniques and the like.

Secondly it appears clear that, particularly in Britain, and with the aid of existing legislation the recession has encouraged a pattern of what might be called 'structured extrusion' from employment. Older workers are forced out of the labour market, women are forced back into the home and at least some prime-age male workers find themselves moving out of secure employment into unstable and inferior jobs. Thirdly, and related to this, it is perhaps worth recalling that thirty years ago Erving Goffman wrote an article which took the relationship between 'con' and 'mark' in a confidence game as the model for the 'cooling out' process by which someone is made to pass with good grace from a desirable status to one that is less so (Goffman, 1952). That article repays careful study by anyone interested in the sociology of redundancy. It seems that policies designed to cope with redundancies frequently function to cool workers out of employment in ways which help to minimize resistance. One hypothesis is that different kinds of workers may be dealt with in different ways; some being provided with a basis upon which they can construct an alternative or compensatory identity, while others, those with relatively low amounts of power (eg. women workers or immigrants), are not judged worthy of the effort. To the extent that workers are successfully cooled out of employment, however, or remain relatively powerless in the face of redundancy, then the less surprising it becomes that a rising tide of social protest has not accompanied increasing levels of redundancy.

Finally, it will be evident that a range of methodological approaches is to be found in the present volume, reflecting in part the quite distinct methodological cultures which exist on either side of the Atlantic. British sociology following its rapid expansion in the 1960s became anti-empiricist and qualitatively oriented in its methodology, while sociology in the US has been dominated by what Bryant (1985) has called 'instrumental positivism' with its emphasis on the development of increasing quantification and

statistical sophistication. Whatever their methodological underpinnings, what these papers share is a
commitment to the detailed empirical examination of
redundancy situations within the framework of a
rigorous structural and processual analysis.

NOTES

1. Dorothy Wedderburn (1968) has noted that the

> use of the word 'redundancy' to describe a situation where the labour force of an enterprise is being reduced by dismissals is unique to Britain. The word does not exist in this sense in France or Germany. Even in the United States there are 'lay-offs' and 'dismissals' but not 'redundancies'.

It can be argued that the term 'redundancy' commends itself because it implies both the superfluity of the worker to the requirements of the enterprise and a degree of permanent separation from the job not captured by the term 'lay-off', which in British parlance signifies a temporary status holding out the possibility of recall.
2. It may be that Martin underestimates the extent to which some forms of 'natural wastage' such as early retirement represent in fact a form of hidden redundancy.

REFERENCES

Benyon, F. and J. Bourgeois (1984) 'The European Community - United States Steel Agreement', <u>Common Market Law Review</u>, <u>21</u>, 305-54

Blackaby, F. (1979) <u>Deindustrialization</u>, Heinneman, London

Blakely, E.J. and P. Shapira (1984) 'Industrial Restructuring: Public Policies for Investment in Advanced Industrial Society', <u>Annals of the American Academy of Political and Social Science</u>, <u>475</u>, 96-109

Bluestone, B. (1984) 'Is Deindustrialization a Myth? Capital Mobility versus Absorptive Capacity in the US Economy', <u>Annals of the American Academy of Political and Social Science</u>, <u>475</u>, 39-51

Bryant, C.A.G. (1985) <u>Positivism in Social Theory and Research</u>, London, Macmillan

Campbell, D.T. and J.C. Stanley (1966) <u>Experimental and Quasi-experimental Designs for Research</u>, Rand McNally, Chicago

Castells, M. (1977) <u>The Urban Question: A Marxist Approach</u>, Edward Arnold, London

Cooke, P. and G. Rees (1984) 'The Social Democratic State in a Radical Region: Development Agencies, Industrial Change and Class Relations in South Wales', in I. Szelenyi, <u>Cities in Recession</u>, Sage, Beverly Hills, pp. 162-91

Fryer, B. (1981) 'State, Redundancy and the Law', in B. Fryer, A. Hunt, D. McBarnet and B. Moorehouse, <u>Law, State and Society</u>, Croom Helm, London, pp. 136-59

Goffman, E. (1952) 'On Cooling the Mark Out: Some Aspects of Adaptation to Failure', <u>Psychiatry</u>, <u>15</u>, 451-63

Gordus, J.P., P. Jarley and L.A. Ferman (1981) <u>Plant Closings and Economic Dislocation</u>, W.E. Upjohn Institute for Employment Research, Kalamazoo, MI

Granovetter, M. (1981) 'Toward a Sociological Theory of Income Differences', in I. Berg, <u>Sociological Perspectives on Labor Markets</u>, Academic Press, New York, pp. 11-48

Hardy, C. (1985) <u>Managing Organizational Closure</u>, Gower, Aldershot

Harris, C.C., R.M. Lee and L.D. Morris (1985) 'Redundancy in Steel: Labour Market Behaviour, Local Social Networks and Domestic Organi- zation', in B. Roberts, R. Finnegan and D.

21

Gallie, New Approaches to Economic Life,
Manchester University Press, Manchester,
pp. 154-66
Harris, C.S. (1984) 'The Magnitude of Job Loss
from Plant Closings and the Generation of
Replacement Jobs: Some Recent Evidence',
Annals of the American Academy of Political
and Social Science, 475, 15-27
Hooks, G. (1984) 'The Policy Response to Factory
Closings: A Comparison of the United States,
France and Sweden', Annals of the American
Academy of Political and Social Science,
475, 110-24
Lee, R.M. (1985) 'Redundancy, Labour Markets and
Informal Relations', Sociological Review,
33, 469-94
Lee, R.M. and C.C. Harris (1985) 'Redundancy
Studies: Port Talbot and After', Quarterly
Journal of Social Affairs, 1, 19-27
Lloyd, P. and J. Shutt (1985) 'Recession and
Restructuring in the North West Region: The
Implications of Recent Events', in D. Massey
and R. Meegan, Politics and Method: Contrast-
ing Studies in Industrial Geography, Methuen,
London, pp. 13-60
Martin, R.L. (1982) 'Job Loss and the Regional
Incidence of Redundancies in the Current
Recession', Cambridge Journal of Economics,
6, 375-95
Martin, R.L. (1984) 'Redundancies, Labour Turnover
and Employment Contraction in the Recession:
A Regional Analysis', Regional Studies, 18,
445-58
Massey, D. and R. Meegan (1982) The Anatomy of Job
Loss: The How, Why and Where of Employment
Decline, Methuen, London
Morris, L.D. (1984) 'Patterns of Social Activity
and Post-redundancy Labour Market Experience',
Sociology, 18, 339-52
Murgatroyd, L. and J. Urry (1985) 'The Class and
Gender Restructuring of the Lancaster Economy,
1950-1980', in B. Roberts, R. Finnegan and D.
Gallie, New Approaches to Economic Life,
Manchester University Press, Manchester,
pp. 48-67
Noble, F. (1981) 'Redundancy Statistics', Employ-
ment Gazette, 89, 260-2
Sayer, A. (1984) Method in Social Science: A
Realist Approach, Hutchinson, London
Sayer, A. and K. Morgan (1985) 'A Modern Industry
in a Declining Region: Links between Method,

Theory and Policy', in D. Massey and R. Meegan, <u>Politics and Method: Contrasting Studies in Industrial Geography</u>, Methuen, London, pp. 147-68

Seglow, P. (1970) 'Reactions to Redundancy: the Influence of the Work Situation', <u>Industrial Relations Journal</u>, 1, 7-22

Thirlwall, A.P. (1982) 'Deindustrialization in the United Kingdom', <u>Lloyd's Bank Review</u>, 22-37

Thomas, B. and C. Madigan (1971) 'Strategy and Job Choice after Redundancy: A Case Study in the Aircraft Industry', <u>Sociological Review</u>, 22, 83-102

Wedderburn, D. (1964) <u>White Collar Redundancy</u>, DAE Occasional Paper, Cambridge University, Cambridge

Wedderburn, D. (1965) <u>Redundancy and Railwaymen</u>, DAE Occasional Paper, Cambridge University, Cambridge

Wedderburn, D. (1968) 'Redundancy' in D. Pym, <u>Industrial Society: Social Sciences in Management</u>, Penguin, Harmondsworth, pp. 65-72

Wood, S. (1980) 'Reactions to Redundancy', Unpublished Ph.D. Thesis, University of Manchester

Wood, S. and J. Cohen (1977-78) 'Approaches to the Study of Redundancy', <u>Industrial Relations Journal</u>, 8, 19-27

Wood, S. and I. Dey (1983) <u>Redundancy: Case Studies in Cooperation and Conflict</u>, Gower, Aldershot

Chapter Two

REDUNDANCY AND CLASS ANALYSIS

C. C. Harris

This paper is concerned with general issues arising out of a study of the post-redundancy labour market experience of a sample of men made redundant from the British Steel Corporation's works at Port Talbot, South Wales in the west of Great Britain. The British Steel Corporation (BSC) is a state owned concern and Port Talbot one of the major plants which produces steel strip in the United Kingdom. In the period 1979-80 the falling market for steel, combined with the arrival of a Conservative administration which enforced what Morgan has described as 'the most stringent cash limits ever imposed on a nationalised industry in Britain' (Morgan, 1983) resulted in a reduction of the plant's labour force from 11,354 to 6654 in nine months and the declaration of 5807 redundancies.

As noted elsewhere (Lee and Harris, 1985), the redundancies were not simply the result of a national decision to make less steel. They were the result of a decision to make less steel in a new way. This involved not only the modernisation of the Port Talbot plant, but also the increased use of contractors rather than direct labour. Informed management sources and the results of an independent study (Fevre, this volume) both estimate the number of contract workers now contributing to steel production as being at least 'in four figures'. That is to say that steel is being produced by at least 1000 contracted labourers as well as with current (1985) established manning of 4808.

The strategy of 'inverse labour hoarding', that is, shedding labour and buying it back in as required (through the use of contractors), would not appear to be confined to British Steel. Indeed it has been claimed as a result of work undertaken by the Institute of Manpower Studies at the

University of Sussex that there has been a distinct movement within British industry in the direction of what Atkinson (1984) has described as the flexible firm: a firm consisting of a core with a minimum established permanent labour force, and a number of peripheral but vital operations which it contracts for as and when required. Certainly BSC has moved in this direction. The matter may be put this way: instead of employing a large labour force a proportion of whom are laid off when times are bad, industry is moving towards employing a small labour force which, via the mechanism of contractors, is augmented when times are better.

This raises the question of why the use of contractors has to be extended for this purpose. In Britain an important factor is the existence of job protection legislation, which gives workers protection against unfair dismissal and the right to redundancy payments as compensation for job loss. These provisions allow the cooling out of those involved (as redundants are) in a status passage to a new and undesired status (Goffman, 1952; Lee, 1985); but they are also a form of compensation for the loss of property; in effect, workers acquire, through satisfactory service in an occupation, the statutory equivalent of customary rights to that employment. As a result the cost of layoffs in redundancy payments (to which both the employer and the state contribute) is a deterrent to achieving flexibility by discharging workers. On the other hand employers are still concerned to ensure employee 'commitment/'involvment'/'loyalty' in relation to the company and dislike creating a second class of direct employees who have 'fixed term' appointments through which they cannot acquire rights in the job. Contracting, where practical, circumvents these difficulties.

A shift in the direction of the flexible firm is likely to result eventually in the increasing redundancy of redundancies, in the sense of lay-offs, since firms will be concerned with expanding small core labour forces rather than reducing large workforces by shedding peripheral members. This implies that 'employment protection' will become a priviledge of core members, and the shift to the flexible firm will result in the exclusion from those privileges of a significant and increasing proportion of the workforce. In the meanwhile, however, redundancies have become an increasingly important feature of the operation of the labour market as the result of the attempt of industry to move towards the 'flexible firm'.

The stimulus to that movement has been the recession of the 1980s. Let it be assumed (though this is doubtful) that the resumption of economic growth (as measured by growth in GNP) will result in the expansion of job opportunities and a return to 'full' employment. If the transition to the flexible firm has taken place in the mean time, that would not mean a return to the labour market conditions of the 1960s and 1970s: the majority of the increased demand for labour would be constituted, not by the expansion of established employment but by the expansion of the demand for contract labour. This transformation of 'the market' would involve a shift of emphasis from the internal to the external market and would result in a far greater proportion of the labour force regularly experiencing periods on the open market; that is regularly experiencing the competitive struggle to sell labour to an employer.

Redundancy, a term which has wider currency in Britain than elsewhere, does not necessarily imply plant closure or labour shedding; it is perfectly consistent with the expansion of employment if that expansion requires a restructuring of the labour process, requires making the product in a new way. The Port Talbot case involved labour shedding under the threat of plant closure, the decision to make steel in a new way and hence the designation of workers as redundant as a result both of a reduction of output and of a restructuring of the labour process in response to external pressures by the product market and the state. However the focus of the term redundancy, created by its connection with 'closure' and 'shedding', needs to be widened by reference not only to the labour process but also to the labour market. Whether or not those made redundant as a result of the decision to contract out operations were actually re-employed by contractors, the expansion of the labour supply by the redundancies ensured fierce competition for work, and hence engendered a supply of workers available and willing to work for contractors. The decision to 'make steel in a new way' could only have been taken in a loose labour market whereby the supply of labour willing to work under those conditions was abundant. The decision and its consequences were conditioned by the state of the market; one of its consequences was to affect the market in a way which ensured the successful implementation of the decision. Once again Port

Talbot is a special case: BSC dominate the local labour market. But even where this condition is not fulfilled it is still the case that the origin of redundancies and their consequences are necessarily conditioned by the market.

The study of redundancy events, therefore, is of critical importance for examining the nature of the connection between product markets, the labour process and the labour market. Hence redundancy is not to be understood as a special area of study in industrial relations or some secular factor which temporarily disturbs the equilibrium of the labour market: it is a type of event the attempt to understand which illuminates <u>processes and relations</u> which are central to the operation of a free market economy. It is also an event involving the <u>redefinition of</u>, and <u>reallocation of people to</u>, places in the social order. As such redundancy events are of central interest to students and theorists of those social phenomena which are apprehended through the concepts of 'social stratification' and 'class'.

OF CLASS AND THE MARKET

While redundancy events have been construed as inflows onto the labour market, and the labour process and product markets have to some extent been ignored, students of class and stratification have tended to concentrate on positions in the process of material production or in the occupational hierarchy to the exclusion of much concern with either product or labour markets. The latter tendency has also affected students of 'labour markets' who have tended to infer the existence of dual or segmented labour <u>markets</u> solely on the basis of evidence of the existence of dual or segmented <u>employment opportunity</u> structures. There is a highly dangerous tendency for any study of economic life to find itself exclusively concerned with what goes on 'inside the factory gate' or with the demand for labour, to the exclusion of any consideration of the relation between markets and production, or of the <u>relation</u> between the two sides of the market which is of the essence of market phenomena.

Similarly students of 'class' in the Marxian sense, have taken too much to heart Marx's remark that to discover the secret of the operation of the capitalist mode of production we must follow the

27

entrepreneur into the workplace. Marx's point was, of course, that it is the workplace that is the site of the labour process through which, under capitalism, surplus value is extracted from the workers' labour. However the discovery of the secret presupposes a definition of capitalism with which even those who disallow Marx's claim to have discovered it must concur, namely that a capitalistic mode of production involves the commoditisation of labour power, and that in capitalist societies the mass of the population subsists by selling its labour power for the means of subsistence.

The central class relation in capitalist societies is then not merely one which subjects wage labourers to what Marx termed the 'despotism of the workplace', it is also one which intrinsically involves what he termed 'the play of chance and caprice in the market' (Marx, Capital I, Ch.14). The worker is subjected to the play of chance and caprice in the labour market. To define the propertyless class (the proletariat) of capitalist society as the wage labouring class implies that before the capitalist can extract surplus value from labour he first has to 'hire the labour'/ 'purchase labour power'. Hence the labour market (ie. in the sense of the mechanisms which bring together the buyers and sellers of labour power) constitutes the central social institution of capitalist society because it articulates/mediates the capital-wage labour relation. To emphasise the centrality to capitalist social formations of this mechanism and relation points us in the opposite direction from that indicated by Marx's claim that the 'secret' of such formations is to be found in the labour process, or, more generally, from that suggested by the view that it is an understanding of the type of way of producing and changes therein that has more explanatory value from the standpoint of economics, sociology and politics than the understanding of market mechanisms. Indeed Marx himself was insistent that market and productive processes cannot be understood in isolation but 'mutually condition one another'.

Unfortunately however the markets that Marx had in mind in this regard were not labour markets but product markets: new markets affect the character of production just as new ways of producing affect the character of product markets. But in spite of his concern with labour, value, price and their relation Marx has relatively little to say about the operation of labour markets as

such. This neglect derives from Marx's concern,
which he shares with other nineteenth-century
writers, with 'the division of labour'. It is well
known that he distinguished two types of this
division, the 'technical' division of labour within
the productive process and the 'social' division of
labour whereby different sectors of society
specialised in the production of different
commodities or types of commodity. The technical
division of labour is clearly central to understanding
any specific instance of the labour process. The
social division of labour directs us to market
processes involving the creation of markets for
products, product differentiation and specialisation
as between enterprises (see Mohun in Bottomore,
1983:132).

The social recognition that 'society' is
composed of different 'classes', which became
widespread in the nineteenth century, involved two
quite different types of distinction: between
categories in some sense higher or lower than each
other and between categories whose members
benefited from the production and sale of different
commodities. The first were denominated by terms
such as 'the lower classes', 'the labouring
classes'. The second were referred to as the
'manufacturing', 'agricultural' classes. The
hierarchical distinction has today been transmitted
into a 'status' order; the latter is retained in
the use of the term 'lobby' as in 'gun lobby',
'farm lobby'. (Though the term 'lobby' is political
rather than economic, lobbies are political
expressions of economic interests as in the archaic
British expression 'he stood for Parliament in the
agricultural interest' implies.)

Marx synthesises and incorporates these two
distinct but related popular senses of 'class' by
regarding them as different expressions of the
'division of labour' and 'private property' and
shows them to be, in general, the outcome of
economic processes, while regarding particular
types of class as definitive of distinctive social
orders. It is in no way to question the utility of
this conceptual achievement in making general sense
of the structure of modern societies to point out
that the emphasis on the division of labour (and
therefore on production) diverts attention from the
fact that the notions of 'market' and 'competition'
are central, not only to the social division of
labour (considered as a process), but also to the
articulation of capital and labour which distinguishes

capitalist societies and is a pre-condition of the labour process.

This neglect of the labour market aspect of the definition of class relations in capitalist society has led to one of the greatest weaknesses in the whole Marxian corpus on class consciousness and action. Wage labourers <u>would no more be</u> wage labourers if they did not sell their labour on the market, than they would be wage labourers if surplus value was not extracted through the labour process. Working class consciousness requires therefore that members of the wage labouring category share the experience of selling their labour (of the play of chance and caprice in the <u>labour</u> market) as well as the experience of alienated labour - of having their life activity and its products owned and controlled by another. In a full employment economy, characterised by labour hoarding firms and large internal labour markets, many workers will not experience themselves as market dependent labour sellers, but as secure in their status as members of work establishments and as being engaged in political struggles with other work groups <u>within the factory</u> to improve their position in the industrial order. The work experience of Marx's wage labourers under those <u>labour market conditions</u>, while providing the opportunity to unite in struggles against capital and its representatives, will not <u>motivate</u> them to do so, since that experience will not be one of being members of a class outside society but of being very much incorporated in it. They will not develop solidarity with other category members since what necessarily and universally unites all wage labourers is the <u>experience</u> of selling their labour for a wage. Even if legally that is what is happening (ie. they are technically rehired at the end of each week) that is not how it feels if you have worked continuously in the plant, as many of the Port Talbot steelworkers had, for more than twenty years.

Redundancy may now be seen as a status passage or life experience which has profound consequences for the political and social consciousness of the worker, but the character of those consequences is not capable of being inferred from the fact of the redundancy or the nature of the redundancy event itself. The significance of the redundancy event will depend not merely upon the labour market outcome for the worker at an arbitrary cut off point in time but upon the character of the redundant worker's labour market experience as encoded in his or her labour market history. The extent, frequency and incidence of redundancy events will therefore be important factors in affecting, in conjunction with labour market conditions, both industrial and social attitudes of workers.

If however it turns out to be the case that there has been a shift in the direction of the flexible firm, redundancies induced by lack of demand in the product market will be less frequent features of the industrial scene, and a new category of workers will come into existence: those who live by being regularly supplied with short-term employments. It is reasonable to infer the coming into existence of such a category once it is recognised that there are forces on both the supply and demand side which will encourage it. Contractors necessarily have more acute problems of labour supply than steady production firms: they have to obtain possibly quite large labour·forces at relatively short notice, a requirement made the more difficult to fulfil the more specialised the labour required. The most economical way of carrying out what Grieco (1985) has usefully termed '_labour_ search' is to pull in as many previously employed workers as possible. The needs of the contractor-employer are likely to generate an irregular series of offers of fixed term employment to persons who have once been in their employ. On the supply side the acceptance of short-term employment is attractive 'while waiting for something better to turn up'. However, it militates against efficient job search thus increasing the chances of subsequent unemployment and hence of the availability of the worker the next time the contractor is looking for labour.

There is however another determinant of the consequences of redundancy which complicates the issue of identifying how the redundancy will be experienced. It is not enough to say that this will depend on the subsequent labour market career, for both the way redundancy is experienced and the character of the subsequent career will be determined by the social identity of the redundants themselves. For 'occupation' and 'class' membership, however great their importance as determinants of social identity, do not by any means exhaust what we mean by that term. Indeed there is a looser usage of the term 'class', as in the phrase (admittedly somewhat archaic) 'they are not our class of person' (as opposed to 'not our class') which, as the term 'person' implies, refers to a wider persona or identity than that given by either the Weberian notion of 'status group' or the Marxian notion of 'class'.

CLASS, 'SOCIAL CLASS' AND LABOUR MARKET BEHAVIOUR

It is no purpose of this contribution to discuss the variety of meanings associated with the term class, but a brief preliminary comment is nonetheless required. Each use of the term has to be understood in terms of the intellectual or practical purpose to which it is put. In one context class has been used to denote hierarchically ranked social strata which emerged in Europe in the nineteenth century in spite of the fact that the political and legal inequalities associated with the old (originally) feudal order had been overthrown. Since this emergent inequality was not derivable from formal hierarchical institutions but arose out of 'civil society', ie. the association of people together to fulfil various 'natural' (ie. physiologically based) needs, this sense - of structured inequality - has always been associated with 'the economic'.

The other sense, the Marxian, is based not on the notion of hierarchy but of differentiation, of a division of labour yielding pairs of logically exhaustive social categories characterised by a logical opposition, a practical interdependence and a mutual antagonism of interests. Throughout history one set of classes has been, it is claimed, the central, structural feature of social life, and one of the pair has dominated the other economically, politically and ideologically.

These two classic senses of the term 'class' are in marked contrast to the notion of estate. Here too the notion of differentiation takes precedence over the notion of superordination, but estates are not defined in logical opposition to one another, they are dependent not on each other but upon the whole of which they form part and any conflict of interest between them, as well as domination by one or other, is a contingent and not a necessary attribute.

In specifying the importance of social identity as a factor in redundancy events and the labour market histories of redundants it is necessary to note that estates and classes in the

Marxian sense are all identity groups as indeed are Weberian 'status groups' (which are stratified in terms of the social honour accorded to their 'styles of life'). We have already noted however that 'class' in the Marxian sense does not exhaust the notion of identity, and would add here that this is equally true of 'status groups' while occupational categories, ranked in terms of reward and honour, are merely constituents of social identity rather than definitive of it.

Now however essential these concepts are for thinking social structure, the type of concept which members employ when making choices between persons - whether for the purposes of marriage, neighbouring, selection for redundancy, permanent employment or employment as contract labour - are less specific and more diffuse. They are conceptions of 'our type of person' and involve conceptions of appropriateness: in the terminology of South Wales 'being a tidy lad', or, for example, the North American designation of some one as 'neat'. People conceive of society for <u>interactional purposes</u> as composed, that is to say, of diffuse identity groups, which are related to the hierarchies of class and status (since these are central components of identity and indeed themselves define members' identity interactionally <u>on occasion</u>), but cross cut or include class and status categories.

We need a term for the array of such member concepts and it has already been furnished to us, together with a seminal analysis by T.H. Marshall (Marshall, 1934 in Marshall, 1950). The term Marshall uses to refer to such diffuse identity groups is 'social class'. No attempt will be made to summarise here what must be one of the best short discussions in the field ever written. What follows is an attempt to convey very briefly what Marshall understands by 'social class'.

'The essence of social class', Marshall writes, 'is the way a man is treated by his fellows ... not the qualities or the possessions that cause that treatment' (Marshall, 1950, p.92). 'The objectivity of social class consists not in the criteria that distinguish it, but in the social relations it produces. Its subjectivity [consists] in the basic need for mutual conscious recognition.' (<u>ibid</u>., p.94). However far it may be the case that 'social classes' differ from one another in terms of objective characteristics and to whatever degree their members share a form of common consciousness or occupy similar positions in an honorific order it is not on the basis of these criteria that they constitute distinct social entities. 'Social class' is therefore a concept which is totally different in kind from the whole array of conceptions through which sociologists have analysed hierarchial differentiation.

Marshall would seem to regard social classes as the interactional precipitates of an historical process which has involved the disintegration of estate societies and their replacement by societies composed of classes and status groups. Any specification of 'social classes' is only intelligible against a background of an historical and structural analysis which deploys conventional class and status categories and which describes the process which precipitates them. However, once in existence 'social classes' condition the further development of that process.

The importance of the social class concept is that it provides a staging post between the specification of social structural features and observed patterns of individual action. Redundancy events and labour market studies require that we understand patterns of individual action in relation to change in structure or in relation to the changed location of persons in a structure or, as in the case of the South Wales study, both.

The reason that Marshall's concept facilitates the structure-action linkage is that his 'social classes' are identity groups in which identity is not reduced to a single component - identity determined by one structural dimension, but in which the relation to structure is maintained: Social classes, Marshall claims, are communities in that they exist 'for the sake of the internal contacts which identity makes possible', are marked by 'the relative self sufficiency of the group for its own purposes' and the boundary between them is defined by an 'attitude of comparison which recognises qualitative differences' (ibid., p.110). These qualitative differences involve members' 'concern not merely with the means but with the ends of life' (ibid., p.95) and hence with 'occupation' in the sense of the proper way for persons of a given class to occupy themselves. Hence 'social class' membership can determine occupational choice by defining what is appropriate to a person of a given identity. Because recognition of that identity 'implies the admission to certain social relationships and therefore ... the offer of a certain Lebenschance, ... social

34

class as distinct from technical and financial endowments, can influence a man's economic Lebenschance. It may affect his selection for certain types of employment' (ibid., p.92).

Marshall's conception of social class entails nothing less than that social class is an important determinant of job search and job acquisition at both normative and relational levels. Conversely the experience of redundancy and unemployment is, because of the threat posed by loss of occupation to social class identity, one that threatens also admission to social relationships with others sharing his previous identity.

Marshall's conception of 'social class' is inadequate in many ways, chiefly because, in his definition of it, there is nothing that necessarily connects it with hierarchy which the term 'class' implies. The notion to which the term refers however, that of diffuse identity group, is, I wish to suggest, of enormous utility for students of industrial life, redundancy and labour market behaviour. Quasi-ethnic and locality categories may be diffuse identity groups in Marshall's sense and, like social class, be understood as the product of the same historical process and as, in turn, conditioning it.

Redundancy, from a Marshallian perspective, constitutes a change at the structural level of a local society which has profound consequences for the identities and relationships of the persons affected by it. This it does by affecting the operation of the labour market at the same time as those made redundant are thrown onto it. What then ensues is a struggle by the redundants on the market, to use their diffuse identities as a means of maintaining those social identities and the social relations constitutive of them. But if not merely the number of different types of positions changes as the result of the redundancy event but new positions appear as the result of the transformation of the labour process, then the identity problems created by the redundancies will not merely be an aggregate of personal troubles but problems associated with a social structural transition out of which new diffuse identity groups will eventually arise.

Controversies arising from plant closures and lay offs certainly constitute public issues; but public issues are not to be confused with the transformation of the collective life of the society which involves changes, as Durkheim pointed

35

out long ago, in the way people are grouped. The concept of 'diffuse identity groups' (Marshallian 'social "classes"') is, I wish to suggest, an invaluable concept which not only sensitises the sociologist to the linkage between personal troubles, public issues and social transitions but refers to a fundamental feature of social reality which is the site of those linkages. As such it bridges the gap between structural statements about class and status and observations of changing behaviour of individuals in economic and political life, and is therefore an invaluable adjunct to class analysis.

Redundancy events are therefore to be understood as events having potential consequences for working class consciousness and organisation by affecting worker experience of the labour market, and they constitute changes in the structure of positions as well as affecting the experience of persons, and hence affect the operation of the labour market. But they also have potential consequences for the social identity of the individuals made redundant and the composition and character of the diffuse identity groups of which the local labour market (in the sense of two sets of persons who are respectively potential buyers and sellers of the same labour power) is made up.

Conversely the post-redundancy labour market career of redundant workers will be profoundly affected not only by their skill and experience (as indexed by their previous position in the technical division of labour in the plant they have left) and their previous work and labour market histories; it will also be affected by their local identity group membership. The actions of redundant workers while on the market are to be understood, not merely as an attempt to regain employment, but also as an attempt to maintain their identity group membership by utilising their social identity and the social relationships it produces in their efforts to obtain the sort of employment which confirms that identity.

A shift towards the flexible firm will therefore not merely mean that more workers have continuous experience of the 'play of chance and caprice in the market' as a result of redundancy events which have changed the available number of permanent positions and generated a demand for contract labour. Such a shift will also constitute a threat to the social identities of some of the redundants, leading those so threatened to employ the resources supplied by their pre-redundancy identity group membership in the attempt to sustain it.

The Port Talbot study revealed that as a result of the shift of BSC in the direction of the flexible firm, the largest single category of redundants had experienced neither permanent unemployment, self-employment, or return to employment but had broken work histories or 'chequered' labour market careers consisting of a series of spells of employment and unemployment. Some workers appeared, that is to say, to have become members of a _peripheral_ workforce supplying the intermittent needs of the new flexible firm. Yet it is not clear why it was those particular workers and not others who had become peripheral workers rather than employed, permanently unemployed, self-employed. Nor is it clear how the position of this category of workers in the class structure should be understood.

The second issue can be resolved, in the terms of this paper, by regarding these peripheral workers as a class fraction whose members are distinguished by their position, not in the productive process, but in the labour market: they share a propensity for obtaining a particular type of position in the productive process. In Marxian terms, this transition from core to peripheral workforce is likely to increase their class _consciousness_ in the sense of their awareness of their dependence on the market, while their experience of competition in the market is likely to decrease their sense of solidarity with other workers and their peripherality will limit their capacity for class organisation.

The first issue can now be rephrased: what are the social determinants of their occupancy of the distinctive labour market position which they share? The answer is of course 'their labour market position' defined this time, not in terms of their chances of obtaining a certain type of employment but, in terms of their location in a local market conceived of as a population subdivided into a plurality of diffuse identity groups. For such membership not only provides information about job opportunities to the worker and information about the reputation of the worker to the employer, it also determines how this information is used: to avoid longer term unemployment by taking fixed term employments - a sort of 'market' tradedown - or the rejection of such work as inconsistent with the worker's social identity and the decision to 'hang in there' until an opportunity for permanent employment turns up.

Redundancy events are therefore implicated in class analysis in two ways. First, they constitute mechanisms/events, linking changes in the product and labour markets with changes in the labour process, which are moments in a process whereby the composition of classes is continually being changed. Secondly, the outcome of those events is conditioned by the structure of the local labour market in the sense of a population made up of identity groups. It is the membership of these groups as well as the objective characteristics of the worker and of the market which is a determinant of the answer to the classic economic question: who gets how much of what, when?

Redundancy and Class Analysis

REFERENCES

Atkinson, J. (1984) 'Manpower Strategies for Flexible Organisations' Personnel Management, 16, 28-31

Goffman, E. (1952) 'On Cooling the Mark Out', Psychiatry, 15, 451-63

Grieco, M. (1985) Information Networks and the Allocation of Employment Opportunities, Unpublished PhD thesis, Oxford University

Lee, R.M. (1985) 'Redundancy, Labour Markets and Informal Relations', Sociological Review, 33, 469-94

Lee, R.M. and C.C. Harris, (1985) 'Redundancy Studies in Port Talbot and the Future', Quarterly Journal of Social Affairs, 1, 19-27

Marshall, T.H. (1933) 'Social Class: A Preliminary Analysis' in T.H. Marshall (1950) Citizenship and Social Class, Cambridge University Press, Cambridge, 66-114

Marx, K.H. (1967) Capital, Vol. I, Lawrence and Wishart, London

Mohun, S. (1983) 'The Division of Labour' in T. Bottomore, A Dictionary of Marxist Thought, Blackwell, Oxford, 131-4

Morgan, K. (1983) 'Restructuring Steel' International Journal of Urban and Regional Research, 7, 175-211

Chapter Three

REDUNDANT POPULATIONS: DEINDUSTRIALISATION IN A NORTH-EAST ENGLISH TOWN[1]

Lydia Morris

We are perhaps most familiar with the term 'redundancy' as applied to individuals shed from the labour-force of an enterprise facing financial crisis, restructuring, or 'rationalisation'. Indeed the study of redundancy has traditionally examined the fate of such workers on re-entering the labour market[2], redundancy thus being conceived of as a moment in an individual's work history, transitional to some other state. Martin Bulmer (1971) has discussed some of the limitations of this 'individual' approach, pointing out that redundancy is a selective process, the nature of which will shape the labour-market prospects of those workers affected. However, these prospects will vary not just according to <u>individual</u> characteristics, but also with the characteristics of the labour market, the nature and number of opportunities for employment, and systems of selective recruitment to these opportunities. To focus on the individual worker might have some advantages at times of full-employment and in a fairly loose and stable labour-market. The study of redundancy in recession, when unemployment is high and when national economies, industrial sectors and individual enterprise may be experiencing radical changes in their basic structure, raises very different sorts of questions which require a broader framework for analysis. Thus the focus of 'redundancy' research must shift away from the isolated experience of· the individual and towards a concern with changes in the demand for labour, and more particularly for different types of labour, and the implications of such change for local social structures.

Decline in heavy manufacturing was first apparent in the U.K. in the 1930s and industrial restructuring has arguably been underway since that

time. A more recent turning point was reached in
the mid-sixties, when workers in manufacturing
began to decline not just as a proportion of the
total employed in the economy as a whole, but in
terms of the absolute number of jobs involved
(Massey, 1984: 133). This process of 'deindustrialisation' has affected some geographical areas more
dramatically than others, and produced what have
been referred to as 'redundant spaces' (Anderson
et. al., 1983); industrial graveyards of fixed
capital, with large unemployed or underemployed
populations.

In her book Spatial Divisions of Labour Doreen
Massey (1984) discusses the process by which social
and spatial changes in the recent past have been
interwoven. She argues that the spatial pattern of
production established in the nineteenth century
was based on access to ports, labour supply, and
coal, and that the national geography of employment
from this time, up until the 1930s, was essentially
moulded by a small group of industries - iron and
steel manufacture, ship-building, and the mining
and export of coal. These industries concentrated
production in a small number of regions, presumably
in response to locational advantage, and:

> It was only when the U.K.'s relation to the
> international economy changed, with its
> decline as a world trading power, that
> production in these industries fell drastically
> and those previously dominant spatial structures
> produced a regional problem. (Massey, 1984:
> 129).

Industrial decline and the movement of capital to
other sectors, and other locations has left large
areas and populations redundant.

Attempts to understand the resultant changes
in social and economic structure have borrowed much
from the sociology of underdevelopment, which has
placed the study of redundancy in a slightly
different context from that discussed earlier.
Social scientists are increasingly required to ask
questions about those populations most affected by
industrial decline, and to focus on redundant towns
or even regions, as well as redundant individuals.
Hartlepool, a town of some 98,000 on the North-East
coast of England, provides us with a classic case.

BACKGROUND TO HARTLEPOOL[3]

The development of Hartlepool from the early 1800s is partly to be understood through its strategic location on the North East coast of Britain. From about 1830 it became established as a port for the export of coal, and soon developed a thriving shipyard. Metal manufacture grew up as a natural adjunct of these activities and thus the town and its workforce acquired their distinctive characteristics; skills built around male employment in construction, engineering and metals, supported by women's domestic services and associated with a rigid traditional sexual division of labour.

Hartlepool's present decline can be traced back to the rundown of ship-building in the late 1950's, an industry which disappeared completely from the town by the early sixties. In 1962 unemployment had reached 15 per cent, although the local economy saw some respite before the onset of recession in the late seventies. Higher levels of public spending, a growth in service sector jobs, and the attraction of new manufacturing industries all contributed to a rise in women's employment, previously low by national standards, whilst also assisting in the temporary maintenance of male employment levels. Opportunities for men were additionally buoyed up by construction work - town centre redevelopment, the completion of a nuclear power station, and a nascent oil and gas industry. By the late seventies all such sources of employment had dwindled, added to which the restructuring of the British Steel Corporation brought the elimination of steel production from Hartlepool. Between 1976 and 1981 total jobs in the town fell by 19 per cent, a loss predominantly borne by the male workforce.

The pattern is by now familiar: a town once dominated by employment in construction, engineering and metal manufacture has passed through a series of transitional stages to emerge with a local economy weakened in every sphere. There have been shifts in emphasis from manufacturing to services, from male employment to female employment, and from full-time to part-time work, whilst alongside these changes the town has, since 1975, known unremitting increases in unemployment.

There have been related changes not only in the amount of employment available, but also in the nature and duration of that employment, in employers' methods of recruitment, in differential access to work opportunities and in the functioning of informal sector activity. In the pages to follow I shall briefly consider the implications of these changes for the social structure in Hartlepool, and examine some of the perspectives available for the understanding and representation of the effects of industrial decline.

THE CHANGING NATURE OF WORK

Employment on a short-term contract basis is not new in Hartlepool, but it was possible in the past to run one contract on from another and thus sustain uninterrupted employment, notably in construction, haulage and maintenance work. Such opportunities seemed plentiful even in the '70s when the oil and gas boom meant a flood of highly paid construction contracts. Although economic decline has undermined the security of long-term employment, the distinction between this 'safe' employment and short-term contract work has become more marked. Sub-contracting in many areas of the economy has fallen off as a result of 'deindustrialisation' with openings in construction, maintenance, transport and haulage much reduced. There has, however, been a change in the relation between these two types of employment, and a number of management strategies at work to produce this effect.

Transport, for example is an area in which the use of contractors seems to be increasing, and will continue to do so with the privatisation of local authority services. Companies which previously maintained their own transport system have been moving towards the use of owner drivers, whilst large haulage companies are themselves increasing the use of smaller scale contractors as a means of trimming their core workforce to a minimum.

Similarly, increased competition between contractors as a result of decline may encourage large enterprise to hive off new areas of maintenance work for sub-contracting. Conversely, increased flexibility in work practice among a core of permanent employees can be used to reduce the amount of maintenance work available for contractors, at a time when inducements to self-employment may have increased the number of firms competing for work in any given area.

It is not yet possible to quantify the effects of these various changes. Data collected at the household level make it clear that recession has meant a fall in employment opportunities over-all, and diminished possibilities of continuous employment achieved through a series of short-term contracts. It may nevertheless be that intermittent employment is rising as a proportion of total employment, whilst falling in absolute terms. There is, however, some indication that preferential access to such employment means a small and privileged section of the unemployed population will have their unemployment broken by spells of temporary work, in contrast to a large and growing concentration of long-term unemployed who lack the skills and contacts necessary to secure such work.[4]

Another aspect of change in the structuring of employment has been the use made of part-time labour. Part-time employment of women in manufacturing has commonly been used to tap an otherwise unavailable labour force in periods of expansion, by providing paid work which can accommodate women's domestic obligations. In decline, such employment serves as a means of coping with reduced demand, but offers in either circumstance a supply of cheap workers with minimal protection against dismissal. The growth in part-time service employment for women at a time when all other employment is falling also suggests at least some substitution of part-time workers for full-time.[5]

THE INFORMAL SECTOR OF THE ECONOMY

Cash-in-hand jobs, also part-time, have traditionally provided a means by which married women could find work that did not disrupt their domestic patterns. During times of high male unemployment such 'informal' work, (i.e. that which bypasses systems of national accounting) will also provide a means of augmenting supplementary benefit without the deductions that formal employment would entail.[6] The availability of informal employment for men seems likely to have increased with recession, as employers take advantage of large numbers of potential employees living on minimal state benefit. This is especially true of the small scale contractor seeking to keep tenders low and the formal workforce at a minimum, and also less likely to be bound by union requirements (Fevre, 1985). Nevertheless, opportunities of informal employment for the unemployed are clearly limited, and as much the object of competition between workers as are

formal jobs. The use of small scale contractors by
larger, established enterprise will mean that the
ultimate beneficiary of much informal employment is
the large, legitimate company, whilst the corollary
of this is that informal employment is to a great
extent dependent on the formal sector of the
economy. Although economic decline and the
consequent creation of a pool of unemployed labour
will produce the conditions under which informal
employment is most likely to flourish, there is a
sense in which such employment will be limited by
the recession, just as are other areas of economic
activity.

In the case of Hartlepool there is evidence,
however, of other kinds of informal activity:

a) There is the provision of services which
depend on the informal network of clients,
and usually on skills acquired in previous
employment, e.g. plumbing, electrics,
joinery, etc. The people offering these
skills may be employed, unemployed or
self-employed though their clients are
usually waged. It is not yet clear whether
there is any increasing tendency for the
practitioners to be found among the
unemployed, offering cheap services to
others in employment.

b) 'Jobbing' is a term used in Hartlepool to
refer to a rather different practice which
is exclusive to those without formal
employment. It depends rather less on
particular skills and contracts, and more
on the ability to persuade potential
clients to have work done - usually
roofing and exterior painting - i.e. jobs
which are visible from the outside thus
signalling prospective customers. Relatively
prosperous areas will be selected for
canvassing, and may well lie outside of
Hartlepool where the potential is reckoned
to be almost exhausted, and where
competition is fierce. This is a case of
the unemployed servicing those in employment.

c) 'Scrapping' is described as the winter
alternative to jobbing, and long hours are
spent scouring tips, roadsides and factory
sites for scrap metal, sold for fairly
nominal sums to local yards. This kind of
scavenging is illegal and only marginally
profitable. It seems to be practised as

much to permit the separation and maintenance of gender roles as for financial rewards. A parallel may be drawn with poaching, and fishing which are used in a similar way, whilst coal-digging provides an example of a rather more lucrative scavenger activity. The slag from pits along the coast is tipped into the sea to be washed up on the beach and sold to local coal merchants. Vendors may be legitimately 'self-employed' but are more probably claiming social security benefit, and almost certainly employing others who do so.

d) In addition to the activities outlined above there is plentiful evidence of systems of mutual aid, in money and in kind, which passes between the employed and the unemployed, and also circulates within these groups. It is not yet possible to say whether exchange across or within employment categories is of more significance, which has the greater long-term viability, or what the role of generational differences could be in mediating exchange.

Despite these varied pursuits, there are large numbers of unemployed people excluded from all possibility of employment of whatever kind, without the skill or ability to exploit such informal opportunities as do exist, cut off from all forms of support in the locality, and totally dependent on benefit.

CONCEPTUALISING INFORMAL ACTIVITY

Development of interest in, and debate about, changes in social structure wrought by the process of deindustrialisation follows on the heels of a long-established literature concerned with 'under-employment' and 'marginality' in third world societies (Nun, 1969; Quijano, 1974; Perlman, 1976). Early work focused on the survival strategies of the urban poor, but became increasingly theoretical in orientation as writers sought to analyse and explain the nature of the relationship between informal activity and the formal sector of the economy. In this context it was considered imperative to discuss unemployment, underemployment and marginality in terms of their position within the total economic structure, rather than as characteristics of particular kinds of individuals living in particular sorts of areas. Thus, the survival strategies of the poor came to be seen as an integral part of the development of a capitalist system.

A definitional point is perhaps appropriate here. The notion of the informal sector in third world countries, where national statistics are notoriously unreliable, is much broader than in the U.K. Thus, the term 'informal' implies something about the scale and organisation of operations rather than their legal status:

> Third world writers have concentrated largely upon employment in small enterprises (including one man businesses) in the fields of artisanal production and trade, which often provides the main source of income for the individuals concerned ... on the whole, then, the term 'informal economy' has tended to be used in Third World literature to refer to small-scale productive or trading enterprises in towns (Bryant, 1982: 3).

For the developed world, a greater confidence in the reliability of official data[7], has restricted our use of 'formal' to the official, legal, recorded activities of legitimate enterprise. The result has been to encourage a somewhat unhelpful distinction between intermittent employment, self-employment, and informal employment; and an equally unhelpful association between informal employment and self-generated 'survival' or reproductive activities. Other difficulties follow from these associations, and conceptual confusion has led many writers to question the validity of the notion of 'the informal', and the utility of equating activities as diverse as clandestine wage labour, petty theft, remunerated personal/household services, and unpaid domestic and communal labour (Connolly, 1985).

For the informal sector as a whole, conceptual unity depends on its being opposed in some way to the formal, but there is considerable variety to be found in analyses of the precise nature of the relationship between the spheres. Ray Pahl (1980), is one writer who has shifted away from viewing informal activity as a·possible alternative to formal work, and towards a position which stresses its dependence upon resources and contacts in the formal sector (Pahl, 1984). Ferman and Berndt (1981) largely endorse this view, but place stress on the inter-dependence of different sectors. Hence, whilst the irregular sector of the economy is dependent upon the formal as a source of goods, it acts as a:

> consumer, distributor and maintainer of products produced in the regular economy, and it is a producer of products sold in the regular economy.

Other writers (Gerry and Birckbeck, 1981) have emphasised the ways in which informal activity can serve the formal sector, paralleling the discussion of informality, marginality and petty commodity production in the third world. Perhaps the most straightforward example of this approach is to be found in the consideration of the small firm which may employ workers 'unofficially' and be contracted to service larger enterprise. Similarly, changes in the structure of formal employment opportunities, the phenomena of intermittent employment, part-time employment and 'informal' employment may be related, as in the present paper, to economic decline and particular management strategies designed to cope with its consequences. In this sense, informal sector activity is but one end of a spectrum of changes in the organisation of production in response to recession.

It is not clear precisely how survival mechanisms, self-provisioning and the delivery of personal services to clients through the informal sector would be accommodated by this approach, though some writers have chosen to focus on the varying relationship between capital accumulation and social reproduction as a means of theorising such activities (Gerry, 1985). Within this framework informal, self-generated employment defrays the costs to the state of maintaining the population of unemployed, whilst the provision of cheap services to those in employment is argued to subsidise wages in the formal sector. In addition, we may take the point made initially by a number of feminist writers[8], that labour performed outside the immediate sphere of production makes a vital contribution to social reproduction through the daily and generational maintenance of the labour force. This has some bearing on how we may conceptualise the workings of different sectors of

the economy, and how to understand the changing
inter-relations which necessarily follow from a
reduction in the number of formally waged workers.

RESERVE ARMY AND SURPLUS POPULATION

Key orienting concepts in the discussion of these
issues have been 'the reserve army of labour' and
'the surplus population', concepts which have been
used in analysing the effects of both deindustrialisation and underdevelopment. The former places
emphasis on relations of production, whilst the
latter is <u>centrally</u> concerned with social reproduction. Friend and Metcalf (1981) have noted the
theoretical distinction between these two concepts.
The reserve army of labour, they maintain, both
supplies labour power when a branch of production
expands, and serves to regulate wages. The surplus
population, they suggest, embraces a wider stratum
of the working class than the unemployed. They
include in their definition casual workers
intermittently employed, part-time workers, participants in the 'black economy', and all those
dependent on state benefits.
    Empirically, the distinction between these two
terms becomes blurred, since we have seen in recent
years that definitions of what constitutes the
labour-force, as opposed to the dependent population
will be influenced by changes in the official
classification for purposes of benefit payment, and
the removal in Britain of certain categories from
the unemployment register.[9] Favouring the term
'surplus population' Friend and Metcalf state:

> This broad definition embraces the majority of
> those living in urban areas who are unemployed
> because they are marginal to the requirements
> of capital in terms of the direct production
> of surplus value during the current long wave
> of recession.

Their statement begs the critical question of
precisely what is meant by 'marginal'; at what
point does a population become 'surplus'?

UNDERDEVELOPMENT AND DEINDUSTRIALISATION

This question has been the subject of some debate,
albeit inconclusive, with reference to third world

urbanization. The point at which a <u>relative</u> surplus
population becomes an <u>absolute</u> surplus is generally
taken to refer to the moment when its presence
becomes inimical to capital accumulation (Quijano,
1974). This stage will be reached under different
circumstances in different societies, and the
nature of the crisis which follows will also be
variable. In many third world societies, for
example, in the absence of adequate state welfare
provision, political concern has focussed on
congested major cities, the threat of social
unrest, and challenge to the established regime as
a result of large concentrations of people living
in dire poverty. A well developed public assistance
system can function to some extent to diffuse the
potential for political instability as a result of
concentrations of unemployment and poverty. It
creates a significant role in <u>consumption</u> for those
excluded from production, but may also trigger off
a new kind of crisis; what O'Connor (1973) has
termed the fiscal crisis of the state. This occurs
where state expenditure on both 'social investment'
and 'social consumption' outstrips state revenue to
an unacceptable degree.

We have already seen doubts cast on the
utility of 'the informal' as a unifying concept for
a varied range of activity. Distinctions of the
sort made above also throw a certain doubt on the
validity of comparisons made between deindustrialising
(or over-developed) and under-developed societies.
Certainly there are striking, if superficial,
similarities - high levels of unemployment and
under-employment, 'irregular' employment existing
outside of a legal framework, informal survival
strategies in part dependent on networks of mutual
aid, etc. ... but these characteristics are
symptomatic of somewhat different causes.

In the case of deindustrialisation the
(relative) surplus population is swelled by
redundant workers expelled from restructured
industry; in third world cities it is swelled by
rural-urban migrants seeking access to industrial
employment, possibly for the first time. Attitudes
to work, and general levels of expectation, will
inevitably be coloured by previous experience of
employment, trade union membership, minimal
material requirements, etc. ... which will differ
between the developed and developing world. But
there is a further important distinction to be
made.

Interest in the (broadly defined) informal

sector of Third World economies has partly stemmed from optimism on the part of governments about its job creating potential through self-employment. The point has been made, however, that in so far as we see the informal sector as harnessed to the needs of capital accumulation then it can have no autonomous capacity to generate employment (Rainnie, 1985). Where a country is experiencing an increase in productive capacity through industrialisation, as are some Third World countries, then there may be related growth of informal opportunities. In the U.K. however, although there has been a reorganisation of production which, in proportional terms, favours the informal sector, self-employment and the 'small' firm, industrial decline would seem to make hopes for a solution to unemployment through self-generated employment largely unjustified.

What the economies of Third World and developed countries do have in common then is simply that both have produced a population providing low cost services to industry and to the regularly employed population of workers, constructing systems of mutual aid based on the communal exchange of goods and services, and investing considerable time and energy in work for 'self-consumption'.

INFORMALISATION AND SOCIAL REPRODUCTION

Mingione (1985), in discussing what he considers to be an increase in informal activity, has made the helpful observation that the place of the informal sector in relation to the total economy will vary with a number of factors: stage of economic development, labour market conditions, and the availability of state assistance. The points of balance between work for 'self-consumption' and work for income will accordingly vary between societies, he argues. Nevertheless, he seems to find no problem in equating the processes occurring in developed and under-developed societies. He traces the emergence of what he terms the relative surplus population in the developed world to a decrease in employment in manufacturing, the failure of service employment to make good the job gap, and the development of labour saving technologies. He also argues, in this context, that production in under-developed countries can never hope to absorb the surplus populations accumulating around the major cities. Crisis of production, he argues, has been accompanied in developed countries by the restructuring of employment opportunities leading to 'fragmentation, Balkanization and the emergence of modern double and informal employment'.

Having made this point, however, he moves on to concentrate not on the realm of production but on the process of social reproduction:

> The umbilical cord of industrialisation and of employment growth had permitted the categorization of the relative surplus population as a reserve industrial labour force, and the under-developed area as a site for future industrial expansion. With its rupture[10], the reproduction of vast, increasingly urban masses seems to be pointless and to presage survival in a poverty to which, at least as far as industrial employment is concerned, there is no solution. (1985: 19)

Essentially he is arguing that the situation facing the modern world has produced rates of unemployment so high that to conceive of the jobless population as a 'reserve army of labour' is no longer useful or appropriate. The crisis in production, he argues, has been transmitted to the reproductive system. In this analysis the informal sector is seen primarily as a way of getting by rather than as a bolster to the formal economy. What follows will be the diminution of monetary income, falling standards of living, increasing work for self-consumption, and 'various forms of informal activities' (unspecified). He also notes the possibility that informalization can, in part, relieve the fiscal crisis of the state discussed by writers such as O'Connor and Gough (1975). In other words, he is suggesting that the costs of reproduction crisis are met by the 'survival strategies' of the poor. Speaking of both developed and underdeveloped societies he suggests that:

> The survival strategies of these two sections of the surplus population are becoming crucial in shaping the present and future problems of societies.

He argues that within the constraints of labour demand, which may be changing in nature with attempts to reduce production costs, households will combine their labour resources - through formal and informal employment, domestic labour and communal exchange - in the construction of a variety of strategies. The resulting patterns will vary with locality, since they represent responses to specific conditions, localised traditions, shifting opportunities etc.

HOUSEHOLD STRATEGIES

In the late 1970s Ray Pahl set out to document the emergence of different household strategies on the Isle of Sheppey in South-East England. The relationship between different categories of work was felt to be changing, to the advantage of the informal sector of the economy; households, it was argued, were increasingly performing their own services and engaging in reciprocal exchange with other households. In other words, <u>people were reclaiming the right to define and organise their work</u>. A number of loosely formulated ideas and assumptions sprang forth (Pahl, 1980). It was suggested, for example, that in the workings of the informal economy the poor may be advantaged because of previously constructed support systems and experience of hardship, and the idea was floated that those with least incorporation into the formal sector might be best placed in the informal - provided they had available the appropriate skills, and a network of contacts through which to exploit them. The reorganisation of work was also assumed to be occurring not simply between sectors and between households but <u>within</u> the home. Household members were, according to Pahl, assessing their situation, their prospects and their needs, and working out an appropriate strategy:

> no longer do we have ... a universal, sex-linked division between the male 'chief earner' in the formal economy and his unpaid and dependent wife engaged in unremunerated housework. Nor is there such a rigidly sex-linked division of labour between men and women in the practice of domestic work.

These early ideas were soon to be questioned by Pahl himself, and by work being carried out in a number of related areas. A critical issue was clearly that of the distribution of opportunities for work, whether formal or informal. The mechanisms of access to work, the social production of unemployment, and the translation of these processes into change at the level of the household and the local social structure were all in need of detailed investigation.

Pahl and Gershuny (1981) began to make the point that unemployment is unequally distributed both geographically and socially, that the decline in work opportunities is borne disproportionately by low skill and low status groups, and that:

> Rather than being able to <u>choose</u> work categories, particular social groups are forced to accept unemployment through specific patterns of incidence in reduction of work opportunities ... high unemployment means related local poverty and hence restricted markets for 'black economy' products and services.

This is simply to recognise that household strategies cannot be understood in isolation from the labour market, but are closely tied to factors <u>external</u> to the home which structure the nature and distribution of 'work' opportunities. Indeed, in contrast to his earlier optimistic work, Pahl's latest writing (Pahl, 1984) concludes that there is a polarisation in society which rests upon differential access to work opportunities in <u>both</u> the formal and informal sectors. Thus, far from being advantaged in the informal sector of the economy, those excluded from the formal are disadvantaged in every sphere.

The major criticism to be made of the approach Pahl developed with Gershuny is that although they stress throughout their work that household strategies should be understood as operating within cultural, social and gender constraints, and as varying with labour market conditions, they take no significant steps towards detailing or theorising this variety. Despite disclaimers to the contrary they also persist in treating the household as an unproblematic unit when a long tradition of anthropological studies, as well as more recent feminist work (Young, <u>et</u>. <u>al</u>., 1981), cautions against it. Nevertheless, their writing has certainly raised some challenging questions about how to integrate studies at the level of the household with analysis of changes in economic structure.

The problem with a household strategy approach to these questions is that in focussing on the everyday experience of individuals in households it may confuse our attempts to distinguish a number of different processes in operation which could help to clarify certain aspects of the reserve army/surplus population debate, the nature of 'informality' and the changing shape of social structure.

Data from Hartlepool have been used so far in this paper to draw attention to two distinct processes of change:

a) managerial strategies for the reorganisation of production to manage decline,
b) development of strategies by the redundant population to maximise their 'reproductive' or 'survival' potential.

This is to make a somewhat artificial distinction between production and reproduction which, whilst not to be understood as a denial of the inter-relation between these two processes, nevertheless enables us to address slightly different questions:

1) How do high levels of unemployment provoke and facilitate a restructuring of production and employment opportunities through the creation of a pool of available labour?
2) Given insecurity or exclusion in relation to the immediate productive process, what other opportunities are available to individuals or households in the creation of survival strategies?

Having established our interest in these two distinct questions we may <u>then</u> raise questions about how household strategies are constructed and what the distributive mechanisms for work opportunities might be.

STRATEGIES OR STRUCTURES?

There has long been considerable research interest shown in the question of how people in receipt of inadequate income survive, and such interest clearly bridges the divide between the sociology of the developed and the under-developed world. Much of this literature focused on the role of the extended family and/or local social networks in the provision of mutual aid and the construction of 'strategies for survival'. In this context social relations have come to be seen as a structured set of arrangements for the provision of goods and services; i.e. as vehicles for certain kinds of economic transaction. They are also the means by which a system of social conventions governing the nature of these transactions, is established and maintained.

It is thus argued that the apparently disorganised nature of life in the ghettoes, slums and shanty towns rests in fact on a highly organised and tightly structured base of informal relations. Around these structures are said to emerge clearly formulated rules and sanctions to regulate the exchanges which flow from informal associations of kinship and friendship. Such linkages form what Ferman and Berndt (1981) term the 'structural underpinnings' of the informal sector of the economy. Pahl's thinking on informal exchanges clearly followed a similar path when he suggested that people who have developed locality-based social networks would be in a stronger position than those who remained dependent on the market (Pahl, 1980). His argument in 'Divisions of Labour' (Pahl, 1984) however, focuses so sharply on the polarisation of households that the nature and significance of links between them is not fully explored and the processes that lie behind the polarisation are never satisfactorily discussed. A similar difficulty can arise from the uncritical application of the notion of the surplus population.

The significance of a web of contacts established through informal social relations could play a part in identifying and clarifying such processes, and certainly need not be confined to the study of the informal sector of the economy. The nature and content of informal exchanges clearly have an important place in the study of certain aspects of formal employment opportunities, notably through the transmission of information, influence and reputation in recruitment. The importance of this kind of analysis is that it illuminates certain aspects of the argument concerning survival strategies, work opportunities, access to supportive resources, etc. Put at its simplest the idea that contacts and resources are differentially distributed according to position in a local social structure raises the question of to what extent survival strategies are structured by factors external to the household. This in turn suggests constraints on the nature and degree of flexibility which it is possible to achieve. In this light Pahl's findings open up questions about the relationship between the social poles he has identified; the characteristics of the area lying between those poles, the structures of support which operate to maintain the division, and the nature of the processes which produced it.

SOCIAL POLARISATION?

We may accept as a basic premiss that there is a process of polarisation at work in society which separates those with work from those without, and that this polarisation extends to areas of informal employment and mutual exchange of services. There is inevitably <u>some</u> degree of polarisation in a society where unemployment has reached 13.4 per cent nationally and stands as high as 25 per cent in some areas, but the detailed implications for the social structure of particular localities remain to be spelt out. In Hartlepool we have seen changes in employment prospects and changes in the organisation of production which have led to intermittent employment patterns within a particular section of the population - those with specific skills and experience, together with the contacts required to gain knowledge of, and access to, available opportunities. Amongst the unemployed they constitute a category with privileged access to employment.

Alongside this phenomenon we have noted the development of self-generated economic activity - either in service provision, or various scavenger activities, and have thus been led to make the following distinctions: between core and peripheral jobs; secure and insecure employment; 'formal' and 'informal' or unofficial work; between different aspects of informal activity which are self-generated rather than employer based; and between the unemployed who have access to such opportunities and those who do not. The implications are that with the category of 'the unemployed' in Hartlepool one finds:

a) a section of the population channelled into temporary, sometimes 'unofficial', employment,
b) a service underclass performing low cost services for those in employment,

      c)   a scavenging unemployed segment driven to scrapping, poaching, coal-digging,

      d)   a system of mutual aid which may cross these and other employment boundaries,

      e)   a truly isolated population of unemployed people.

These divisions, whilst representing different types of activity, carry no necessary implications for the emergence of distinctive or exclusive social groupings, their inter-relations or relative fixity. What would appear to be the case is that the existence of a 'redundant' population has facilitated a shift in employment patterns, whilst also fuelling the provision of low cost services to the employed and bolstering consumer demand for goods. This population, however, will be internally differentiated by access to temporary employment, varied capacity for producing self-generated survival strategies, and differing resources in the form of communal support patterns. Whilst the study of deindustrialisation has advanced to some extent by borrowing from a pre-existing literature on Third World societies, conceptualisations in terms of 'reserve army', 'surplus population', or indeed social polarisation, can only begin to open the way to more detailed mapping of locally specific changes in the composition of 'redundant' populations.

NOTES

1.   This paper is based on research carried
out in my capacity as New Blood lecturer at the
University of Durham.
2.   For a discussion of relevant material see
Wood and Cohen, 1977-8.
3.   A fuller account of this background data
is to appear in a forthcoming ESRC publication.
4.   Findings in S. Wales reported a similar
pattern of intermittent employment in contracting
firms, with opportunities channelled through
informal networks of contacts (Morris, 1984).
5.   Part-time employment reduces the cost to
the employer by cutting the National Insurance
contribution.
6.   In Britain a man claiming Supplementary
Benefit will have his allowance reduced in line
with his wife's declared earnings.
7.   A confidence now somewhat shaken as
difficulties associated with estimating the size of
the black economy become apparent.
8.   A position developed in the extensive
literature now referred to as the 'Domestic Labour
Debate'. For a review see Harris, 1983, Ch. 10.
9.   Observer 15.9.85, 'Tampering Hides 1m.
Jobless, says Labour'.
10.   i.e. the 'umbilical cord'.

REFERENCES

Anderson, J., S.Duncan and R. Hudson (1983)
    Redundant Spaces in Cities and Regions,
    Academic Press, London
Bryant, J. (1982) 'An Introductory Bibliography of
    Work on the Informal Economy in Third World
    Literature' in J. Laite, Bibliographies on
    Local Labour Markets and the Informal Economy,
    SSRC, London
Bulmer, M. (1971) 'Mining Redundancy: A Case Study
    of the Workings of the Redundancy Payments Act
    in the Durham Coalfield, Industrial Relations
    Journal, 2, 3-21
Connolly, P. (1985) 'The Politics of the Informal
    Sector: a Critique', in N. Redclift and E.
    Mingione, Beyond Employment, Blackwell,
    Oxford, pp. 55-91
Ferman, L.A. and L.E. Berndt (1981) 'The Irregular
    Economy' in S. Henry, Can I Have It In Cash?,
    Astragal Books, London, pp. 26-42
Fevre, R. (1986) 'Contract Work in the Recession'
    in S. Wood and K. Purcell, The Changing Exper-
    ience of Work, Macmillan, London
Friend, A. and A. Metcalf (1981) Slump City, Pluto
    Press, London
Gerry, C. (1985) 'The Working Class and Small
    Enterprises in the UK Recession' in
    N. Redclift and E. Mingione, Beyond Employ-
    ment, Blackwell, Oxford, pp. 288-316
Gerry, C. and C. Birkbeck (1981) 'The Petty
    Commodity Producer in Third World Cities' in
    F. Bechhofer and B. Elliott, The Petite
    Bourgeoisie, Macmillan, London, pp. 121-5
Gershuny, J. and R.E. Pahl (1981) 'Work Outside
    Employment' in S. Henry, Can I Have It in
    Cash?, Astragal Books, London, pp. 73-88
Harris, C.C. (1983) The Family in Industrial
    Society, Allen and Unwin, London
Massey, D. (1984) Spatial Divisions of Labour,
    Macmillan, London
Mingione, E. (1985) 'Social Reproduction and the
    Surplus Labour Force' in N. Redclift and
    E. Mingione, Beyond Employment, Blackwell,
    Oxford, pp. 14-54
Morris, L.D. (1984) 'Patterns of Social Activity
    and Post-redundancy Labour Market Experience',
    Sociology, 18, 339-52
Nun, J. (1969) 'Superpoblacion Relativa, Erjercito
    Industrial de Reserva y Masa Marginal' Revista
    Latinoamericana de Sociologia, 5, 178-235

Pahl, R.E. (1980) 'Employment, Work and the Domestic Division of Labour', <u>International Journal of Urban and Regional Research</u>, <u>4</u>, 1-19

Pahl, R.E. (1984) <u>Divisions of Labour</u>, Blackwell, Oxford

Perlman, J. (1976) <u>The Myth of Marginality</u>, University of California Press, Berkeley

Quijano, O.A. (1974) 'The Marginal Pole of the Economy and the Marginalised Labour Force', <u>Economy and Society</u>, <u>3</u>, 393-428

Rainnie, A. (1985) 'Small Firms, Big Problems', <u>Capital and Class</u>, <u>25</u>, 140-68

Wood, S. and J. Cohen (1977-78) 'Approaches to the Study of Redundancy', <u>Industrial Relations Journal</u>, <u>8</u>, 19-27

Young, K., C. Wolkowitz and R. McGillagh (1981) <u>Of Marriage and the Market</u>, CSE Books, London

Chapter Four

REDUNDANCY AND THE LABOUR MARKET: THE ROLE OF 'READAPTATION BENEFITS'[1]

Ralph Fevre

Between June and December 1980 total employment at the Port Talbot works of the British Steel Corporation (BSC) in South Wales fell from 11,202 to 6,342 as a consequence of BSC's 'Slimline' programme. A further 641 jobs were lost in the following three years bringing the total reduction under Slimline to over five thousand. Slimline was local management's response to a national strategy which was intended to reduce employment throughout BSC. At Port Talbot the cumulative effect of Slimline and the other programmes implemented between 1979 and 1985 was to cut total employment from 12,500 to 4,800. Most of the job losses, including the bulk of the reductions under Slimline, led to redundancies. What makes these redundancies remarkable is not so much their scale, but the fact that some of the people who were made redundant - at Port Talbot and elsewhere in BSC - found work back at BSC, not as BSC employees, but as the employees of private contractors. In other words, when they made people redundant in 1980 BSC managers brought in contractors and some of the redundants went back into the steelworks with contracting firms. Over a thousand jobs were created in the contracting firms, i.e. there was one contracting worker for every four or five BSC employees. How many of these jobs were filled by people made redundant from BSC?

As in other aspects of research into BSC's use of outside contractors, there is no easy answer to this question. In the years after Slimline BSC managers were reluctant to disclose information about contractors. Trades Union sources were also either reluctant or simply did not have access to such data. Both BSC management and some Trades Union sources believed that disclosure could prove

embarrassing and therefore much of what follows
relies on sources which, although reliable, cannot
be acknowledged. Fortunately, some helpful data
were produced by two sample surveys. The second of
these, consisting of a sample survey of households
in Port Talbot, will be discussed towards the end
of this chapter. The first survey, beginning soon
after the redundancies were implemented, took the
form of a survey of a sample of those workers who
were made redundant by BSC in 1980. Three waves of
interviews were used to establish the subsequent
labour-market experience of the redundants. (See,
for example, Harris et al., 1985; Lee, 1985). The
results of these interviews gave some information
on the number of jobs with contractors filled by
people made redundant by BSC.

Just under ten per cent of all respondents to
the survey of those made redundant from BSC had
some experience of work with private contractors at
the steelworks after redundancy; however, 55 per
cent of the total sample had no work at all in the
two years after their redundancy. The proportion of
these redundants who had contracting experience
among those who had ever worked after redundancy
was therefore much higher: over 20 per cent of all
the redundants who found work had had at least one
spell with a BSC contractor.

If the sample of redundant steelworkers was
representative of all those made redundant in 1980,
then about 550 of the people made redundant as a
result of Slimline worked for a contractor back at
the steelworks at some time in the following two
years. They were joined in later years by workers
made redundant after Slimline. Among other reasons,
the fact that subsequent reductions in employment
could no longer be facilitated by improved
productivity (since potential gains in productivity
had largely been exhausted with Slimline), meant
that the proportion of these later redundants who
found work with contractors was even higher than 10
per cent (or 20 per cent of those redundants
finding work). I would therefore estimate that, in
total, up to 1,000 of those made redundant by BSC
between 1979 and 1984 had at least one spell of
work with a contractor back in the steelworks.

Almost all of the jobs given out to
contractors after 1980 consisted of work once done
by people BSC made redundant. To put it another
way, it was the redundants' jobs that went out to
contractors. The redundants themselves explained
what had happened in their interviews during the

63

redundancy survey:

> Done away with our janitor's job and gave whole job to contractors. (Janitor)

> Department closed and went out to contract labour. (Mobile Workshop employee)

> Whole department closed down and was taken over by contractors. (HGV lorry driver)

> The whole section finished. Work went to contractors. (Painter, Civil Engineering)

> Whole department except for Chief Surveyor was made redundant. Went to outside firm on contract. (Senior Surveyor)

> If I remained I thought I would have to take a cut in wages and whole section went shortly afterwards to contractor. (Mobile Plant operator)

> Department closed down and it was put out to contract. (Internal transport driver)

> My job went. Contractors took it over. (Burner)

> The whole job went out to contract. (Crane driver)

> The whole Morfa Bank went out to contractors. (Plant operator, Morfa Bank stockyard)

> My whole section went. Our work was given to contractors. (Labour foreman, hot strip mill)

> The job was coming to a close and being given to contractors. (Slag tipper, blast furnace)

Explanatory comments on some of the redundant steelworkers' questionnaires showed that in a small number of cases ex-BSC workers found jobs with contractors because their jobs were immediately taken over by contracting firms which made a direct approach with an offer to stay on with their new employer. This was most common amongst drivers of all kinds, mobile-plant operators and janitors. As a manager of a contract cleaning firm explained to me: 'I'm an ex-steelworker myself and, to be honest with you, they're just laying them off and the contractors are taking them on.' Other workers were taken on (more or less immediately) to work for contractors in the same job or department - for example, men who had worked in the blast furnaces as electricians or boilermakers, and fitters in heating and ventilating. At BSC's works at Llanwern near Newport (also in South Wales) ex-BSC workers in catering, mobile plant and cleaning performed the same work for contractors. One of the (Trade Union) Works' Committee members added that 'unfortunately, a lot still think they are working for BSC.'

In some cases the redundant steelworkers 'got their jobs back', although not always the same jobs. Thus one redundant might go back to the steelworks, as a contractors' employee, to do work which was once done by a colleague at BSC. The colleague s/he replaced might perhaps be doing her/his old job, but as a contracting worker. Thus a man who had been a bricklayer's labourer·at BSC might be employed as a rigger in his new life as a contracting worker. In general, however, there was some correspondence between the kind of work redundant steelworkers found with contractors and the kind of work they used to do as BSC employees.

It seems that BSC still needed the labour of at least some of those workers that had been made redundant. In fact there was an agreement with the steel unions that the contractors should recruit BSC redundants wherever possible. The Slimline document of 15 May 1980 stated:

> It will be management's concern where contractors are selected, ... that their immediate manpower needs are identified and where vacancies exist, to use their best endeavours to ensure that Port Talbot Works' employees are recruited.

According to one of the union negotiators, this clause was the only concession the Trade Unions managed to extract from management in return for their signatures to the Slimline Agreement. BSC had first been asked to guarantee that contractors would take on redundant BSC workers, but it seems that the personnel department at Port Talbot would only accept the watered-down version which finally became part of the Agreement. It does not take close inspection to see that the final agreement allowed the Corporation a wide degree of latitude and, indeed, a representative of the contracting employers explained that the clause was merely 'a sop to the Union'. He added, however, that BSC had asked contractors on large new projects to show preference for <u>local</u> workers (although not necessarily redundant steelworkers). Even some Trade Union officials were ambivalent about the recruitment of ex-steelworkers by contractors. Thus at <u>Llanwern</u> the Trades Unions had asked contractors to give priority to ex-BSC people, but, as one official added, 'there's personalities to consider, it's not always a good thing ...'. In fact those redundants who found jobs at BSC Port Talbot with contractors owed their good fortune less to a clause in the Slimline Agreement than to the existence of what was popularly known as 'make-up pay'.

ECSC READAPTION BENEFITS

In 1973, soon after Britain joined the Common Market, BSC had discussions with the EEC about the possibility of financial help to ameliorate the worst effects of the cutbacks in employment then being considered. The establishment of the European Community began with the common organisation of the European coal and steel industries into what became known as the European Coal and Steel Community (ECSC). The treaty which constituted the ECSC, signed by the member countries in Paris in April 1951, included the following provision. The ECSC would:

> at the request of the interested governments, participate in the study of the possibilities of re-employment, either in existing industries or through the creation of new activities, of workers set at liberty by the evolution of the market or by technical transformations.

Furthermore, where such changes led to 'an exceptional reduction in labour requirements in the coal or steel industries, creating special difficulties in one or more areas for the re-employment of the workers released', the ECSC would:

> grant non-reimbursable assistance to contribute to:

- the payment of indemnities to tide the workers over until they can obtain new employment;
- the granting of allowances to the workers for reinstallation expenses (sic);
- the financing of technical retraining for workers who are led to change their employment. (European Coal and Steel Community, 1951)

Since BSC, even in 1973, was planning to reduce output in order to fulfill the UK's obligations as a member of the ECSC, they were able to claim EEC assistance to soften the blow resulting from their efforts to rationalise productivity and Sir Melvyn Rosser, a member of the BSC Board, writing in the trade journal British Steel (Winter 1973-4, p.21), was able to announce that:

BSC has a sensitive, social conscience ... it has successfully argued the case for enhanced benefits for Welsh and other steelworkers under the terms of the proposed European Coal and Steel Community Readaptation Aid Convention.

Of course, ECSC cash did not arrive in great quantities until seven years later when it was warranted by the large number of redundancies being implemented by BSC at Port Talbot and elsewhere. BSC then told the workers who were going to be made redundant that:

Under the European Communities (Iron and Steel Employees Readaptation Benefits Scheme) Regulations 1979 the Government has introduced a scheme for the payment of benefits to certain steelworkers who lose their jobs as a result of particular reductions in activity caused by market conditions in the steel industry.

and that

The British Steel Corporation has agreed to extend similar benefits to other of its employees as defined in agreements between the Corporation and the Trade Unions representing those employees. (BSC, 1979)

The 1979 Regulations were difficult to understand.[2] So difficult, in fact, that one of the tasks of the counsellors employed by BSC to advise redundant workers was the explanation of the rules for make-up pay. If they could make sense of these explanations and of the literature provided by BSC, prospective redundants would discover that they could receive ECSC money in four different ways. Firstly, they might be assisted to retire early (see Bytheway, this volume). Secondly, they might get cash help if they retrained. Approved training gave redundants benefits equal to their previous earnings less tax for a maximum of 52 weeks. Thirdly, workers who were unemployed after redundancy benefited. No matter what their entitlement to State earnings related supplement (ERS, since abolished by the Conservative Government) they received at least 90 per cent of State ERS on top of unemployment benefit for 52 weeks of unemployment[3]:

> There is a maximum of 52 weeks during which benefits, made up of State ERS and Schemes ERS equivalent, may be paid during unemployment. These weeks, however, need not be continuous providing they fall within the overall period of entitlement of 78 weeks following the date of redundancy. (BSC, 1979)

Redundants received the same benefits if they did not register as unemployed because they were sick. Finally, redundants who found a job or became self-employed had their earnings made-up to 90 per cent of their 'previous earnings' at BSC for a maximum of 78 weeks: 'previous earnings' were the average of all normal earnings, excluding non-contractual overtime and payments relating to abnormal working conditions, for the 13 weeks ending four weeks before redundancy. Current earnings were calculated on a similar basis, but over four weeks for those who had become employees and six months for the self-employed.

Not all redundants were eligible for these benefits, however, and some groups (for example, those made redundant under other programmes) may not have benefited from the ECSC provisions. To qualify, a redundant had to be under 65 (60 for women) at the date of redundancy and to have been working 16 hours or more a week for BSC for at least 52 weeks. Furthermore, s/he had to have worked at the same plant for at least 52 weeks before the beginning of the change in circumstances which led to her/his redundancy. Finally, s/he must:

> have been made redundant as defined by the
> Redundancy Payments Act 1965; now incorporated
> in the Employment Protection (Consolidation)
> Act 1978[4]

and

> If you are receiving compensation under the
> Iron and Steel (Compensation to Employers)
> Regulations 1968 make-up under the Schemes
> will be adjusted so that your total income
> does not exceed your previous earnings in the
> Corporation. (BSC, 1979)

Even if the redundant worker satisfied the
criteria for make-up of pay or benefits, s/he was
not paid make-up if absent from their new
employment. Furthermore, s/he might lose entitlement
if the new job was left 'through misconduct or
without just cause'. The unemployed lost make-up of
benefits:

> For any day on which you are unemployed, but
> are not registered for employment and you are
> not certified as such; or if you are
> disqualified or disallowed from receiving
> State Unemployment Benefit. (BSC, 1979)

There were some alterations to the Schemes in
later years. The maximum period of make-up of
unemployment benefit was extended to two years for
the over-55s and the level of make-up they received
was changed. The under-55s received a maximum of
£16 per week for 52 weeks. The maximum period of
make-up of _earnings_ was extended to two years for
the over-55s and 130 weeks for the over-60s. This
is all terribly confusing of course, and it is
probably wise to conclude by highlighting the
aspect of make-up which is of most interest in the
present discussion: providing they had not already
used up their entitlement while unemployed or on
another job or while retraining, ex-BSC workers
(under 55) who found employment with contractors
back at BSC would have their pay made up to a
maximum of 90 per cent of their BSC earnings.

Make-up Pay and Redundant Steelworkers
In April 1984 the Steel Committee of the Trades

Union Conference (TUC) heard that contractors at
BSC's plant at Ravenscraig in Scotland were simply
taking over the jobs of men made redundant by BSC
and re-employing them at lower wages. They further
heard from the Trades Unions at Ravenscraig that:

> Redundant workers are readily employed by
> contractors because the men, knowing their
> wages will be made-up ... and cushioned by
> redundancy pay, are ready to accept low wages.

ISTC, the main steel union, had heard something
similar from officers and officials in Scotland a
year before:

> Currently the tendency has been to re-employ
> BSC employees at low rates in the knowledge
> that the members will receive ECSC make-up.

But this 'tendency' was not confined to
Scotland: a manager of one of the contractors at
Port Talbot explained that, since 1980, some
contracting firms had paid a 'nominal' sum to their
new employees. The redundant steelworkers accepted
low wages because they were glad to have work and
their pay was made-up. Of course not all of the
ex-BSC workers who found employment with contractors
had their pay made-up. Some had used up their
entitlement while unemployed, re-training in other
jobs, and in a few cases their wages in their new
jobs were too high to require make-up to reach 90
per cent of their earnings at BSC. Nevertheless,
three quarters of contracting workers in the survey
of BSC's redundant workers received make-up.

Make-up Pay and the Contractors

Clearly a great deal of ECSC assistance was given
to redundant steelworkers, and this assistance had
a profound effect on the local labour market of the
settlement most affected by the redundancies, Port
Talbot. Indeed, this was what make-up pay was
designed to do, to 'readapt' workers who were no
longer needed to changed conditions in the labour
market. What comes to mind immediately is the
possibility that make-up money actually created
employment, especially in the contracting firms
which found work at BSC. By providing a subsidy to
these employers, make-up money ensured that the
contractors could pay lower wages and would
therefore recruit more workers for a given wage

bill. Furthermore, if the subsidy was passed on to
BSC in the form of lower tenders for contract work,
then BSC would be encouraged to create more work
for the contractors and hence more contracting
jobs.

In fact, the ECSC subsidy was not the reason
that BSC brought contractors into the Port Talbot
works. The proof of this statement can be found, in
part at least, in the record of outside contractors
at BSC after Slimline. After 1980 the Trades Unions
quickly realised that using contractors was
frequently not cheaper than using BSC employees,
i.e. that BSC had not increased their use of
outside contractors because they were cheap. For
example, in 1981 a local official of the National
Union of Blastfurnacemen at another steelworks
complained that

> The BSC obviously claim that the economics of
> the exercise are for the good of the industry,
> but personally I think it is total madness and
> that the Steel Committee (of the TUC) should
> be making an in-depth study into this subject!

Workers at BSC frequently complained that the
contractors' work was poorly done and they believed
that the standard of work done by contractors
should be considered when costing the use of
contractors against direct employees. Poor standards
were also mentioned by representatives of firms
which had traditionally done contract work for BSC
Port Talbot. Some of these firms had been
supplanted by firms with 'lower standards' and
there was obviously a large element of self-interest
in their complaints; as there was in the complaints
made by BSC employees that the maintenance work
done by contractors was not up to pre-1980
standards when much of the work had been carried
out by BSC workers. They even claimed that using
contractors had affected production. It is
impossible to establish to what extent contractors
were to blame for production breakdowns, but it is
interesting that these should be mentioned at all
since BSC Port Talbot's record was widely reported
as having improved dramatically. (Although, as I
have recorded elsewhere (Fevre, 1986), because of
the breakdowns the workers themselves often found
such reports a source of amusement).

Support for claims by BSC workers that the
standards of contractors' work was poor came from
the contracting workers themselves. Several told

stories of BSC workers being brought in to rectify mistakes made by contractors. These stories were later confirmed by Trade Union sources and Union officials at another BSC plant (at Llanwern) explained that this was one of the reasons they did not like BSC workers and contracting workers to work next to each other:

> We need the contractors to be responsible for themselves. We don't want to be blamed if the contractors cock it up. It's an insurance.

We will return to the question of productivity at BSC Port Talbot after Slimline, but what of the assumed relationship between the use of contractors and lower labour costs? Clearly, BSC would <u>expect</u> to reduce its total labour costs where contractors were used only occasionally because it would no longer have to provide money to pay the wages of workers who were permanently on site, but it is not clear that all the sums came out in favour of using contractors. It might, for example, have been cheaper to use existing BSC employees <u>on overtime</u> to do a one-off job which was intended for a contractor. The Trade Unions at BSC Port Talbot were able, during the years after Slimline, to convince BSC Management that they should not put certain jobs out to contract by showing that the work would be done at a lower cost by BSC employees. In other cases, the workforce was convinced that contracting was more costly, but failed to make their case through the Trade Unions or were unable to dissuade management from bringing in contractors. It may be that management will only keep the work 'in house' if the Unions are prepared to make additional concessions. Nevertheless, BSC employees suspected that the Corporation frequently decided in favour of contractors without a proper comparison of costs. An ex-BSC worker interviewed by Griselda Leaver[5] explained that:

> This business of contractors ... it's going to bump their costs up in the end ... Well, before I worked for Leeris I had been involved in dealing with the contracted labour at BSC. Now, we paid Leeris £3.78 per hour for a labourer, so when I went to work for Leeris myself I thought forty hours times the best part of £3.78 ... less stamps and that ... it would be a good deal ... But when I got it I was only on £1.40 an hour ... the rest had

gone to the contractor ... so I went along and
asked him 'What's going on here ... £1.40 an
hour ...?'and he said 'What's wrong with
that?' ... so I said 'We paid you £3.78 when I
was in the Abbey' ... so he said 'I'll give
you extra as long as you don't tell the rest
of the men' ... I got the extra ... He was
charging BSC £3.78 and paying £1.40 ... and
I'd have to pay my stamp from that.

Finally, my earlier studies of the use of
contractors in other industries (Fevre, 1980) had
suggested that contractors might be able to save
their clients' money by reducing capital and
supervision costs. It is, however, not certain that
the increased use of contractors reduced BSC's
capital costs. Many of the contractors on the BSC
site used BSC tools and machinery together with
other BSC facilities (for which they might or might
not be charged) and it was commonly believed that
contractors had bought BSC plant and equipment,
including transport, at knock-down prices. Furthermore,
BSC had only recently abandoned the practice of
directly employing people whose sole responsibility
lay in the supervision of contractors and their
employees.

If using contractors was not cost-effective,
why then did BSC substitute contractors for direct
employees in 1980? It is likely that the increased
use of contractors in BSC followed from the
pressure to reduce direct employment created by the
Government.[6] By late 1979 the BSC Board had made
suggestions about how the various BSC plants might
go about reducing employment in line with
Government directives. One of the ways they thought
this might be accomplished was by the increased use
of outside contractors in place of BSC employees.
This suggestion was put into writing by BSC's Chief
Executive, Mr. Robert Scholey. In his report Return
to Financial Viability : Presentation of South
Wales Options, considered at a Board meeting on 17
January 1980, Mr. Scholey argued for 'the freer use
of contractors where operationally and financially
desirable' (Reprinted in House of Commons Committee
on Welsh Affairs, 1980).

The possibility of using contractors on a very
large scale had been present in BSC's thinking for
two decades (see Upham, 1980). In the 1960s steel
executives began to visit Japan to observe the
extensive use of contractors in Japanese steelworks.
BSC were impressed by the level of contracting-out

73

in their supposedly more efficient competitors:
other steel producers, even some European plants,
had more contract workers than direct employees.
Nevertheless, even in the period immediately
preceding the announcement of the redundancies in
1980, BSC appeared to be treating the contracting
option with caution (Hicks, 1980). It was not yet
agreed that the 'Japanese' solution could successfully
be applied in the UK. The possibility of extending
that part of the work of a steel plant which might
be covered by outside contractors was obvious, but
- unlike the idea of concentrating steelmaking on
large coastal sites - the increased use of
contractors never became part of the grand design
for the development of steel production in the UK.
This did not, of course, mean that BSC did not use
outside contractors at all. Contractors were used,
but not to anything like the same extent as in
Japan. In early 1979, then, contractors still
remained 'just an option'.

Towards the end of 1979 the BSC Board told
managers of their large integrated plants that they
must quickly reach a plan for reducing employment.
The Board suggested that where reductions in
employment would not be facilitated by reduced
output, local plants might consider increasing
their use of outside contractors. Local managers
were given very little time to make their plans
because the BSC Board was under pressure from the
Government. Given the pressure to draw up a plan
very quickly, the BSC Board were no longer worried
about the relative costs of increasing their use of
contractors, and the same applied to local
managers.[7] For example, they had little time to
request quotes from likely contractors which might
allow them to consider the relative merits of
direct labour versus contractors before they put
their plan before the BSC Board. Indeed, it is
highly unlikely that local managers knew even how
many contractors' workers they would need in any
part of the works (or in total). In simple terms,
each member of the Port Talbot Mangement Committee
was asked to arrive at the lowest possible
employment figure for the part of the plant that
they were responsible for. In arriving at a figure,
each manager knew that they could rely on the use
of contractors to keep the plant running. They
assumed that BSC would have a free hand if they
wished to bring in contractors, just as they
assumed management would have a free hand if it was
considered necessary to introduce flexible working

practices. There were areas of the steelworks -
cleaning and internal transport being the most
obvious - where it must have been known from the
start of the exercise that contractors would take
over all of the work. But in other cases managers
can have had little clear idea of the mix of direct
labour and contractors which would be required,
especially since they could not anticipate the full
effect of flexible working on the productivity of
those BSC employees who remained after the
redundancies.

In subsequent months, after the BSC Board had
accepted Port Talbot's Slimline plan, local
managers made some enquiries about costs and, as a
result, made minor alterations in their plan. For
example, they decided not to contract out all
catering at Port Talbot. There were, however, no
major changes in the Slimline plan for total
employment at BSC to be reduced to 5,401 workers.
Port Talbot, like the other BSC plants, was forced
to substitute contractors for direct employees when
this was not necessarily the cheaper alternative.
BSC still wanted the work done, but, because of
Government pressure, did not want the workers who
did it to appear in the count of BSC employees. In
many cases workers were simply shifted off the BSC
payroll onto the contractors' payrolls. It was
immaterial whether the cost of the work they did
had increased or fallen in the process. In fact, we
have no way of making this calculation since BSC's
accounts do not allow us to isolate payments to
contractors let alone estimate the longer-term
costs of bringing in contractors. Furthermore,
there is good reason for scepticism about the basic
- i.e. not costed - productivity improvements
claimed by BSC. Whether by intention or good
fortune, BSC's figures give a much too optimistic
interpretation of improvements in productivity.
These figures cannot be taken at face value since
comparisons of output per head before and after
1980 do not take account of contractors' employees.[8]
If we do a rough and ready calculation, without any
attempt to allow for part-time workers, productivity
at BSC Port Talbot works out at 184 tonnes of steel
per employee (including staff) in 1979 and 380
tonnes per employee in 1984. But if we add the
maximum BSC estimate of the number of contracting
workers to the official number of BSC employees,
productivity in 1984 drops to 270 tonnes per person
per year. The productivity improvement between 1979
and 1980 is of the order of one hundred per cent
without the inclusion of contractors, but less than

75

fifty per cent if contracting workers are included.

Make-up Pay and the Local Labour Market

Using contractors allowed BSC to reduce direct employment as required by the Government. BSC did not introduce contractors in order to reduce costs and so any subsidy to the contractors was irrelevant to their decision. But this does not complete our investigation of the effects of make-up on the local labour market. We know that redundant steelworkers were able to get jobs with contractors because their wages were made-up, but what effect did make-up have on other workers in the local labour market? In fact, make-up pay meant that the burden of unemployment resulting from the redundancies was experienced by a variety of workers, and not simply those who were made redundant. Make-up pay spread the unemployment resulting from BSC's cutbacks around the local labour market.

Port Talbot's labour market has always been unbalanced as a result of the over-dependence of the town on manufacturing and especially iron and steel. Although the town had always had an unusual mix of employment opportunities, for three decades after the Second World War it had jobs (mainly jobs for men it must be admitted) to spare. In fact, Port Talbot had so much employment that it could afford to lose jobs throughout the 1970s without a large rise in unemployment. Mass unemployment (of officially 16 per cent) arrived only late in the day when the Slimline redundancies were implemented in 1980. Port Talbot's good fortune in the post-war period largely followed from the fact that successive governments were prepared to use the British steel industry as a form of regional aid (c.f. Morgan, 1983) to areas which had insufficient employment to keep their residents in work. This would have been the case in Port Talbot, but for government support for steel-making in the town, a fact which could no longer be disguised in 1980 when the redundancies were implemented.

A full analysis of the figures for the crucial (1980-82) period when the effects of make-up could be expected to show up in the statistics provided by the Department of Employment is available elsewhere (Fevre, 1985). However, in broad terms it would be fairer to conclude that to begin with the industrial distribution of unemployment in Port Talbot reflected the distribution of employment in the town. The greater the volume of employment in an industry, the greater was the volume of reported unemployment under that industry heading. Only in vehicles, and food, drink and tobacco, did unemployment appear to be lower than we might expect from the employment figures for those industries. The redundancies in metal manufacture therefore had a substantial impact on Port Talbot's unemployment figures and accounted for the largest absolute increases in unemployment as well as in redundancies. Even though Port Talbot's manufacturing industries as a whole shed jobs during this period, it was the steel redundancies that had the most dramatic effect.

The largest batch of BSC redundancies were notified in January 1980, but were implemented from March onwards while their greatest impact was in the last six months of the year: according to BSC figures only ten per cent of the final total of the redundancies had been implemented by 12 June 1980, but over 60 per cent had been implemented by 11 September and over 80 per cent by 11 December 1980. Most of the rise in unemployment over the whole period 1979-82 occurred in the latter half of 1980. The direct effect of the redundancies was to double male unemployment in the Port Talbot Employment Area (EOA) and add perhaps five percentage points to the rate of unemployment (if rates were calculated for EOAs). In fact, the level of unemployment in metal manufacture suggests that something like two thirds of those made redundant by BSC and residing in Port Talbot reached the unemployment register and independent research confirms that this proportion is about right (see Lee, 1985). This, then, is the first point of interest: a third of the redundants did not join the unemployment register after redundancy.

The second point of interest concerns trends in unemployment for workers who had not been made redundant by BSC, since many of the unemployed were not ex-BSC workers. Of course total unemployment in metal manufacture (1500 workers) was only the most obvious effect of the Slimline programme. Some workers may have become unemployed as a result of reduced demand from BSC for the goods and services provided by other local employers, however, this example does not exhaust the induced effects on the local labour market. Unemployment in the 'unclassified by industry' category increased by 60 per cent in 1980. This heading included people without previous work experience, and about one in three of this group were school-leavers. The effect of rising unemployment on the younger workers in Port Talbot - especially those with little or no employment experience - can be seen in the official figures on unemployment categorised by age and by the length of time out of work (see Fevre, 1985). Before 1980 'permanent' unemployment (over a year) was only a significant problem for the older unemployed, but by 1982 this was no longer the case. The third and final point of note in the unemployment figures is the _fall_ in unemployment amongst steelworkers in the months after the redundancies. The steel redundancies may have caused most of the massive rise in unemployment in 1980, but employment was maintained at this level while many redundants left the register. Many left soon after joining: flows _off_ the register were highest in 1980 and the level of unemployment in metal manufacture declined from the end of 1980.

All three of these features of the local labour market - the redundants who _didn't_ join the register, the non-steelworkers who did, and the steelworkers who left the register - were at least in part the consequence of make-up money. Make-up money ensured that redundant steelworkers were able to 'displace' the unemployment created by job losses at BSC onto other less advantaged groups of workers. 'Displacement' does not necessarily imply the displacement of employees from their jobs by other workers. Here in fact, we have a special case of a more general phenomenon; the displacement of _unemployment_ from one section of the population to another: the composition of the unemployed workforce in Port Talbot was not radically changed by the redundancies in the way we might have expected. It seems likely that the burden of unemployment on the most disadvantaged sections of the working class was actually intensified when more favoured groups lost their jobs.

There were, of course, other contributing factors. Some ex-steelworkers 'retired' early, and others found places on special programmes, including training programmes. Some may also have transferred to sickness benefit. There may also have been labour shortages which could only be satisfied when the level of unemployment increased making available workers with the required skills or training. But none of these factors would account for the increased proportion of non-steelworkers on the register or for the _massive_ flows off the register in 1980. Even though jobs

with outside contractors at BSC were created, these
came nowhere near to balancing the loss of steel
jobs in 1980, let alone the other job losses at
this time. There was no net increase in jobs in
Port Talbot, yet redundant steelworkers found jobs,
either with the contractors or with other local
employers. They therefore did not join the
unemployment register or left it sometime after
redundancy. Since unemployment did not fall as a
result, some workers were suffering unemployment in
their place. This would also explain the flow of
workers who had not been made redundant by BSC onto
the register.

Even in jobs with contractors at the
steelworks there was no automatic mechanism to
ensure the redundants were first in line. What gave
the redundants an advantage was, of course, access
to make-up money. But for ECSC assistance, it is
doubtful whether the redundants would have been
well-placed to find work, even with contractors at
BSC. For the most part, it is likely that other
workers would have been prepared to accept lower
wages than these ex-steelworkers. Yet make-up money
reversed this position: it allowed the redundants
to accept low wages and hence displaced unemployment
to other groups in the labour market. Make-up, at
least in the initial stages (see below), helped to
ensure that redundants would get jobs with
contracting firms. It goes a long way towards
helping us to account for the fact that not all the
redundants joined the unemployment register; that
many of the redundants left the register; and that
other workers became unemployed in their place.
Concrete proof of displacement arising from the
payment of make-up money is, of course, difficult
to find; however, fluctuations in vacancy statistics
may reflect the fact that redundants from BSC found
jobs which could have been taken by other workers.
The speed at which vacancies notified to the Job
Centre were filled increased in 1980 and it was
during this period that Port Talbot's largest
increase in school-leaver unemployment occurred
(although the highest ratio of notified to unfilled
vacancies was reached in June 1981). Furthermore,
the reduction in numbers of notified vacancies may
have resulted, in part, from the recruitment of BSC
redundants in place of notification. (Notified
vacancies were at their lowest level in December
1980).

CONCLUSIONS

It is very difficult to believe that, when the idea of make-up money for ex-steelworkers was being devised, the ECSC was aware that they were creating a modern equivalent to the Speenhamland system of poor relief so reviled by historians of nineteenth-century England. As with Speenhamland, ECSC money allows employers to pay unusually low wages and it is this consequence of make-up pay which explains the unusual labour market created in Port Talbot after the redundancies. The transference of the unemployment which would have been the fate of the redundants to less advantaged workers was therefore an <u>unintended</u> consequence of make-up pay. Clearly it is not a <u>necessary</u> consequence of this sort of income maintenance strategy since the use of minimum wage clauses where make-up was paid would ensure that the redundants receive no advantage in the search for jobs[9], nevertheless, the early misuse of make-up pay had lasting and damaging effects for all the workers involved.

Readers should <u>not</u> conclude that make-up money gave the redundants a chance of alternative (to BSC) <u>permanent</u> employment. Work with contracting firms is by definition insecure and many of the redundants who went back to the steelworks could only expect to work for a few weeks at a time, sometimes only for a few days or even one shift. They would become unemployed once more until their next short spell with a contractor.[10] The household survey of Port Talbot showed that men with experience of work with BSC contractors (over 20 per cent of the whole sample) were four times as likely to be in receipt of unemployment benefit and three times as likely to be living on supplementary benefit at the time they were interviewed.

In time the redundants exhausted their eligibility for make-up pay, but by this time the damage had been done. Wages were not increased in order to compensate for the loss of make-up. Senior Trade Union officers explained that BSC would not allow any increase in contractors' tenders to allow for a larger wage bill and employers who did attempt to do this lost their contracts. Ex-BSC employees of the contracting firms complained, but most stayed on. As one Union official commented, by this time they were prepared to 'work for a bowl of rice'. In other words, make-up money not only helped to spread the effects of the BSC redundancies across the whole labour market, but it also helped to ensure that in the longer term being in work was not much better than being unemployed. The availability of make-up money lowered wages in the first two years after the redundancies and wages proved to be 'sticky', as the economists say, after the make-up money ran out. Make-up money was therefore responsible for lowering the incomes of a proportion of the working population of Port Talbot. A policy which was designed to maintain incomes after redundancy actually succeeded in lowering the wages of redundants and non-redundants in the longer term.

So much for the unintended consequences of make-up. We can conclude with a few words on its intended effects. In the first place, it is debatable whether - as the official name for make-up, 'readaption' or 'readaptation' benefits, implies - the efficiency of the local labour market was improved where these benefits were paid. But there was some readaption nevertheless. The younger workers were readapted to life on lower wages and the older workers were readapted to life without work (usually in the form of 'early retirement'). In both cases make-up kept BSC redundants out of the ranks of the long-term or permanently unemployed as reckoned by the official agencies. This was as intended, but was it intended that other workers joined the long-term or permanently unemployed in place of the redundants? It could be concluded that make-up was intended to get the redundants off the unemployment register - although not necessarily for good - at whatever cost.

This was not the only intended consequence of make-up, however. Make-up was undoubtedly of help to BSC in publicising its 'sensitive social conscience' at a time of mass redundancies. Furthermore, make-up helped BSC to secure their workers' compliance with the redundancies and the rest of the Slimline programme. The reader must decide whether either of these are laudable aims and judge the (apparently enlightened) policy of paying make-up money accordingly.

NOTES

1. This paper is based on three chapters of my forthcoming book, How Many People Work at BSC? I would like to thank all my colleagues associated with the Steel Project for their help at all stages in the production of this paper, but especially Bill Bytheway and Ray Lee for their comments on the effects of make-up pay during the redundancy process. Any mistakes, of course, remain my own.

2. My colleague at Swansea, Bill Bytheway, suggests in a personal communication that prospective redundants were less confused by the detail of the make-up regulations than by the reasoning that lay behind them. Their main grievance was the lack of rationality; they couldn't understand the 'why' of many regulations. Readers might like to bear in mind the redundants' grievance when considering the 'intended effects' of make-up listed at the end of this paper, especially those which were not explained at the time.

3. c.f. a maximum of 26 weeks on State ERS.

4. Note that BSC had its own schemes for some workers who did not qualify for ECSC assistance because of the cause of their redundancy although these workers were still required to have been made redundant.

5. Griselda Leaver was a co-worker on the Steel Project at University College of Swansea. I am grateful to her for allowing me to reproduce this quotation. Details have been altered to preserve confidentiality. 'Leeris' is a fictional name for a real company.

6. See How Many People Work at BSC?

7. See How Many People Work at BSC?

8. But note that BSC's increased use of contractors has at least made their productivity figures comparable to those quoted by overseas producers.

9. See How Many People Work at BSC?

10. See How Many People Work at BSC?

REFERENCES

British Steel Corporation, (1979) <u>Changing Your Job</u>

European Coal and Steel Community (1951), <u>Treaty Instituting the European Coal and Steel Community</u>, Paris

Fevre, R. (1980) <u>Sharing the Burden</u>, unpublished paper

Fevre, R. (1984) <u>Contract Work in the Recession</u>, paper presented to the Annual Conference of the British Sociological Association, Bradford

Fevre, R. (1985) <u>Employment and Unemployment in Port Talbot : a Reference Paper</u>, University College of Swansea

Fevre, R. (1986) 'Contract Work in the Recession' in K. Purcell, <u>et</u>. <u>al</u>., <u>The Changing Experience of Work</u>, Macmillian, London

Fevre, R. (forthcoming) <u>How Many People Work at BSC?</u>

Harris, C.C., R.M. Lee, and L.D. Morris, (1985) 'Redundancy in Steel : Labour Market Behaviour, Local Social Networks and Domestic Organisation' in B. Roberts, R. Finnegan, and D. Gallie, <u>New Approaches to Economic Life</u> Manchester University Press, Manchester pp. 154-66

Hicks, C.A. (1980) 'The Use of Contractors for Maintenance : Benefits and Pitfalls' in <u>Minimizing the Cost of Maintenance</u>, The Metals Society, London

House of Commons Committee on Welsh Affairs (1980) <u>Minutes of Evidence</u>, Session 1979-80, HMSO London

Lee, R.M. (1985) Redundancy, Labour Markets and Informal Relations' <u>Sociological Review</u> <u>33</u>, pp. 469-94

Morgan, K. (1983) 'Restructuring Steel : The Crises of Labour and Locality in Britain, <u>International Journal of Urban and Regional Research</u>, <u>7</u>, pp. 175-201

Upham, M. (1980) 'British Steel : Retrospect and Prospect', <u>Industrial Relations Journal</u>, <u>8</u>, pp. 5-21

Chapter Five

REDUNDANCY AND THE OLDER WORKER

Bill Bytheway

INTRODUCTION

> ... I think it is very good for the young
> people to be able to go somewhere and mix with
> other young people in the same situation as
> themselves. I would be interested to know if
> there is a similar place for my age group. I
> have been unemployed for three years. I am 58
> years old, still very active and live on my
> own. I am not old enough to join the old age
> group so what can the forties and fifties
> people do with their time? ...
>
> Hopeful,
> South Wales Evening Post,
> 27th November 1985.

One dominant focus of studies of the labour market
has been concerned with the transitions of the
individual into it from school and out of it upon
retirement. Both transitions are essentially age
specific, tradition and legislation stipulating a
narrow range of chronological ages in respect of
each. Between the two transitions the individual is
seen to follow certain patterns in which age is
conceptualised as a key variable rather than as a
structuring dimension. This process may lead the
worker through a certain occupational career, or it
may lead to unplanned alternations from job to job
or between employment and unemployment. Generally
speaking, however, such employment patterns are not
seen to be related to retirement and the
post-retirement period through anything more than
the occasional incidental statistical correlation.
Thus retirement has been seen to be something quite
distinct from unemployment, to the extent that the

status of the individual is thought to be
completely transformed upon ceasing to be an
unemployed worker and becoming a retired pensioner
- even though there may be virtually no change
involved in everyday activities.

Redundancy, however, is beginning to change
this situation. Wood's study (1980) of the early
retirement of managers illustrates well the
ambiguities of 'voluntary' redundancy, and the
secretive way in which some managers organise
retirement through this means. Wood has argued
strenuously that studies of the 'redundancy
situation' should not assume that redundancies are
an inevitability: those threatened with redundancy
might emerge in many different guises one of which
is retirement.

However not only is it just the enormous
increase in redundancies[1] that is bringing about
change. In Britain, the 1965 Redundancy Act
introduced government aid to redundant workers in a
way which has positively encouraged redundancy on
the basis of age. This, together with high levels
of unemployment, fosters the popular belief that
with age the chances of becoming re-employed are
substantially reduced. As Parker (1982) found, the
older a worker, the more he or she believes age to
be the biggest hardship in obtaining another job.
Makeham (1980) and Jolly et. al. (1980) have shown
that this belief is in fact well-founded (see also:
Office of Population Censuses and Surveys, 1980, p.
94). Surveys such as Daniel and Stilgoe (1977) and
Colledge and Bartholomew (1980) have not only
confirmed the high unemployment rates of older
workers and their longer average durations of
unemployment, but also the fact that considerable
proportions of those over 55 have reported that
they are no longer looking for jobs.

Daniel suggests that about a third of the
people in his follow-up study who were registered
as unemployed in 1973 had experienced a subsequent
three years that 'could be most usefully conceived
of as a transitional phase between economic
activity and inactivity' (p.60). At the time of the
re-interview in 1976, 34 per cent of those aged
55-60 and 54 per cent of those 60-64 were not
seeking full-time work. Half of the latter
explained this on the grounds of age. Thus there is
a critical problem of distinguishing between those
who seek and those who do not, between those who
are unemployed and economically active and those
unemployed and economically inactive. Given that

there is in most local economies a small
specialised labour market for elderly people (car
park attendants, cleaners, shop assistants, etc.)
it has become effectively impossible to divorce the
study of retirement from that of the labour market.

Since older redundant workers are perceived to
be on the point of leaving the labour market,
however, they do not excite the interest of
students of employment (see, for example, Greenwood
and Pearson, 1979, Blake et. al. 1979, Carmichael
and Cook, 1981). There has been a similarly narrow
approach adopted to the study of retirement.
Because 65 years is the statutory minimum age for a
retirement pension, and because this indeed has
been the average age at which people have withdrawn
from full-time work, little attention has been paid
to variations in retirement age. It is generally
presumed that 'early retirement' occurs unambiguously
only with sickness or choice. More recently,
however, there has been a growing recognition
within retirement studies that how a worker becomes
retired may not be an overnight transformation, but
may be a lengthy process extending over several
years and involving subtle changes in subjective
self-definition as well as in administratively
defined social status. Parker (1980), for example,
found in his pilot work that some prefer to
describe themselves as semi-retired or partly
retired. However, one in nine of those he
interviewed who were retired said they might
undertake paid work in the future. Studies of the
political economy of old age, notably Walker (1981)
and Phillipson (1977), have argued effectively that
the timing of retirement is determined by economic
forces as much as by legislated chronological ages.
Two French studies have highlighted the problems
that arise from a premature cessation of work
(Cribier 1981, Gaullier 1982), and Altmann (1981)
has focussed attention upon the income of the early
retired.

Paralleling this research interest have been a
number of developments regarding retirement
policies. Most notable in the United Kingdom is the
decision of the Social Services Committee of the
House of Commons to inquire into 'The Age of
Retirement'. This followed considerable pressure to
have a degree of flexibility introduced that might
allow the retirement process to be better attuned
to the retiree's circumstances (as noted in
'Growing Older', 1981, para. 32). There are,
however, many conflicting views on this question,

ranging from the commitment of Age Concern to USA-like legislation prohibiting age-discrimination prior to the age of 70 years, to pressure from the heavy industry unions for a substantial reduction in the minimum pension age. There has been pressure also for flexible timing and for phased retirement (EEC 1980a), and concern over the continuing discrimination between the sexes (EEC 1980b). It is clear that the Commission of the European Communities is seriously concerned not just because of the major implications for employment and the labour market, but also because of the substantial variation between member states in retirement legislation.

The Job Release Scheme (Makeham and Morgan, 1980) is a modest initial step towards instituting early retirement at the national level in the United Kingdom. Recently it has been extended (April 1982) and now includes certain specified categories of men aged 60. As it is further extended and as similar schemes become more established in particular industries and occupations, then it is reasonable to suppose that certain social redefinitions will begin to emerge. It is one thing for the occasional worker to retire 'early' given an inducement coupled with uncertain health, it is quite another for withdrawal from a local labour market to become the norm for all those over the age of 55 years or so. It can no longer be handled discretely and individually: a new social grouping comes to acquire an identity within the community (Gaullier 1982).

Casey and Bruche (1983) provide a detailed comparative analysis of national policies in regard to older workers. They compare France, the United Kingdom, the Netherlands, Sweden and the USA under the following headings:

a) Work adjustment through changed working conditions and job transfers.
b) Work adjustment through reductions in working time.
c) Dismissal protection.
d) Unemployment compensation.
e) Reintegration of unemployed older workers.
f) Early retirement.

In examining the overall policy mix of each of the five countries, they conclude that the United Kingdom has almost no policy for older workers. Policy is limited to the period immediately prior to statutory retirement age and, in certain respects, policy is informal rather than statutory. Referring to the 1966 Redundancy Payments Act, they conclude that:

> a seniority-based redundancy payments system also provides employers with the means, in certain circumstances, to put longer serving workers out.

As they point out, the Act sanctions age-specific payments in order to prevent employers being discouraged from hiring older workers because the overall objective is to stimulate the flow of labour from declining to growing industries. In the context of an increasing surplus of labour, this has led to agreements between management, unions and workers to encourage older workers to volunteer for dismissal.

Despite a 1969 amendment intended to counter this trend, the Act has established the practice of pressing older workers into retirement:

> ... the interest of employers to buy themselves conflict-free redundancies and to assume that, when running down their labour force, they can rid themselves of particularly their least productive workers leads them, in many cases, to offer severance terms well in excess of those required by the law and for some workers to complement these payments by provisions for receipt of an early company pension.

It is ironical that one of the few significant statutory provisions in the UK has had a major effect that was never intended. This has established a link between redundancy and early retirement that has been widely accepted. Despite this outcome, Casey and Bruche are still able to conclude that:

> to some extent the deficit in public policy is filled by arrangements for early pensioning made by individual companies seeking to run down their labour forces, but the levels of benefits paid is, in general, rather lower and a good many of such early retirees still register as unemployed in order to supplement their incomes by claiming public aid.

There is a clear indication here that the transition of some workers in the UK into retirement is a long, complex and uncertain process.

Casey and Bruche show that France, in contrast to the UK, emphasises compensation and early retirement. In early 1979, only 38 per cent of French males aged 60 to 64 were economically active - by far the lowest of the five countries that they compare. The corresponding UK figure was the highest at 76 per cent. Reflecting this, Gaullier (1982) has described in detail the emergence in France of a new class of pre-retired economically inactive men. In the Netherlands there is considerable emphasis placed upon work adjustments to protect older workers. At the same time, however, there are substantial compensations for the older unemployed worker and this effectively promotes early retirement. Sweden is similar to the Netherlands but with added emphasis upon reduced work-times (partial retirement) and job security (Blyton, 1984).

The USA is found to be similar to the UK in the lack of official policies. Casey and Bruche examine the Age Discrimination in Employment Act, and find that in reality the older worker is still vulnerable to dismissal on the grounds of lower productivity. Substantial reintegration efforts are made through the inclusion of the older unemployed on job creation programmes.

REDUNDANCY IN PORT TALBOT

The analysis of Casey and Bruche demonstrates the need to study the consequences of policies of individual companies in the UK. Thus it was particularly timely that a cohort of older redundant workers should be available for study. The Economic and Social Research Council was already funding the larger study of workers made redundant in 1980 by the British Steel Corporation from their Port Talbot works under its Slimline Plan but, as with other manpower studies, this centred upon the impact of redundancy on those continuing in the labour market, something which inevitably implied the study of migration, mobility and alternative economic activity.

It is clear that the Corporation took a decision to reduce overall manning levels and accomplished this through the offer of a major redundancy programme that was particularly attractive to older workers. There was no offer of work adjustments to protect older workers (although this had clearly been practised in the past), of partial retirement or of reintegration efforts through job creation. The primary effect of Slimline for older workers was to <u>induce</u> voluntary early retirement.

Slimline brought three sources of finance to those aged 55 years or over. There was the <u>redundancy payment</u>, <u>Readaptation Benefit</u> (popularly known as 'make-up money') and the <u>works pension</u>. There are of course many qualifications affecting particular instances but this is the basic pattern: a single payment upon redundancy in 1980 (varying considerably but on average of the order of 1 to 2 years' wages), make-up money for two years thereafter (bringing income up to 90 per cent and 80 per cent of previous earnings) and a works pension for the remainder of their lives (again varying considerably in amount but approximately £20 to £30 per week). There are two major variations on this pattern. The first is 'the pension option': in 1980 redundant steelworkers could choose to plough their make-up money into a boosted works pension. The second affects those over 63 years of age: their make-up money finishes at the age of 65 years, when they become eligible for the state retirement pension.

It is fairly clear from the way in which Slimline was organised that those aged 55 years or over were being encouraged ('readapted') to leave not just the steelworks but also the labour market. The make-up money was paid <u>automatically</u> - there would be no financial gain during the first two years in obtaining employment (assuming refusal of the pension option and ignoring the improbable prospect of employment at higher rates of pay than 90 per cent of final earnings). In contrast, those under 55 only received make-up money when they obtained new employment - a strong incentive to find work (indeed <u>any</u> work irrespective of pay and conditions). Secondly, those 55 or over were immediately eligible for the works pension whereas those under 55 have to wait until they are 65 (unless they had a proven disability). These contrasts in themselves (similar to earlier arguments that had encouraged the older worker to volunteer for redundancy) created a certain moral obligation upon those 55 or over not to seek work - to do so would deprive a younger unemployed man to whom work would bring greater financial advantage. Thus the redundancy process described by Harris,

Lee and Morris (1985) as assortative extends beyond the bounds of the steelworks.

THE SAMPLE

Any research project has two starting points: an idea and a source of data. In reporting the results of the research back to the respondents (Bytheway 1985a), I described the idea as follows:

> Being made redundant towards the end of your working life forces you to think hard about your circumstances, and in particular about the prospects and reality of retirement. It is a major change in your position in society: last week you spent much of your time on the site in a largely sheltered environment, following certain routines, working jointly with other people and knowing that a wage or salary will follow in due course; this week you are on your own in the outside world competing, insofar as you are able and interested, with many others for scarce employment opportunities, reorganising your domestic life and household budget, and thinking about an unfamiliar and complicated future in which one of the few certainties is that (God willing) you will be eligible for your retirement pension - a permanent regular source of income - on a certain date in a few years time.

Thus my main objective was to study the transition of redundancy in the context of the approach of 'normal' retirement age: to examine the ways in which it was an ageing experience.

Data had already been collected through the much larger research project on the effects of the 1980 Slimline Plan upon Port Talbot and the surrounding area, (Harris, Lee and Morris, 1985). For this there were three waves of interviewing of a sample of 752 redundant employees (i) during the summer of 1981, (ii) during the summer of 1982, and (iii) at the end of 1982. This was differentially weighted towards younger workers but nevertheless included 121 men who were aged 55 years or more when made redundant and who had been interviewed in the third wave. Of these I interviewed 108 between May and July 1984[2]. The interview was taped and was guided by a proforma that covered various aspects

of the interviewee's working life, the effects of
redundancy, and his present circumstances.
   The 108 interviewed men have three characteristics in common:

   1)   They are all male[3],
   2)   They were born between 1916 and 1926
        inclusive,
   3)   They were working for the BSC at the Abbey
        Works in Port Talbot at the beginning of
        1980 and were made redundant during the
        course of that year.

Most, 86, were works employees of BSC, eleven were
staff and eleven were management. There were 18
Trades Union officials. Owner-occupiers made up 57
per cent of those I interviewed and 38 per cent are
in council housing. There are very few who are in
lodgings or privately rented accommodation. Nearly
half the sample were born in West Glamorgan, the
county in which the steelworks is located. About a
third were born elsewhere in Wales, primarily in
Mid Glamorgan. Of the 18 from outside Wales, ten
were from England, four from Scotland, two from
Ireland and two from Europe. Thus only 83 per cent
were born in Wales compared with 88 per cent of the
whole Steel sample. This indicates that immigration
into the area is more characteristic of this older
generation of steelworkers. It should be noted,
however, that 22 per cent spoke Welsh compared with
only 14 per cent in the whole sample and this
reflects differences between the generations of
Welsh-born people.
   In the 1930s, when the 108 were young boys
becoming young men, there were two steelworks in
Port Talbot, both dating back to the First World
War. There were also half a dozen tinplate and
other metal works. Other important sources of
employment were the docks, the collieries up the
Afan and Goytre valleys, the local retail and
service industries and the railways. All were
struggling under the effects of the recession, but
all were to benefit significantly in terms of
employment by the rearmament programme.
   Port Talbot has experienced two expansions: in
the nineteenth century and in the 1950's. The
cohort for this study were in their late twenties
and thirties at the time of the latter. Their
working lives date back to the origins of the Abbey
works in 1946 to 1951. The large majority, 78,
entered the workforce of the Steel Company of

Wales between the end of the War and 1960. Twelve had started in the steelworks in Port Talbot before the War, and 18 had been taken on during the course of the 1960s and 1970s. There is a connection between starting work in the Abbey and moving into their present homes. A fifth moved in within the first two years of their employment.

Except for those who have arrived in the area more recently, they have observed (and many were engaged in) the construction and expansion of the strip mill. Five new furnaces were opened during the course of the 1950s. They will have seen the development of the Abbey in the context of their personal lives, their local communities and, to some extent, in the part that it has played in British industry. More generally, all were young adults, some with young families (but some still too young to vote), when the Labour government came to power in 1945. In 1981, just over half said they had voted Labour in 1979 and would vote Labour again 'tomorrow'. It is fair to suppose that the large majority will have voted Labour at the 1945 election and that they will have had firm expectations of the future of the newly nationalised industries such as steel - expectations that will not have included redundancy in 1980.

Their approach to adulthood and the labour market was affected by the War and this varied greatly since their ages in 1939 ranged from 13 to 23. Several told me tales of how the War had affected the course of their lives. About half of those born outside South Wales came to the steelworks because in the course of the War they had met and married a South Wales woman. Similarly their earlier experience and memories of the depression varies with age. The older men, for example, recounted their experience of intermittent work in the metal industries during the 1930s. They were the only ones who before 1980 had ever experienced unemployment. For these reasons, age is an important variable - quite apart from the approach to statutory retirement age.

POST-REDUNDANCY CAREERS

Appended to this paper is the basic matrix outlining the post-redundancy careers of the 108 ex-steelworkers. The three dimensions of the matrix are: status immediately following redundancy, current status in 1984, and certain characteristics of the intervening period. Taking each of these in turn we obtain the percentage distributions shown in Tables 5.1 and 5.2. These show that only a small minority had work when made redundant, almost one in four have since worked but only half of these are currently working.

In regard to 1980 a distinction has been made between those who were actively looking for work and those who were not but who nevertheless described themselves in the interview as unemployed. These two groups account for one half of the sample, and rather more than twice as many were looking as were not. In 1984 it was difficult to make the same kind of distinction since so many had been unemployed for a long period. Perhaps half a dozen could be described as actively looking for work but this was not the same kind of activity as looking immediately after redundancy. The redundancy process entails certain expectations about alternative work, and some came out in 1980 confident that there was work to be found. Six months later they were still available and still 'on the lookout', but they had learnt much about life outside the steelworks and, four years later, those who were available for work had, broadly speaking, settled into a routine which presumed that their only chance of being offered paid employment lay in a dramatic change in the national economy. Similarly, because of the very different financial circumstances, not looking and being available in 1980, is different to being of the same status in 1984.

Table 5.1: Percentage Distributions:

	1980	1984
In work	2	12
Looking	36 ⎤	
	⎥	24
Not looking/ unemployed	16 ⎦	
Ill/disabled	24	37
Retired	22	27
Total	100	100

Table 5.2: Percentage Who Have:

Ever worked	23
Ever refused work	7
Looked after ill wife	8
Passed 65th birthday	18

As Table 5.1 shows there has been a substantial increase in the numbers of the ill and disabled in the intervening period: from one in four to over one in three. Likewise there has been a 20 per cent increase in the number of the retired, although this is more than accounted for by those who have passed the age of 65 years.

Turning to the non-exclusive categories of Table 5.2 we see that seven per cent have at some point refused the offer of work. To these might be added a similar number who have resigned from work subsequently obtained. These men, given the payments that arose from redundancy and faced with unsatisfactory work, felt able to say no. Eight per cent have been involved in nursing a sick wife. This last group is included in the basic matrix because it was the one domestic circumstance which involuntarily removed redundant workers from the labour market. Finally, Table 5.2 shows that nearly one in five were over 65 years of age when interviewed in 1984.

Variations in outcome are summarised in Table 5.3. The most striking fact that emerges is that all those who are presently in work were actively looking for work when first made redundant. There was only one individual (now retired) who has been in work since redundancy who did not initially look for work. Thus no redundant worker found work as a result of only actively seeking it when his make-up money ran out in 1982. Although some explained that they had not looked for work because there would be no financial gain from taking work whilst receiving make-up money, it would seem that none had subsequently filled the gap between make-up and state retirement pension by seeking work at that time.

Table 5.3: Summary Percentage Transition Matrix

1980	1984 In work	Available	Not in Work and: Ill or disabled	Retired	Total
Looking (inc. In work)	32	29	29	10	100 (41)
Not looking: unemployed	-	35	18	47	100 (17)
Ill/disabled	-	19	77	4	100 (26)
Retired	-	12	21	67	100 (24)

The second feature of Table 5.3 is the stability of the states of ill/disabled and retired. The large majority of those who enter these states upon redundancy remain in them. Rather less striking but more interesting are the outcomes for those who were unemployed and available in the labour market. Setting aside those who found work, fairly similar proportions of those who looked and those who did not are still available. Of those who have dropped out of the labour market, however, substantially more of those who did not look are now retired compared with those who looked. Conversely, the latter are comparatively more likely to withdraw because of illness or disability. Rather than a causal explanation such as 'looking makes you ill', this suggests that not looking is a first step towards retirement, and that unsuccessful attempts to find work are followed by successful applications for Invalidity Benefit, a source of income for those who are too ill or disabled to be able to undertake paid employment.

WORK

The figures reported in Tables 5.1 to 5.3 are compatible with Harris's conclusion that a significant number of redundant steelworkers have subsequently experienced a chequered career of alternating employment and unemployment (1984). Below we examine in rather more detail their post-redundancy employment histories. What should be said at the outset is that a post-redundancy chequered career at the age of 58 is not the same thing as it is at 38. Firstly, the Slimline plan, as argued above, was designed to 'readapt' the younger man through positive inducements to participate actively in the labour market. It would seem that it was decided that it was crucial to get him into work and enjoying the kind of income that he had been used to. The effects of this was to stimulate the local contractor firms into creating essentially temporary employment with low wages that were made-up by the Corporation (see Fevre, this volume). It may have been intended, and in reality the more perceptive of the redundant workers realised, that this was at best a holding operation whilst better, more secure employment was sought and found. Having obtained temporary work, some may have left this in order to have the time to seek something more satisfactory and, if frustrated, may have accepted a second temporary arrangement. Thus Slimline, itself, will have directly induced chequered careers.

In regard to the older worker, this outcome was not intended. Slimline was orientated to the expectation (and the belief) that he would (and should) take his 'early retirement'. He was being readapted to a life without paid work. It was essentially the initiative of the particular worker and the interest of the employer that led to the development of chequered careers for these men. Secondly, there is a difference between the 58 year old and the 38 year old because of their different positions in their working lives. The younger man may have ten or twenty years behind him in the steelworks, but he still hopes to be able to invest twenty years and more in an alternative setting. If he were to succeed he may subsequently view his time in the steelworks in much the same way as those whom I interviewed who had worked in the coal mines for ten or twenty years and who had moved to the Abbey when the local pit had been closed. These men had strong memories of the mines, were by and large relieved to have 'escaped', and viewed the 1984 miners' strike (and the contentious role of the steelworkers) with considerable interest and occasional passion. Thus, for the younger man, the hope is that 1980 and the readapting years will constitute a midlife change of direction and the establishment of a second career which they may yet come to see as their main life's work.

The 58 year old, in contrast, hopes for seven more years of employment at most. Whatever becomes of this, his main occupation in life will have been working in the Abbey. This is what he will look back upon in his old age. Nor is it just a question of the number of years spent working there. Many of the older workers actually helped to build the steelworks and they had been led to think of their employment there as a job for life. Much of their life has been engaged in shift work in teams, and consequently theirs has been a shared experience and, in particular, they shared the assumption that they would be there until they retired at 65. How then have some come to acquire a post-redundancy chequered career?

Just as it is important to remember that redundancy in 1980 affected and threatened many more than those who were actually made redundant, so it is necessary to appreciate that many of those who were made redundant subsequently sought and were considered for employment quite apart from those who actually gained it. In other words there is an important difference between those predisposed to taking work and actively seeking it, and those who actually obtain it. That said, the accounts of the 25 who obtained employment are highly pertinent to an understanding of the experience of older redundants on the labour market. This is because expectations and aspirations within the network of redundant workers is largely based upon knowledge of successes in the labour market, and because success for the individual radically changes his own predispositions and expectations.

Table 5.4: Employment Status at Time of Wave 1 Interview

Employment Status		
Work to go to upon redundancy		2
Looked for work:		
and found it:	full-time	4
	part-time	3
and not found it:	unemployed	14
Undertaken a retraining course		1
Not looked for work:	unemployed	1
		25

Twenty-five of the 108 men obtained employment in the course of the four years between redundancy and interview. Their employment status at the time of the Wave 1 interview in 1981, is described in Table 5.4.

This indicates that only a minority - nine - had obtained work within the first year or so. The remainder, however, were not among those who were not looking for work - it was not the withdrawal of make-up money that had spurred them into looking for work. Rather, they had been looking for work without success during most of the first year. Several reported that they had applied for a large number of jobs and others described how they had actively sought work. DA, for example, unemployed for twelve months after redundancy, said he had started looking for work as soon as he heard about the redundancies although he knew there was not much about. He eventually found work by going to the local town council offices and asking if there were any vacancies.

The distribution of the length of time between redundancy and first job is shown in Table 5.5.

Table 5.5: Length of Time Between Redundancy and First Job

	Months
0 - 6	7
7 - 12	7
13 - 18	6
19 - 24	3
25 - 30	1
DK	1
	25

At the time of the interviews in 1984 the precise status of some respondents was unclear. The classification shown in Table 5.6 is based upon their responses to three lines of enquiry. One was about the redundant's present employment status, the second about their interest in the hypothetical offer of employment and the third about when they had retired or expect to retire. These specific questions were frequently overtaken by rather more biographical accounts of their experiences.

Table 5.6: Status in 1984

	Under 65	65 and over
Employed	12	1
Expecting employment	2	
Looking for employment	2	
Not looking because of illness/disability	5	
Retired	2	1
Total	23	2

The two shown in the table who were <u>expecting</u> work had particular jobs in mind and in both cases this related to work that they had already undertaken since 1980.

The two who are <u>looking</u> for work in 1984 are FB and BR. FB is single and lives in Porthcawl, a holiday resort six miles from Port Talbot. He had obtained seasonal work during each of the previous three summers but, in 1984, he deferred to the needs of a younger man. Although nearly 65, he continues to walk round Porthcawl looking for employment and has picked up occasional 'hobbles' (unofficial paid work) such as digging gardens. His labour market behaviour, characterising several others, is heavily influenced by the view that older men should make way for younger men: at all stages in the redundancy process, the younger man is seen to have the greater moral claim upon available work (Bytheway, 1985b).

BR, working in a large components factory, was made redundant for a second time in August 1983. He is keen to obtain further work because being employed at BSC for only nine years, he has a smaller pension than most. He has also invested all his redundancy money in the purchase of his council house. In 1984, this is showing substantial structural faults and he is involved in legal negotiations with the council. Before BSC, he had spent much of his working life as a draper but, without capital, he is unable to return to that line of business. He has applied for five or six jobs but has not been encouraged by what is available at the Job Centre. Although FB and BR are both looking for work, their motivations and their approaches to the labour market are very different. BR is stuggling to maintain a chequered career which started well before his redundancy from the steelworks.

Of those not looking because of ill-health, two claim they are still available for work, even though they have no expectations of returning to employment. The other three are clearly out of the labour market. Two, and possibly the third, resigned from their post-BSC employment because of ill-health. There are three who had found work after redundancy, but who now consider themselves retired. One has effectively retired through ill-health and another is over 65 years of age. The third said that he had done 'a bit of contracting in timber' since redundancy. He gave this up through ill-health but he still maintains a certain trade in horticultural goods. In response to the question about retirement he answered:

> Semi-retired. More or less you can say I'm retired. I don't intend to go through no business books.

Thus most of those who had entered the job market upon redundancy, who had found employment, and who had since left it, had done so primarily as a result of ill-health rather than retirement. Yet, despite leaving the job market, a few of these men are still prepared to undertake certain forms of paid work. They illustrate well the reality of Daniel's 'transition phase between economic activity and inactivity'. This phase may extend over several years and is characterised by (i) subtle changes in job-seeking initiatives and routines, (ii) changing expectations based upon common knowledge and first-hand experience and (iii) changing estimations of the value of work determined by changes in income (make-up money, etc.), (iv) changes in domestic circumstances and (v) the approach of state pensionable age. It would be a mistake to assume that changes in this phase are all one way. Whilst it is true that there are certain statutes and biological processes that are 'inevitable', a chequered career which seemingly leads the ageing man out of the 'active' labour market is still characterised by periodic ups and downs.

The thirteen who are presently employed include nine who are in full-time employment in 'proper' jobs. Out of the whole sample of 108 ex-steelworkers, these nine are those who, it might be said, have made no progress towards retirement since redundancy, other than through being four years older. The other four who are employed are significant in that they illustrate resistance to the inevitability of economic inactivity.

> CV is employed by a garage as a car cleaner. Immediately after redundancy he had found work as a storekeeper for a large chain store. Later he had six months retraining as a painter. He was disappointed that this did not lead to employment and after twelve months on the dole, took his present job in April 1983. Sometimes he is full-time, sometimes part-time, working as a jack-of-all-trades. He turned down another job he was offered because he didn't like the hours. He intends to resign when he's about 63 and then undertake paid work as a painter as and when he feels inclined.

> EM is employed on a job creation scheme - his second such job. Both have drawn upon his interest in local history. Although he would like to see the local council funding it as a 'proper' job, he expects to end up being occupied in voluntary local historical research. He has learnt from bitter experience that part-time temporary lecturing and election polling booth employment create no useful supplementary income.

> EJ is 59 and is one of the few who has seriously entered the state of self-employment. After two years of actively looking for employment, he invested his redundancy money in a project in the Potteries. This failed but it led him, in October 1983, to set up his own local pottery business. He sees 1984 as being a make or break year.

> WD is past his 66th birthday and is employed delivering bread. He says he is retired now and the job is only a pastime. Previously he had resigned himself to being retired after he had left a job under the Job Release Scheme but, after ten months, he had grown bored at home. Without telling his wife, he had answered an advertisement in the paper to obtain his present job.

Nine of these thirteen employed workers have no plans to retire from their current work. EJ, the potter, for example, has no intention of finishing at 65. His wife's exasperated comment was:

> As far as he's around, he would never retire. Because he's a workaholic. Is that the word? He can be sat there now half dead. And he can get up in an hour's time when everybody's tired and ready for bed and he's ready for work. You know ... I think they should put down men of his type. Don't laugh, I've seen it. Like old bulls, they should shoot them.

These men believe that work keeps you fit and most have plans to stay in paid employment past their 65th birthdays: 'I don't want anyone to tell me I'm too old to work.' To some extent they share the freedom of having <u>chosen</u> to work, rather than the need to undertake paid employment. DW is a good example of this. He has had two jobs since 1980. The first he gave up because of his poor hearing. The second lasted nearly two years and was with a contractor on the BSC site. In the ten months since he used to think of himself as retired, but the answer on the day of the 1984 interview was 'semi-retired' because the following day he was starting a new contract. Later in the interview he summarised his attitude as:

> To me, it's great. I don't have to set that little alarm every night to go to bed, you know, and this sort of thing. Oh, no. I think early retirement's great.

This implies that if it was early retirement that he entered when he took redundancy, this does not exclude active participation in the job market.

In contrast to the above, there were four who were expecting retirement at 65 or earlier. One runs his own small haulage business and is looking forward to closing it when he is 'able to retire at 65'. In the meantime he needs the income. The other three have jobs from which they will be compulsorily retired at 65, if not before. Only one said that he was looking forward to his retirement.

UNEMPLOYMENT

The appendix shows that of 39 who had looked for work, 22 were taken on and 17 have remained out of work since 1980. Of these, eight are still available, seven are ill or disabled and two are retired. Five of the eight have consciously given up looking for work - generally after about two years of unemployment. One said he had tried 'a bit harder' after his Unemployment Benefit had finished but to no avail. The other three are not now actively looking. They had fairly clear ideas about particular jobs they might have obtained - one believed he would have got a job in a private quarry but his contact there had just left. Another was approached, but when interviewed felt under pressure to make way for a younger person and, in some indignation, had withdrawn his application. One, like several others, had been conscious of trends in the local labour market: 'I gave up after eighteen months. People were coming out all the time. It was hopeless'. Four are presently on Invalidity Benefit but are still available for light work. When asked about retirement, there was a reluctant admission that they are now in effect retired: 'no more jobs' was the usual explanation. Yet they expressed their disappointment vividly: 'Retired? Got to now. Tried to battle against it. There's years of work left in me now.' Another said he feels retired, but will only call himself retired at 65. He remarked ambiguously that he will do hobbies once he's passed that age.
    The seven who are now ill or disabled are little different from those who had never looked for work (see below). It was not so much that they were fit when first made redundant before becoming invalids. Rather they were keen to stay in work despite their ill-health:

> The doctor disapproved. With Invalidity Benefit there was no need for me to work. But I wanted to and went for a few interviews. When age was mentioned: sorry, no way. It was a bit humiliating.

The two who are now retired are both over 65 years of age.
    Turning to the fifteen who said that they had not looked for work, Table 5.3 indicates that there is a tendency for them to claim retirement in 1984 rather than illness or disability, and this

reflects the situation they were in in 1980 and 1981: they were available for work, registered unemployed and willing to consider offers, but they knew there was little available and they did not have the need to obtain any. They used to look in the paper, but noticed the 'situations vacant' column diminishing and eventually gave up bothering. Those who are still available are those who have always been ready to consider an offer, but who have been quite likely to refuse. They are 'too young' to be retired. Three of the six were managers at the Abbey - their health is good, there is no pressure to obtain work and they are happily engaged in alternative pursuits. Of the three now ill, one did not look for work because of the advice of the doctor: 'They seem to want to put you on the sick' he said.

The seven who did not look and who are now retired, look back and see their retirement to have started in 1980. The one who refused the offer of a job also outlined the problem of status:

> Retired? Yes but when people tell me "Are you retired?", I tell them "unemployed", see. Technically, I'm unemployed. I do. I do draw people up, mind. Although I consider myself retired I'm unemployed technically.

ILLNESS AND DISABILITY

Of the 26 who described themselves as sick in 1980 (ill or disabled), five claim to be available for work in 1984. One of these still expects to obtain work. Two were not fit enough for the climbing tasks that they had had to undertake in the steelworks. Despite illness and disability, they would like some light work. Two others had wives who were also ill and who needed them to finish in 1980. One of these wives is now fully dependent upon her husband and for him, it is not so much a case of being available as liking to think that he might have been available had she not been so disabled. The fifth, the youngest of the five, is interested in work because of boredom. Three of these five had comparatively serious complaints. Rather than suffering minor or temporary conditions and being generally available, these are disabled people who could only consider suitable 'light' work. There may be others among the ill and disabled who would similarly be available for such work but who did not say so.

The most significant distinctions to be made among the 26, concern the level of disability and the date of onset. A total of seven were not significantly ill or disabled when made redundant. They developed conditions shortly thereafter - two cases of heart disease, three operations, pleurisy and hypertension. None are now seriously disabled. The impression they gave was that their experience of illness has made them decide to withdraw from the labour market, to retire on the grounds of ill-health. In two instances the receipt of Invalidity Benefit and the implied state of being under doctor's orders seemed significant.

Twelve were moderately disabled when made redundant and, of these, three have become more seriously disabled since. One lost a leg in the Second World War and had been employed by BSC as a registered disabled person. He is becoming increasingly disabled by arthritis. Five made a direct connection between their disability and difficulties they had had in undertaking their work at the Abbey. A major problem had been that of working on the gantries when suffering from arthritis or balance problems. These men would have expected to have been offered a ground level job as had others in similar circumstances before 1980, but for them the Slimline offer coming shortly after the relieving twelve week national steel stike was a timely opportunity. Some had had hopes of finding light work outside. Seven were severely disabled when they took their redundancy. They were not capable of any kind of work and would have been forced into ill-health induced early retirement irrespective of the redundancy proposals.

It was clear that many of the 108 have engaged in serious activity in the 'illness and disability market'. Just as a prospective employer might be persuaded to 'take you on' and you thereby receive a regular income, so the same is true of your doctor. There is a gap between the end of make-up money and the beginning of the state retirement pension that can only be filled (in the absence of paid employment) by Invalidity Benefit. Financially, it is an important source of income. I have not interviewed local doctors about their interpretation of the regulations regarding this benefit. In authorising the benefit, it is undoubtedly the case that the patient has a condition (more than likely several) which can be and is being treated. The doctor may feel that it will not be good for the patient's health to need to seek work when there is so little chance of being successful. Some doctors may indeed see Invalidity as an early retirement pension. Whatever the case, the fact remains that about a third of those I interviewed were in receipt of Invalidity. Because it is an important source of income, it followed that their health is an important feature of their post-redundancy lives over and above the simple matter of keeping well.

RETIREMENT

The appended basic matrix shows that there were 24 who reported in the 1980 Wave 1 interview that they were retired and that, of these, three in 1984 were available for work, six were ill or disabled and the remaining 15 are still retired.

None of the three who have remained available for work indicated that there had been a significant change in their position. It was more a case that in their early retirement they have continued to be available should an unexpected opportunity arise. There is also a fourth presently disabled who also said that if he were offered 'a nice little number' he would take it. The other four of the disabled reported a variety of conditions: a prostate operation, diabetes, arthritis and a serious stroke. The latter two were disabled prior to redundancy (and consequently they could equally be classified as sick or disabled in 1980). The diabetes was diagnosed shortly after redundancy - taken in part because he did not feel well and was looking forward to retirement. In all five instances, it was not so much a case that these disabled retirees had ceased to be retired, only that their disabilities are now a major handicap. The other fifteen include seven with medical conditions of some significance, so ill-health or disability is a feature in the retirement careers of about half of this group.

The common characteristic of these 24 redundant workers was a certain readiness to adopt the status of being retired upon being made redundant in 1980. The term 'early retirement' had been much used in that year and undoubtedly at that time they had come to associate themselves with that status. A number described their position unambiguously: 'Free now', 'That's the end of the day', 'Once finished, finished', and 'My working life was over'. About ten made it clear that they had decided in 1980 that this was it - their retirement. For the other, it was more a case of a retrospective judgement, some had been to the Job Centre without expectations and some might well have stayed on at the steelworks given the opportunity. It is only with hindsight that they now recognise 1980 to have been their retirement.

There are four ways in which the dynamics of the retirement career are made apparent. Firstly, as many as fourteen are receiving Invalidity Benefit. As indicated above, this reflects to a large extent the level of disability and illness in this generation of steelworkers and this has a dynamic that is not unrelated to work and unemployment. Income after redundancy has highly complex and structured patterns of change. Life in early retirement has to be funded either by drawing upon the securities created by the redundancy payment or by receiving some regular substitute for the short-term make-up money.

The second source of change is in the domestic world, typically changes in the circumstances of wives. One of these 24 had lost his wife since 1980 and another three had wives who were ill. As has been indicated, wives' illnesses were most influential upon the course of the redundant workers' lives. The wives of two others have since ceased work and the wife of another is regularly away from home to tend to her elderly mother. One other has been divorced since being made redundant. In all these instances, domestic change has seriously changed the course of retirement (and in some instances has been caused by redundancy). The retired man may find that much of his time is taken up with domestic matters, or that the financial balance of his domestic circumstances has changed drastically and he has to rethink his decision to be retired.

The third aspect of the retirement career is the familiar question of occupation. Two of these men have since had successful careers in local politics. This has occupied much of their time and, in incidental ways, created supplementary income. Two others have also taken on employment-like occupations. Of the others, eight drew attention to their efforts in the garden, five mentioned traditional leisure pursuits, and five indicated that much of their time was taken up in assisting their adult children with home improvements or with childminding.

Finally there is the simple matter of age.

Thirteen of these, the retired, were into their sixties when made redundant. As a group, they were older on average than the whole sample. Those who were in their sixties were nearer retirement in more ways than simple chronological time. Most thought that the age of 60 was a more appropriate statutory pension age than 65. It is after all the statutory pension age for women. Unemployment benefit and social security regulations are different for men over the age of 60, and the Slimline programme accorded certain additional benefits to some of those over the same age. Perhaps most important of all, the individual is 'in his sixties': the decade of retirement.

Many of those interviewed indicated that they had carried out fairly detailed calculations to help them decide to volunteer. They had worked out that there was little to be gained financially over and above a certain age: one said that 61 was 'ideal' and another that: 'If I stayed, I'd be working for nothing'. Consequently it was easier for those over 60 to abondon the prospect of further continued employment. Those who were under 60 who described themselves as retired were either reasonably secure (eg. had been either staff or management), had working wives, or were suffering from disability. One final comment upon these 24 retirees. Most made some reference to 'making way' for younger men. Having decided to do so in taking redundancy, it naturally follows that they would tend to do so in the wider labour market, and several did indicate that they had retired in order not to deprive a younger person of employment.

CONCLUSION

A frequent conclusion of empirical sociological enquiry is that things are not as simple as they might appear to be. It was inevitable from the start of the present research that this would be one of its 'findings'. In fact it might be said that it is not really so very complicated. The following is a listing of conclusions.

    1) In preparing the Slimline plan, the BSC recognised the problematic and distinctive circumstances of older workers and instituted special arrangements for those who had passed their 55th birthdays.

    2) These arrangements were designed to ease

the older worker out of the labour market.

3) Management, unions and popular opinion established a moral principle that older workers should make way for the younger generation. Most of the older workers accepted this 'in principle'.

4) Those made redundant had little experience of life in the labour market and competed, if at all, ambivalently or ineptly.

5) The motivation to seek and take paid employment remains strong even if largely inhibited by the lack of opportunity.

6) About half undertook a search for jobs. Of these, half were unsuccessful, and their search petered out after a year or two.

7) A quarter were successful and most entered a chequered career of intermittent low-paid employment.

8) The two primary alternatives to continuing participation on the labour market, are illness or disability and retirement.

9) The status of being ill or disabled is sanctioned through the family doctor and leads to the receipt of Invalidity Benefit. It frequently relates to previous working conditions and experiences.

10) The status of the retired is informally induced and self-ascribed. It is not incompatible with paid employment.

11) The older worker's post-redundancy career is significantly constrained by age: his basic problem is managing his approach to pensionable status. There are three alternative 'scenarios': economic activity in the labour market, invalidity and retirement. He may or may not take direct action in pursuing a particular scenario. It is possible to detect aspects of all three scenarios in a worker's post-redundancy career.

This list of eleven conclusions is a fair summary of what the study has revealed of the redundancy process of the 'typical' individual worker. In considering the effects of redundancy upon older workers in general, however, this study has a certain relevance. It is limited to the effects upon men, previously employed on a largely secure and long-term basis in heavy industry, and to local labour markets characterised by an unemployment rate of about one in six. In such circumstances redundancy is a major push or inducement towards early retirement, one that throws the social order of the worker's life into serious disarray. In the particular case of the Slimline plan at the Abbey works in Port Talbot, a 'job for life' that was based upon shift work and continuous production and that had been scheduled to terminate on a particular day in the future, had suddenly 'dissolved' leaving the redundant worker high and dry and uncertain about how to proceed.

I have deliberately avoided questions of 'adjustment'. Most of those whom I interviewed appeared to have coped well, but several told tales of the domestic disasters that had followed redundancy. It may be that this is just part of the modern folklore of Port Talbot, or it could be, for example, that the five whom I could not contact had suffered such consequences, and it may be that there were others whom I had interviewed who had not declared the full facts. Consequently it may well be that there is a fourth scenario: the personal disaster. What was made clear to me, however, by those I interviewed was that finishing was a great release. The shift system, the continental hours, which ran through every public holiday meant that their lives had been largely dictated by the routines of the steelworks. Many reported substantial problems in orientating themselves to a new sleeping pattern in the months following redundancy. For some there was a 'rediscovery' of the family: old acquaintances were renewed and new ones formed. There were frequent references to grandchildren and to brothers, daughters, etc. who had migrated to Australia and the US not to mention Scotland. For others, there was the time to consult the doctor about some niggling complaint - most had chest and hearing problems and complained of arthritis, and they related this to their working environment. Thus after thirty years or so of continuous employment in heavy industry - incidentally in an enormous plant that employed 15,000 people at one time - they had found themselves prematurely discharged to a new life that was characterised by unprecedented choice and devoid of direction. This was the impact of redundancy upon the older worker.

NOTES

1. The number of redundancies has increased
   fourfold in Wales between 1974 and 1979
   (Welsh Office, 1980).
2. Five of the sample of 108 had died since
   1982, three refused to be interviewed and
   there was no response by five to my
   efforts to contact them. Of the 108,
   eleven refused to have the interview taped
   and two interviews were substantially
   abbreviated because of disability. The
   average interview took 44 minutes and all
   but six were more than 20 minutes in
   length. I am grateful to the ESRC for
   supporting this research.
3. There were only six women in the larger
   sample who were 55 years of age or over.
   It was decided that it would be inappropriate to include them in this study since
   they were so few in number.

REFERENCES

Altmann, R.M. (1981) 'Incomes of the Early
    Retired', Journal of Social Policy, 11,
    355-64
Blake, C., I.L. Buchanan, M.J. Tooze and P.G.
    Chapman (1979) Redundancies in Dundee,
    Scottish Economic Planning Department,
    Edinburgh
Blyton, P. (1984) 'Partial Retirement: Some
    insights from the Swedish Partial Pension
    Scheme', Ageing and Society, 4, 69-84
Bytheway, W.R. (1985a) Induced Voluntary Early
    Retirement, Working Paper, University College
    of Swansea
Bytheway, W.R. (forthcoming) 'Making Way: The
    Disengagement of Older Workers' Proceedings
    of British Society of Gerontology
Carmichael, C.L. and L.M. Cook (1981) Redundancy,
    Re-employment and the Tyre Industry, Manpower
    Services Commission, London
Casey, B. and G. Bruche, (1983) Work or Retire-
    ment?, Gower, London
Colledge, M. and R. Bartholomew (1980) 'The Long-
    Term Unemployed: Some New Evidence',
    Department of Employment Gazette
Cribier, F. (1981) 'Changing Retirement Patterns
    of the Seventies: an Example of a Generation
    of Parisian Salaried Workers', Ageing and
    Society, 1, 51-72
Daniel, W.W. and E. Stilgoe (1977) Where are they
    now? A Follow-up of the Unemployed, PEP,
    XLIII, No. 572
Department of Health and Social Security (1981)
    Growing Older, Her Majesty's Stationery
    Office, London
European Economic Community, (1980a) Community
    Guidelines of Flexible Retirement, CEC Com
    (80), 393
European Economic Community , (1980b) Discrimin-
    ation in Occupational Pension Schemes,
    EEC Commission working paper
Gaullier, X. (1982) 'Economic Crisis and Old Age:
    Old Age Policies in France', Ageing and
    Society, 2, 165-82
Greenwood, J. and R. Pearson, (1979) 'Redundancies
    and Labour Displacement: Effects within a
    Local Labour Market', Industrial Relations
    Journal, 10, 22-29
Harris, C.C., R.M. Lee and L. D. Morris, (1985)
    "Redundancies in steel: labour market

behaviour, local social networks and domestic
organisation' in: New Approaches to Economic
Life (Eds. Roberts, B., R. Finnegan, and D.
Gallie), Manchester University Press,
Manchester

Jolly, J., S. Creigh and A. Mingay (1980) 'Age as
a Factor in Employment', Research Paper No.
11, Department of Employment, London

Makeham, P. (1980) 'Economic Aspects of the
Employment of Older Workers', Research
Paper No. 14, Department of Employment,
London

Makeham, P. and P. Morgan (1980) 'Evaluation of
the Job Release Scheme', Research Paper No.
13, Department of Employment, London

Office of Population Censuses and Surveys, (1981)
General Household Survey, 1979, Her Majesty's
Stationery Office, London

Parker, S. (1980) Older Workers and Retirement,
Office of Population Censuses and Surveys,
London

Parker, S. (1982) Work and Retirement, George
Allen and Unwin, London

Phillipson, C. (1977) 'The Emergence of Retirement', Working Papers in Sociology, No. 14,
University of Durham

Social Services Committee, House of Commons (1983)
Age of Retirement, Her Majesty's Stationery
Office, London

Walker, A. (1981) 'Towards a Political Economy of
Old Age', Ageing and Society, 1, 73-94

Welsh Office, (1980) Digest of Welsh Statistics,
No. 26, Cardiff

Wood, S. (1980) 'Managerial Reactions to Job
Redundancies Through Early Retirements',
Sociological Review, 28, 783-807

APPENDIX The basic matrix (Numbers).

		In Work	Status in 1984 Available	Not in work Ill/disabled	Retired
Status in 1980 (immediate post- redundancy)					
In work	T	1		1	
	A	1		1	
Looking	T	12	12	11	4
	A	12	4	4	2
	B	2	1	1	1
	C	–	–	1	–
	D	1	–	–	3
Not looking/ unemployed	T		6	3	8
	A		–	–	1
	B		–	–	1
	C		1	–	2
	D		–	–	–
Ill/disabled	T		5	20	1
	A		–	–	–
	B		1	–	–
	C		1	1	–
	D		1	4	1
Retired	T		3	6	15
	A		–	–	–
	B		1	–	–
	C		–	1	2
	D		1	–	9
Total	T	13	26	41	28
	A	13	4	5	3
	B	2	3	1	2
	C	0	2	3	4
	D	1	2	4	13

Characteristics of 1980-1981 period.
Key: T   Total
      A   Ever been in work
      B   Ever refused work
      C   Looked after ill wife
      D   Past 65th birthday

Chapter Six

ETHNIC INEQUALITY IN LAYOFF CHANCES: THE IMPACT OF
UNIONISATION ON LAYOFF PROCEDURE[1]

Daniel B. Cornfield

With the growth of the U.S. labour movement through
the 1940s and the emergence of the civil rights
movement in the 1950s and 1960s, alternative
strategies for labour allocation in business
enterprises have come in conflict with one another.
While civil rights advocates espouse affirmative
action policies to ensure equality of employment
opportunity for minorities, labour unions champion
the use of seniority-based labour allocation
procedures. In advocating the use of seniority,
unions contributed to the bureaucratisation of
business enterprises. The virtual demise of the
union hiring hall by the end of World War II
shifted control of hiring into the hands of
management. In order to limit particularistic and
capricious managerial decision making, unions
argued for the use of seniority (i.e. amount of
continuous service in the company) - an objective,
universalistic and quantifiable rule - as the basis
for selecting workers for promotions, transfers,
layoffs and recall. Moreover, unions could demand
strict managerial adherence to bureaucratic
procedures through collective bargaining and the
written labour contract, the possibility of binding
outside arbitration in worker grievances alleging
contract violation, and the ultimate strike threat.
    However, combined with discriminatory hiring
practices of managements, bureaucratic labour
allocation decision making has contributed to
ethnic inequality in worker layoff chances. With
privileges typically accruing to the more senior
workers, ethnic groups of workers, such as blacks,
who had been barred from employment by discriminating
managements tend now to have less seniority than
favoured ethnic groups and, therefore, to be the
'last hired and the first fired' (U.S. Commission

on Civil Rights 1977). This is not to deny the long-standing, cooperative relationship between the civil rights and labour movements. At least since the 1950s, the two movements participated together in civil rights demonstrations and in union organising campaigns among low-wage blacks, contributing to both the passage of civil rights legislation and the improved livelihoods of newly unionised blacks (Marshall 1967; Barbash 1973; Wilson 1978; Foner 1982).

The conflict over the divergent goals and outcomes of affirmative action and seniority-based layoff procedures is reflected in the 1984 U.S. Supreme Court case, Firefighters Local Union No. 1784 v. Stotts. In a 1980 consent degree which was established to rectify past racial discrimination in hiring, the Memphis, Tennessee Fire Department agreed to hire and promote more black employees. In 1981, faced with projected budget deficits requiring layoffs, the Memphis Fire Department announced that it would use the City's 'last hired, first fired' seniority-based procedure for laying off employees. Plaintiff Carl Stotts sought an injunction barring the strict use of seniority in laying off workers, arguing that the gains made by recently hired and promoted black employees would otherwise be in jeopardy. The lower courts agreed with the plaintiff. However, in a 6-3 vote, the Supreme Court reversed the lower courts, arguing that the City was not contractually obliged to depart from its seniority-based layoff procedures because layoffs were not mentioned in the consent decree; and that Title VII of the 1964 Civil Rights Act did not authorize remedial alteration of seniority systems except with regard to identifiable victims of past discrimination (Supreme Court Reporter 1984).

Notwithstanding any effects of seniority-based labour allocation procedures on the ethnic differential in layoff chances, little is known about how labour allocation decision making in non-union work settings affects this differential and how the determinants of this differential in unionised and non-union settings may differ. Indeed, in the absence of a union and the strike threat, management is more likely to opt for performance criteria over seniority and to engage in non-bureaucratic, particularistic behaviour when laying off workers (U.S. Bureau of Labour Statistics 1972: Weeks 1976; Cornfield 1983). Therefore, the purpose of this chapter is to

examine the effect of unionisation on the
<u>determinants</u> of ethnic inequality in layoff
chances. After discussing the historical relationship
between unionisation and bureaucratisation, I
develop hypotheses and test them on the unionised
and non-union work forces of Emco (pseudonym), a
U.S. telecommunications corporation.

UNIONISATION AND BUREAUCRATISATION

With the emergence of national and international
markets, the subsequent increasing size of business
enterprises, and unstable supplier and consumer
markets, many firms by the 1930s had developed
structures that were similar to the ideal-typical
bureaucracy depicted by Weber (1969). Business
enterprises integrated backwards, forwards and
horizontally through mergers and acquisitions,
spawning a new managerial class, large administrative
staffs, increased divisionalisation and numerous,
more specialised jobs (Bendix 1956; Chandler 1962,
1977; Blair 1972; Nelson 1975).
    Unionisation also promoted bureaucratisation
in the early twentieth century (McNeill 1978). With
wide fluctuations in the business cycle, labour
turnover rates, and employment, unions and large
corporate managements alike sought to regularise
employment by rationalising labour allocation
decision-making (Slichter 1919, 1941; National
Industrial Conference Board 1930; Slichter, Healy
and Livernash 1960; Commons 1934; Vollmer 1960).
Through collective bargaining, unions helped to
spin a web of written, seniority-based labour
allocation rules in many contracts, arguing for the
fairness and predictability embodied in these
universalistic and quantifiable decision-making
rules (Selznick 1969). Some large corporations also
favoured seniority rules because they facilitated
the administration of large, impersonal firms
(Vollmer 1960). Seniority-based labour allocation
rules were first used in the large railroad
companies during the late nineteenth century and
had become widespread in the mass production
industries by the 1930s (Mater 1940; Berger and
Piore 1980). Today, seniority-based labour allocation
rules are most commonly used in unionised
enterprises and large enterprises (Vollmer 1960;
U.S. Bureau of Labor Statistics 1970, 1972; Weeks
1976).

ETHNICITY, UNIONISATION, AND LAYOFF CHANCES

The successive waves of different immigrant groups to the United States throughout the nineteenth and twentieth centuries led them to occupy different positions in bureaucratising business enterprises and to acquire different amounts of seniority with their employers. Just as the new generations of each ethnic group moved outward from their original, inner city residences when the next ethnic groups arrived in the inner city - the process of ecological succession described by the early Chicago sociologists (Park and Burgess 1925) - ethnic groups also moved through formal career paths in corporate 'internal labour markets' (Spilerman 1977), accumulating seniority in the corporation along the way. Access of some ethnic groups, such as blacks, to corporate career ladders and their subsequent capacity for accumulating seniority were affected by employer discrimination in hiring. Hence, despite their relatively long duration of residence in the United States, blacks have gained access to bureaucratic career ladders and some seniority only in recent years especially after the passage of civil rights legislation in the mid-1960s (Wilson 1978; Alvarez and Lutterman 1979; Fernandez 1981; Davis and Watson 1982).

In a local labour market area, the occupational distribution of worker ethnic groups and the ethnic differential in seniority levels are often a function of variation across ethnic groups in their duration of residence in the area and past patterns of employer hiring behaviour. For example, in his study of the South Chicago steel mill community, Kornblum (1974) shows that the mill workers of Northern European descent, the first group to have arrived in the area, tended to occupy the highest-status jobs and to be the most senior employees; workers of Eastern European descent, the next group which migrated to the area, held medium-status jobs and were the next most senior employees; and black and Hispanic workers, who had either recently arrived in the area or had been barred from employment by discriminating employers, worked in the lowest-status jobs and tended to be the least senior employees. In short, patterns of immigration, employer hiring behaviour, and the seniority-based promotion rules used in the mill led effectively to the upward succession of some ethnic groups through the mill job hierarchy.

Unionisation, the rationalisation of labour

allocation decision making, the successive immigration of different ethnic groups, and the subsequent ethnic stratification of workers by occupation and seniority constitute the historical and institutional legacy which informs my hypothese about ethnic inequality in worker layoff chances. These processes and institutions may have promoted the upward succession of some ethnic groups through the status hierarchies of corporations. However, they periodically interrupted this succession when worker ethnic groups were laid off in times of economic recession or rapid technological change.

It will be helpful to define a layoff before proceeding to the hypotheses. A layoff is an employee termination which is initiated by the employer because the employee's job is deemed to be superfluous to the functioning of the enterprise. Employees may be laid off involuntarily or voluntarily. Involuntary layoffs occur when the employer unilaterally terminates employees. Voluntary layoffs, which have become increasingly common in recent years (Cornfield 1982, 1983; Lee 1985), occur when the employer intends to reduce the number of jobs and solicits volunteers for termination by providing them with incentives. A layoff differs from a firing or discharge in that the latter occurs when an employer is dissatisfied with the performance of a specific employee and fills the vacancy with another employee.

Given differences in ethnic group occupational distributions and seniority levels, my hypotheses develop the assertion that ethnic inequality in worker layoff chances is more or less attributable to these differences among ethnic groups, depending on the unionisation status of the work force. Therefore, I begin with hypotheses that I have presented elsewhere (Cornfield 1983) on determinants other than ethnicity and unionisation of inequality in worker layoff chances. The first hypothesis is that workers in jobs directly involved in the production process, or in jobs that are indirectly involved but whose work volume depends on the volume of production, are more likely than other workers to be laid off. The work volume of jobs directly involved in production - production jobs - varies with product-demand in the market. Therefore, these jobs are more likely to be deemed superfluous in periods of declining demand than non-production jobs, such as office clerical jobs, whose work volume is relatively constant and independent of changes in demand (Cornfield 1981, 1983; Schervish

1983).[2] However, non-production jobs whose work volume depends on that of production jobs, such as supervisors of production workers, are likely to be deemed superfluous when production jobs are eliminated during a decline in demand. Also, production jobs are more vulnerable to elimination from technological change because technological innovations in industry have been largely directed toward improving production efficiency. Therefore, supervisory and other non-production jobs which monitor production are indirectly but, nonetheless, highly vulnerable to elimination from the introduction of increasingly self-monitoring and self-correcting multi-purpose production technologies (Cornfield 1983).

The second hypothesis is that workers whose personal characteristics correspond most closely to the procedural criteria for laying off workers are more likely than other workers to be laid off. For example, in firms which lay off workers in reverse order of seniority, worker seniority is expected to be negatively associated with layoff chances. Similarly, in firms which solicit voluntary layoffs by providing greater incentives (e.g. severance pay and early retirement benefits) to more senior and older employees, seniority and age are expected to be positively associated with layoff chances.

The third hypothesis pertains only to cases of voluntary layoffs: workers who are less committed to their jobs and to their employers are more likely than other workers to volunteer and, therefore, to be laid off. Although worker commitment data are unavailable for the empirical analysis below, data on worker characteristics, income, education, sex and marital status, which turnover research has shown to affect the likelihood of quitting, are available. While turnover research demonstrates consistently a negative association between income and quitting chances, research findings on the education, sex and marital status effects are ambiguous (Price 1977). Therefore, I have no a priori reason for hypothesizing effects for these variables on layoff chances. I expect a negative association between income and layoff chances when a firm implements a voluntary layoff procedure.

These three hypotheses suggest that in the absence of discriminatory layoff decision-making, ethnic inequality in layoff chances is a function of differences between ethnic groups in their occupational employment distributions, the

correspondence between their personal characteristics
and the procedural criteria for laying off workers,
and, in the case of voluntary layoffs, their
individual traits which may motivate them to
volunteer. Therefore, I present the fourth
hypothesis as three sub-hypotheses:

4a. Ethnic groups which are disproportionally
employed in production jobs and other
vulnerable jobs are more likely than
others to be laid off;

4b. Ethnic groups whose personal characteristics
correspond most closely to the procedural
criteria for laying off workers are more
likely than others to be laid off;

4c. In the case of voluntary layoffs, ethnic
groups whose individual traits most
closely correspond to those which promote
volunteering are more likely than others
to be laid off.

How might unionisation affect the <u>determinants</u>
of ethnic inequality in layoff chances that are
described in hypotheses 4a-4c? In the absence of a
union, a written labour agreement and the ultimate
strike threat, management will have greater
flexibility in determining the number and types of
jobs to be eliminated and the procedures for laying
off workers. Moreover, a non-union employer is more
likely to invoke particularistic, non-bureaucratic
criteria for laying off workers because of the
absence of a written agreement and mechanisms, such
as the strike threat, for compelling strict
adherence to bureaucratic layoff procedures, as
discussed above.

Assuming that non-union employers are more
likely than unionised employers to invoke non-bureaucratic layoff procedures, they are also likely to
have allocated and promoted employees to jobs in a
less bureaucratic fashion before implementing
layoffs. In a non-union firm, ethnic groups may not
have passed through the job hierarchy in the
orderly manner described by Kornblum (1974) above.
Given the subsequent difficulty in assessing the
likelihood of non-random, occupational employment
distributions among the ethnic groups of a
non-union work force, I present no hypothesis on
the impact of unionisation on the <u>occupational</u>
<u>determinants</u> of ethnic inequality in layoff chances
described in hypothesis 4a. Similarly, I have no <u>a</u>
<u>priori</u> reason for positing a unionisation effect on

how the determinants of volunteering, in turn, affect ethnic inequality in layoff chances as outlined in hypothesis 4c.

However, stricter managerial adherence to bureaucratic layoff procedures is more likely in unionised settings. The impact of any bureaucratic layoff rules on ethnic inequality in layoff chances, as in hypothesis 4b, is likely to be greater in unionised than in non-union settings. Therefore, the fifth and final hypothesis is that differences between ethnic groups in the correspondence between their personal characteristics and the procedural criteria for laying off workers will have a greater impact on ethnic inequality in layoff chances in a unionised work force than a non-union work force.

LAYOFFS AT EMCO

The Emco corporation (pseudonym) is a multi-locational, U.S. telecommunications carrier. Over half of its 2500-member work force is unionised. In 1976, faced with declines in its market share and profitability, Emco automated further its production technologies, closed some of its branch operations, consolidated departments and laid off over 10% of its total work force (Cornfield 1982, 1983).

The voluntary layoff procedure used at Emco was established through collective bargaining but was applied to unionised and non-union employees. Under this procedure, employees were given seniority-based incentives to volunteer for layoff. The amount of severance pay was tied directly to company seniority, with more senior volunteers receiving greater severance pay then less senior volunteers. Management selected volunteers in direct order of seniority. The most senior volunteers were chosen first and the least senior volunteers were chosen last. Although involuntary layoffs were permissible in the absence of volunteers, 96% of the layoffs were voluntary. Also, volunteers over the age of 55 received early retirement benefits, in addition to severance pay.

Data and Variables

The analysis below is based on over 100 interviews I conducted with Emco personnel and other managers, union officials, and non-supervisory employees and Emco personnel record data. The data are the 1976 unionised and non-union Emco work forces. The dependent variable in the logistic regressions[3] below is the natural logarithm of the odds of an employee being laid off. Four sets of independent variables are used in the regressions. First, ethnicity variables were created for the different ethnic groups at Emco in order to determine ethnic inequality in layoff chances.[4] Each is a dichotomous variable indicating employee ethnic descent (yes = 1). The percentage laid off for each ethnic group is shown in descending order of magnitude by unionisation status in Table 6.1.

Table 6.1: Percentage Laid Off at Emco by Unionisation Status and Ethnicity

Unionised Workers			Non-union Workers		
Ethnicity	%	N	Ethnicity	%	N
Puerto Rican	23.1	65	German or		
Irish	16.5	109	Scandinavian	11.1	144
Eastern European	16.1	62	British	9.9	243
British	16.0	250	Eastern European	9.7	62
German or			Afro-American	8.1	62
Scandinavian	15.9	126	Asian	6.7	74
Afro-American	12.3	243	Irish	6.3	95
Jewish	12.0	75	Hispanic	5.8	69
Asian	11.0	145	Italian	5.5	200
Italian	10.8	195	Other European	1.8	167
Other European	8.8	57	All Workers	7.2	1116
Other Hispanic	4.3	93			
All Workers	13.2	1420			

Second, in order to test hypotheses 1 and 4a, dichotomous job variables were created, indicating whether an employee was employeed in a given occupation (yes = 1). For the unionised work force, one variable was created for each of the clerk, operative, technician, service, custodian, warehouse worker and office clerical occupations. The layoff chances of employees in the first three occupations, which are production jobs, are expected to exceed that of the latter four which are ancillary to actual production (Cornfield 1983). For the non-union work force, the job variables indicate employment in one of the supervisor, assistant, professional, salesperson, manager and office clerical occupations. Under the first hypothesis, the layoff chances of employees in the first three occupations are expected to exceed that of the latter three because the tasks of the former are more closely connected to production activity than the latter (Cornfield 1983). Finally, for both work forces, the variable 'headquarters' was created in order to indicate whether the employee worked at Emco headquarters (yes = 1) or in a branch operation, given the closing of some branch operations. The layoff chances of branch operation employees are expected to exceed that of headquarters employees.

Third, procedure variables were created to test hypotheses 2, 4b and 5. Given Emco's seniority - and age-based voluntary layoff procedure, procedure variables indicate employee seniority at Emco (in years) and whether the employee was over the age of 55 (yes = 1). Each is expected to be positively associated with layoff chances under the second hypothesis.

Fourth, turnover variables are included in order to test hypotheses 3 and 4c. Under the third hypothesis, income (in U.S. dollars and including overtime pay) is expected to be negatively associated with layoff chances. As discussed above, no hypotheses are presented for the effects of sex (female = 1), marital status (married = 1), and education (0 = less than 8 years of school; 1 = 8 years of elementary school; ...; 7 = Master's degree; 8 = Ph.D.).

Findings

The results of the logistic regressions of the odds of being laid off for the unionised and non-union work forces are presented in Tables 6.2 and 6.3, respectively. The same stepwise method was used in the regressions for these two work forces. The job, procedure and turnover variables, in this order, were successively and cumulatively added to the model containing only the ethnicity variables. The twofold purpose of this method is: 1) to determine the effect of each independent variable on the odds of layoff net of the effects of the other independent variables; and 2) to discern those independent variables whose inclusion in the model most reduces the magnitudes of the ethnicity variable coefficients. Thus, model 1 (column 1, Tables 6.2 and 6.3) contains only the ethnicity variables. For each work force, the ethnic group with the lowest percentage laid off in Table 6.1 is omitted as the benchmark ethnic group whose layoff chances are compared to those of each of the other ethnic groups in the model (the omitted ethnic groups are other Hispanics and other Europeans for the unionised and non-union work forces, respectively). The job variables are added to model 1 in model 2 (column 2, Tables 6.2 and 6.3). The occupation with the lowest percentage laid off is omitted as the benchmark occupation (these omitted occupations are office clerical workers for both the unionised and non-union work forces). The procedure variables are added to model 2 in model 3 (column 3, Tables 6.2 and 6.3) and the turnover variables are added to model 3 in model 4 (column 4, Tables 6.2 and 6.3).

Given the twofold purpose of the stepwise method, I begin by describing the findings on the net effects of the job, procedure and variables, followed by a description of the effects of including the latter variables on the magnitudes of the ethnicity variable coefficients.

The findings in model 4 in Tables 6.2 and 6.3 support the first hypothesis on the effects of job variables for both the unionised and non-union work forces. For the unionised work force (Table 6.2), clerks, operatives, and technicians were more likely ($p < .05$) to be laid off than office clerical workers, while service workers, custodians and warehouse workers were no more likely to be laid off, irrespective of the other variables; for non-union employees (Table 6.3), supervisors, assistants and professionals were more likely than office clerical workers to be laid off, while managers and salespeople were no more likely to be laid off. For both work forces, employees at Emco headquarters were less likely to be laid off than their counterparts employed in branch operations.

The model 4 findings support the second hypothesis on the effects of the procedure variables for the unionised work force. Seniority and age are significantly and positively associated with layoff odds. For the non-union work force, however, the seniority coefficient is statistically insignificant but the age coefficient is both significant and positive. The model 4 findings also address the effects of the turnover variables. For the unionised work force, the income coefficient is significant and negative, as expected, but the coefficients of the other turnover variables are

Table 6.2: Logistic Regressions of the Odds of Being Laid Off, Unionised Work Force (N=1336)

Independent Variables	Regression Coefficients			
	(1)	(2)	(3)	(4)
Ethnicity Variables				
Puerto Rican	.743*	.730*	.714*	.624*
Irish	.606*	.579*	.161	.177
Eastern European	.602*	.626*	.225	.237
British	.558*	.475*	.183	.204
German or Scandinavian	.607*	.554*	.294	.297
Afro-American	.405	.493*	.485*	.475
Jewish	.369	.340	.044	.074
Asian	.327	.068	.179	.101
Italian	.368	.439	.186	.157
Other European	.329	.317	.021	.035
Job variables				
Clerk	–	1.240*	1.020*	.934*
Operative	–	.797*	.704*	.718*
Technician	–	.511*	.486*	.544*
Service	–	.295	.186	-.245
Custodian	–	.060	-.105	-.319
Warehouse worker	–	-.099	.070	-.091
Headquarters	–	-.295*	-.350*	-.230*
Procedure variables				
Seniority	–	–	.032*	.040*
Age	–	–	.755*	.729*
Turnover variables				
Income	–	–	–	-.00009*
Marital status	–	–	–	.009
Sex	–	–	–	-.138
Education	–	–	–	-.052
Constant	2.080	3.390	1.140	1.570
Improvement chi-square[a]	13.808	68.824*	104.532*	11.634*
df	10	7	2	4

*p < .05

Note: a. indicates improvement over previous model in fit between observed and expected frequencies; for model in column 1, improvement over constant-only model (not shown); for model in column 2, improvement over model in column 1; etc.

Table 6.3: Logistic Regressions of the Odds of Being Laid Off, Non-Union Work Force (N = 1065)

Independent Variables	Regression Coefficeints			
	(1)	(2)	(3)	(4)
Ethnicity variables				
German or Scandinavian	.915*	.799*	.788*	.795*
British	.897*	.743*	.832*	.837*
Eastern European	.880*	.833*	.688*	.661*
Afro-American	.808*	.665*	.864*	.803*
Asian	.696*	.338	.536	.621
Irish	.648*	.653*	.562	.578
Hispanic	.696*	.332	.647	.598
Italian	.568*	.665*	.756*	.739*
Job variables				
Supervisor	–	1.380*	1.070*	1.120*
Assistant	–	1.610*	1.440*	1.340*
Professional	–	1.230*	1.100*	1.160*
Salesperson	–	.020	-.276	-.260
Manager	–	.818	.438	.584
Headquarters	–	-.819*	-.847*	-.789*
Procedure variables				
Seniority	–	–	.026*	.021
Age	–	–	.858*	.882*
Turnover variables				
Income	–	–	–	-.00005
Marital status	–	–	–	.182
Sex	–	–	–	-.181
Education	–	–	–	-.275*
Constant	2.150	4.410	3.980	5.890
Improvement chi-square [a]	16.247*	69.780*	61.859*	8.926
df	8	6	2	4

*p < .05

Note: a. See Table 2, note a.

insignificant. For the non-union work force, only the negative education coefficient is significant.

Turning to the second purpose of the stepwise method and tests of hypotheses 4a-4c, let us first examine the findings for the unionised work force in Table 6.2. Model 1 (column 1) contains only the ethnicity variables. Although this model constitutes

an insignificant (p > .05) improvement in fit over
the constant-only model, five of the ten ethnicity
coefficients are significant (p < .05). Employees of
Puerto Rican, German or Scandinavian, Irish,
Eastern European or British descent were significantly
more likely to be laid off than employees of other
Hispanic descent, the omitted benchmark ethnic
group. The employees of the other ethnic backgrounds
were no more likely than employees of other
Hispanic descent to be laid off. Comparing the
ethnicity coefficients of model 1 to those in model
4 (column 4) shows that with the addition of the
job, procedure and turnover variables, the
coefficients of four of these five significant (in
model 1) ethnicity variables are reduced to
statistically insignificant magnitudes in model 4,
while only the Puerto Rican coefficient remains
significant, but 16% smaller, in model 4. The four
other coefficients that are significant in model 1
are from 51% to 71% smaller in model 4.

Hypotheses 4a-4c are examined in columns 2
through 4 in Table 6.2. The job variables are added
to the model in model 2 (column 2, Table 6.2). The
inclusion of the job variables significantly
improves the fit but the five significant ethnicity
coefficients remain significant in model 2 and the
Afro-American coefficient becomes significant. The
significant improvement in fit that results from
the addition of the procedure variables in model 3
(column 3) reduces four of the five significant
ethnicity coefficients in model 1 to insignificant
magnitudes, while the Afro-American and Puerto
Rican coefficients remain significant. Finally,
adding the turnover variables in model 4 (column 4)
significantly improves the fit, reduces the
Afro-American coefficient to an insignificant
magnitude, and reduces by 13% the Puerto Rican
coefficient which remains significant. In sum, the
reduction in magnitude of the significant ethnicity
coefficients of model 1 in model 4 is mainly
attributable to the inclusion of the procedure
variables in model 3. Therefore, these results
provide the most support for hypothesis 4b but
yield little support for hypotheses 4a and 4c.

The findings for the non-union work force are
shown in Table 6.3. Model 1 (column 1) contains
only the ethnicity variables. All of the ethnicity
coefficients in model 1 are significant, indicating
that, with the significant improvement in fit over
the constant-only model, each of these employee
ethnic groups was more likely to be laid off than

employees of other European descent, the omitted benchmark ethnic group. Comparing the model 1 ethnicity coefficients to those in model 4, which includes the job, procedure and turnover variables, shows that seven of the eight ethnicity coefficients are from 1% to 25% smaller in model 4, the Italian coefficient is 30% larger in model 4, and only the Asian, Irish and Hispanic coefficients are insignificant in model 4.

Models 2 through 4 in Table 6.3 indicate which of the job, procedure or turnover variables most accounts for the reduced coefficient magnitudes in model 4 for the non-union work force. Adding the job variables to model 1 in model 2 significantly improves the fit, reduces the Asian and Hispanic coefficients to insignificant magnitudes, lowers the German or Scandinavian, British and Afro-American coefficients by 13% to 18%, reduces the Eastern European coefficient by 5%, and increases the Irish and Italian coefficients. With the significant improvement in fit which accompanies the inclusion of the procedure variables in model 3, the Irish coefficient becomes insignificant, the Asian and Hispanic coefficients remain insignificant, the German or Scandinavian and Eastern European coefficients are reduced by 1% and 17% respectively, and the British, Afro-American and Italian coefficients are larger. Finally with the addition of the turnover variables in model 4, which insignificantly improves the fit, the Asian, Hispanic and Irish coefficients remain insignificant, the Eastern European, Afro-American and Italian coefficients are reduced by 2% to 7%, and both the German or Scandinavian and British coefficients are increased by 1%. Thus, for the non-union work force, any reductions in ethnicity variable coefficients in model 4 compared to model 1 are largely attributable to the inclusion of the job variables in model 2. Therefore, these results provide weak support for hypothesis 4a but little or no support for hypotheses 4b and 4c.

The findings for the unionised and non-union work forces may be comparatively summarized as follows:

1. the job variables were significantly associated with layoff odds for both work forces, supporting the first hypothesis;
2. while both procedure variables were significantly and positively associated with layoff odds for the unionised work

force, age, but not seniority, was significantly and positively associated with
layoff odds for the non-union work force;
the second hypothesis is more strongly
supported for the unionised work force;

3. for each work force, three of the four
turnover variables were insignificantly
associated with layoff odds, with income
and education having significant negative
associations with layoff odds for the
unionised and non-union work forces,
respectively; the third hypothesis is
partly supported for both work forces;

4. the reductions in the magnitude of the
ethnicity variable coefficients which
accompanied the inclusion of the job,
procedure and turnover variables were
greater for the unionised work force than
for the non-union work force; also, more
ethnicity variable coefficients were
rendered insignificant by the inclusion of
these variables in the unionised work
force models than in those of the
non-union work force;

5. for the unionised work force, reductions
in the magnitudes of the ethnicity
variable coefficients were mainly attributable to the inclusion of the procedure
variables; for the non-union work force,
any reductions were mainly attributable to
the inclusion of the job-variables; for
the unionised work force, these results
strongly support hypothesis 4b and provide
little support for hypotheses 4a and 4c;
for the non-union work force, hypothesis
4a is weakly supported and hypotheses 4b
and 4c receive little support.

These comparative findings support the fifth
hypothesis. For the unionised work force, ethnic
inequality in layoff chances was largely attributable
to the procedure variables; for the non-union work
force, procedure variables had little effect on
ethnic inequality in layoff chances. Thus, in the
unionised work force, ethnic groups which tended to
have more seniority and to be older were more
likely than their less senior and younger
counterparts to be laid off. For the non-union work
force, the causes of ethnic inequality in layoff
chances are less apparent in these quantitative
data.

Some managers reported in my interviews that perceived employee incompetence and personal incompatibility were criteria used by managers in some cases to select volunteers for termination from the non-union work force. However, it is impossible to assess the net impact of these criteria on layoff chances because of the absence of appropriate data. While some managers could have discriminated against some ethnic groups when selecting volunteers from the non-union work force, the ethnic differences in layoff chances in Table 6.3 suggest that this was unlikely. Non-union employees of Afro-American descent, the ethnic group against whom employer discrimination would be typically waged in the U.S., had lower odds of being laid off than non-union employees of British descent and comparable odds to those of non-union employees of German or Scandinavian descent, net of the job, procedure and turnover variable effects.

Assessing other possible correlates of ethnicity and layoff chances for the non-union work force is complicated further by the voluntary nature of the layoff procedure. In addition to being motivated by the incentives of the layoff procedure, non-union volunteers may have also been motivated by turnover variables other than those included in this study and for which data are unavailable. These may include, among many others, on-the-job interpersonal relations with coworkers and the availability of alternative employment in the local labour market area (Price 1977). The latter could lead to ethnic differences in the likelihood of volunteering. Assuming geographical variation in both employment opportunities and the residences of ethnic groups, ethnic groups who disproportionately resided in areas abounding with employment opportunities could have been more likely to volunteer for layoff than their counterparts in economically depressed geographical areas.[5]

Discussion

The findings suggest that unionisation affected the determinants of ethnic inequality in layoff chances at Emco. Given ethnic variation in seniority and age in the unionised work force, the seniority - and age-based incentives for volunteering in the layoff procedure were the main determinants of ethnic inequality in layoff chances among the unionised employees. However, these incentives had a negligible impact on the ethnic inequality in layoff chances among the non-union employees. Therefore, the findings suggest that the stricter adherence to bureaucratic rules for laying off workers for the unionised work force led to a greater impact of these rules on ethnic inequality in layoff chances in the unionised work force than in the non-union work force.

What, then, were the determinants of ethnic inequality in layoff chances among the non-union employees? Unfortunately, the absence of data and the voluntary nature of the Emco layoff procedure render the affirmation of these determinants virtually impossible. The decisions of both employees and management affected layoff chances under the voluntary layoff procedure. Turnover variables other than those included in the study could have motivated some ethnic groups to volunteer with a greater likelihood than other groups, as discussed above. The negligible seniority effect in the non-union work force suggests that managers did not closely adhere to the seniority rule when selecting non-union volunteers for layoff. Moreover, I was not informed of any other written, quantitative, universalistic rules used by management to select non-union volunteers. This implies that what criteria were used by management for selecting non-union volunteers were of a non-bureaucratic and particularistic nature. In sum, ethnic inequality in layoff chances among non-union employees may have resulted from different propensities of ethnic groups to volunteer and from less bureaucratic, less universalistic managerial decision making in the non-union work force than in the unionised work force.

The divergent findings for the two work forces suggest, then, that the same management invoked a more bureaucratic and universalistic set of labour allocation rules in the presence of a union than in its absence. Therefore, while bureaucratic universalism contributed to ethnic inequality in the layoff chances of unionised employees, non-bureaucratic particularism may have led to such inequality among the non-union employees.

CONCLUSION

The Emco case suggests that unionisation affects the degree of bureaucratic universalism in the determinants of ethnic inequality in layoff chances. In a unionised work setting, such inequality results from the application of bureaucratic, universalistic layoff procedures to a work force whose ethnic groups characteristically differ in terms of the procedural criteria for laying off individual workers. In a non-union setting, ethnic inequality in layoff chances is more likely to be the consequence of non-bureaucratic, particularistic managerial decision making. This implies that in the presence of the ultimate strike threat, the management of a unionised firm will adhere more strictly to universalistic procedures, thereby generating more predictable patterns of ethnic inequality in layoff chances, than the management of a non-union firm. [6]

This assertion can receive further corroboration or falsification in future layoff research if the findings of the Emco case are compared to those in other organizations which vary simultaneously among at least two relevant dimensions. The first is the type of layoff procedure deployed, whether involuntary or voluntary. Fewer actors participate under the former procedure, while employees, in addition to management and possibly a union, participate under a voluntary procedure. Therefore, future research on voluntary layoffs ought to include such factors as employment conditions and availability of alternative employment which motivate and facilitate quitting.

The second dimension is unionisation. The procedures and criteria for laying off workers, such as seniority and employee performance (merit), as well as managerial adherence to them ought to be compared in unionised, partly unionised and non-union firms. These comparisons may show how unionisation affects not only the degree of universalism in the determinants of ethnic inequality in layoff chances, but also which criteria lead to more or less inequality in layoff chances.

In sum, inequality in life chances results not only from the legacy of bureaucratic work place structures (i.e. rules) which developed along with the increasing size, complexity and unionisation of business enterprises in the early twentieth century. Such inequality also derives from the capacity of management to consistently engage in bureaucratic decision making within a bureaucratically structured enterprise. While unionisation contributed to business enterprise bureaucratisation, it also tended to reinforce, if not compel with the strike threat, the continuation of bureaucratic managerial decision making within bureaucracies. This suggests that bureaucratic structure is a necessary but insufficient condition for the perpetuation of bureaucratic decision making; and that the potential for worker disruption of profits through unionisation and the strike threat compels the managements of a bureaucratic enterprise to engage more consistently in bureaucratic decision making. Therefore, inequality in life chances is more likely to result from predictable patterns of bureaucratic decision making in a unionised firm than in a non-union firm.

It would seem, then, that the challenge for the labour and civil rights movements is not only developing mutually acceptable, universalistic rules which reconcile the divergent goals and outcomes of affirmative action and seniority-based labour allocation procedures. A greater challenge, perhaps, is limiting the impact of capricious managerial decision making on ethnic inequality in layoff chances by introducing such universalistic rules in non-union work settings.

NOTES

1. I am gratefully indebted to the Emco corporation (pseudonym) for permitting me to do the research and providing me with data and to Doris Davis for typing the manuscript. The material in this project was prepared under the partial support of a grant from the Stouffer-Star Fund of the University of Chicago and Grant No. DD-80-17-010 from the National Council on Employment Policy (NCEP). Researchers undertaking such projects under NCEP sponsorship are encouraged to express their professional judgment freely; therefore, points of view or opinions stated in this document do not necessarily represent the official position or policy of NCEP.

2. In Britain, some employers contract for labour on a temporary basis in order to adjust the work force to changes in product demand. Termed the 'ancillary employment structure' by Lee (1985), such labour contracting often results in the reemployment of laid off production workers with the same employer but with employment conditions which are inferior to those prior to layoff.

3. Logistic regression is useful for analysing variation in a dichotomous dependent variable. Each regression coefficient is the amount of change in the natural logarithm of the odds of a 'success' with respect to the dependent variable which is associated with a unit change in the given independent variable, net of the effects of the other independent variables in the model. Interpretation of logistic regression coefficients is similar to that of coefficients in an ordinary least-squares multiple regression equation. For further discussion of logistic regression, see Pindyck and Rubinfeld (1981).

4. Ethnicity was determined by analyses of surnames, birthplaces, foreign languages spoken, and the EEO records maintained by Emco. No surnames are included in the magnetic tape. The surname analysis has three weaknesses. First, people change surnames to hide their ethnicities. The other data helped overcome this problem. Second, by virtue of paternal transmission of surnames, only the father's ethnicity can be obtained. Third, the adoption by the wife of the husband's surname obscures the wife's ethnicity. Maiden names were analysed for married women and married women whose maiden names were unavailable were coded as 'not ascertainable'. Only 1.5 percent of the cases were

coded as 'not ascertainable'. For further discussion of problems related to the retrieval of ethnicity-related data, see Featherman and Hauser (1978: 523-28).

5. For example, with the post World War II suburbanization and Southward and Westward shift of population and businesses in the U.S., employment opportunities in the growth areas often exceed those in the declining central city areas of Northeastern metropoli. Therefore, the rate of volunteering for layoff and of quitting, more generally, among ethnic groups who disproportionately reside in suburban areas in the South and West are likely to exceed that of ethnic groups who disproportionately reside in declining areas.

6. Unionisation may also affect gender inequality in layoff chances. In a non-union setting, non-bureaucratic decision making may facilitate the application of sexist criteria for laying off workers. In a unionized firm, the application of seniority rules could adversely affect women workers. For example, if past patterns of sex discrimination in hiring led to a gender differential in seniority, such that women workers tended to be less senior than men workers, the layoff rate of women workers would exceed that of their male counterparts with the implementation of a 'last hired, first fired' layoff procedure.

REFERENCES

Alvarez, R. and K. Lutterman (eds.) (1979) _Discrimination in Organizations_, Jossey-Bass, San Francisco

Barbash, J. (1973) 'The Emergence of Urban Low-Wage Unionism' in _Proceedings of the 26th Annual Winter Meeting of the Industrial Relations Research Association_, Industrial Relations Research Association, Madison, pp. 275-83

Bendix, R. (1956) _Work and Authority in Industry_, University of California Press, Berkeley

Berger, S. and M. Piore (1980) _Dualism and Discontinuity in Industrial Societies_, Cambridge University Press, Cambridge

Blair, J. (1972) _Economic Concentration_, Harcourt Brace Jovanovich, New York

Chandler, A. (1962) _Strategy and Structure_, The M.I.T. Press, Cambridge

Chandler, A. (1977) _The Visible Hand_, Harvard University Press, Cambridge

Commons, J. (1934), _Institutional Economics_, Macmillan, New York

Cornfield, D. (1981) 'Industrial Social Organization and Layoffs in American Manufacturing Industry' in I. Berg (ed.). _Sociological Perspectives on Labor Markets_, Academic Press, New York, pp. 219-48

Cornfield, D. (1982) 'Seniority, Human Capital, and Layoffs: A Case Study', _Industrial Relations_, 21, 352-64

Cornfield, D. (1983) 'Chances of Layoff in a Corporation: A Case Study', _Administrative Science Quarterly_, 28, 503-20

Davis, G. and G. Watson (1982) _Black Life in Corporate America_, Anchor Press/Doubleday, Garden City

Featherman, D. and R. Hauser (1973) _Opportunity and Change_, Academic Press, New York

Fernandez, J. (1981) _Racism and Sexism in Corporate Life_, D.C. Heath, Lexington

Foner, P. (1982) _Organized Labor and the Black Worker 1619-1981_, second edition, International Publishers, New York

Kornblum, W. (1974) _Blue Collar Community_, University of Chicago Press, Chicago.

Lee, R. (1985) 'Redundancy, Labour Markets and Informal Relations', _Sociological Review_, 33,3, 469-94

McNeill, K. (1978) 'Understanding Organizational

Power: Building on the Weberian Legacy',
Administrative Science Quarterly, 23, 65-90
Marshall, F.R. (1967) Labor in the South, Harvard
University Press, Cambridge
Mater, D. (1940) 'The Development and Operation
of the Railroad Seniority System',
Journal of Business of the University of
Chicago, 13, 387-419
National Industrial Conference Board (1930) Lay-Off
and its Prevention, Studies in Industrial
Relations, No. 155, National Industrial
Conference Board, New York
Nelson, D. (1975) Managers and Workers, University
of Wisconsin Press, Madison
Park, R. and E. Burgess (1925) The City,
University of Chicago Press, Chicago
Pindyck, R. and D. Rubinfeld (1981) Econometric
Models and Economic Forecasts, second edition,
McGraw-Hill, New York
Price, J. (1977) The Study of Turnover, Iowa State
University Press, Ames
Schervish, P. (1983) The Structural Determinants
of Unemployment, Academic Press, New York
Selznick, P. (1969) Law, Society, and Industrial
Justice, Russell Sage, New York
Slichter, S. (1919) The Turnover of Factory Labor,
D. Appleton, New York
Slichter, S. (1941) Union Policies and Industrial
Management, The Brookings Institution,
Washington, D.C.
Slichter, S., J. Healy, and E.R. Livernash (1960)
The Impact of Collective Bargaining on Manage-
ment, The Brookings Institution, Washington,
D.C.
Spilerman, S. (1977) 'Careers, Labor Market
Structures, and Socioeconomic Achievement',
American Journal of Sociology, 83, 551-93
Supreme Court Reporter (1984), 104, 2576-610
U.S. Bureau of Labor Statistics (1970) Seniority
in Promotion and Transfer Provision, Bulletin
No. 1425-11, U.S. Government Printing Office,
Washington, D.C.
U.S. Bureau of Labor Statistics (1972) Layoff,
Recall, and Worksharing Procedures, Bulletin
No. 1425-13, U.S. Government Printing Office,
Washington, D.C.
U.S. Commission on Civil Rights (1977) Last Hired,
First Fired: Layoffs and Civil Rights, U.S.
Government Printing Office, Washington, D.C.

Vollmer, H. (1960) Employee Rights and the Employ-
    ment Relationship, University of California
    Press, Berkeley
Weber, M. (1969) 'Bureaucracy' in H.H. Gerth and
    C.W. Mills (eds.), From Max Weber: Essays in
    Sociology, Oxford University Press, New York,
    pp. 196-244
Weeks, D. (1976) 'Compensating Employees: Lessons
    of the 1970s', Conference Board Report No.
    707, Conference Board, New York
Wilson, W. (1978) The Declining Significance of
    Race, University of Chicago Press, Chicago

Chapter Seven

WOMEN AND THE REDUNDANCY PROCESS: A CASE STUDY[1]

Claire Callender

The aim of this chapter is to untangle the web of complex social processes involved in a redundancy situation. In particular it will examine these processes by charting the experiences of a group of women who lost their jobs as a result of a partial closure.[2] The chapter will attempt to highlight some of the gender-specific dynamics associated with redundancy and additionally consider the impact of legislation upon the processes involved. It will also challenge the notion that women are particularly acquiesent in redundancy situations by showing that there exists a range of factors which in fact militate against their collective action.

THE STUDY OF THE REDUNDANCY PROCESS

The majority of studies on redundancy concentrate upon the <u>consequences</u> of redundancy rather than the <u>process</u> and workers' responses to that process. Redundancy, therefore, is understood in an unproblematic way and its occurrence taken for granted and left unquestioned. It is viewed as an end product rather than as an ongoing interactive process between both management and workers. Wood and Cohen (1977) and Martin and Fryer (1973) have ably demonstrated the limitations of the existing approaches to the study of redundancy, arguing forcibly that the consequences of redundancy cannot be examined in isolation from the redundancy situation, and that it is important to examine the actual redundancy process: analyses must examine the social production of redundancy - the way it is legitimised and opposed, and 'the dynamic, processual and potentially conflictual nature of redundancy situations' (Wood 1977, 54). Martin and

Fryer have further suggested that there is a need
to incorporate in any analysis the attitudes and
meanings which redundants themselves attribute to
their actions and to their social situation. As
they assert (1973, 22) 'understanding behaviour
within the labour market involves understanding the
meaning of work and jobs and of the relation
between these and the social structure'. In a
similar vein Wood and Cohen (1977) stressed the
need to examine workers' aspirations, the role of
institutions in influencing these aspirations and
how they are shaped by redundancy.

WOMEN AND REDUNDANCY

Another glaring omission of analysis to date has
been its failure to consider how redundancy - and
redundancy processes - affect women. Even the most
recent studies, such as those in Port Talbot and
Sheffield (reported in this volume), exclude
redundant women from their samples, for apparently
methodological reasons, whilst the few studies
which do incorporate women are either gender-blind
or gender-bound, i.e. they assume that women's
experiences are either (a) the same as men's or (b)
that they can be explained solely in terms of the
sexual division of labour and women's domestic
role. These assumptions need to be questioned
because they distort our understanding of the
issues and reinforce existing assumptions. More
recent studies which have been specifically
concerned with women and redundancy have fallen
into the old analytical mode described above and
have underplayed the actual redundancy process,
concentrating instead on post-redundancy experiences
(Coyle 1984, Martin and Wallace 1984).

      Such studies aside, however, the main trend
remains to ignore women. A redressing of this
imbalance is the first reason behind an imperative
to include women in surveys of redundancy. The
second is that redundancy must be understood within
the context of the labour market and how it
operates. Although some women's experiences of
redundancy may be similar to men's, the demand and
supply of their labour is not the same since women
exhibit distinctive characteristics within the
labour market and their experiences and relations
to waged labour are different from those of men
(Martin and Roberts 1984).[3] Furthermore, women's
domestic roles and the dominant familial ideology

are both likely to affect their responses to redundancy. However, their experiences cannot be explained solely in terms of their family role just as men's experiences cannot be understood solely in terms of their economic role. In other words, we have to examine the specificity and reality of women's experiences.

A third reason why it is important to examine women and redundancy is in order to enhance our understanding of women's vulnerability to unemployment. There is considerable debate on the extent to which women (or at least certain categories of women workers) are particularly susceptible to unemployment in comparison to male workers. [4] Part of the specificity of women's vulnerability to redundancy and unemployment may be explained by the mechanics of the redundancy process.

Fourthly, prevailing concepts of work in Western societies not only reflect a male notion of employment and work but also ideas about who should have access to that employment (Callender 1985b). The actuality of women's redundancy - as revealed through empirical and analytical study - challenges this dominant concept and raises the issue of how far women's right of access to paid employment has in fact been secured (despite the fact that women workers are vital to the economy, and despite the narrow political assumptions embedded in the demand for the 'right to work' (Beechey 1982)). These issues have increased in importance because of the recession and the emergence of 'New Right' ideologies which have encouraged and legitimated economic and social policies designed to persuade women back into the home (David 1983). Analysis of women's redundancy would reveal much.

The fifth reason for examining how redundancy affects women is that the redundancy process represents the realisation of the interests of the powerful and is an outcome of the conflict of interests between the employer and the employee. This is the distinguishing feature of the employment relationship:

> Under capitalism it is capital's ability unilaterally to terminate its relation with specific labour, thus preventing workers from realizing subsistence through that relation by the sale of their labour power, that characterises the class conflict of dismissal ... it is the manifestation of class conflict in the instance of redundancy that merits

attention. (Fryer 1981, 141)

By studying the redundancy of women, therefore, we can also see the way gender relations interact with both class conflict and the relations of capital. Moreover, we can examine the stereotypical images portrayed of women in a redundancy situation as passive, fatalistic and acquiescent workers (Daniel 1972).

THE LEGISLATIVE PROVISIONS

To return to the actual process of redundancy, a further context which must be considered is the legislation governing redundancy. In Britain, this is primarily the concern of the 1975 Employment Protection Act (amended in 1979) which sets out procedural rules largely concerned with questions of notification and consultation, and guidelines for tribunals and courts in assessing appeals.[5] The emphasis of the Act is thus upon establishing proper procedures rather than stipulating the nature of the procedures. The 1978 Employment Protection (Consolidation) Act (amended in 1984, 1985, and 1986) outlines substantive rules relating to the compensation of those declared redundant, which secure and codify the rights of workers to financial remunertion. The payments are calculated on the basis of the worker's age, length of continuous service and pay. These statutory minimum redundancy payments can be supplemented by additional, privately negotiated ex-gratia payments which lie outside the scope of the legislation.

Elsewhere I have examined the substantive rules governing statutory compensation and the ways in which redundancy payments affect women workers and make them vulnerable to redundancy (Callender 1985a). I have argued that the legislation is both disadvantageous to women and discriminates against them because it is based upon a male dominated conception of work and so fails to consider the position of women in the labour market - a market which by its very nature leads to gender inequalities. By contrast, the concern of this paper, is primarily with the procedural rules which govern redundancy.[6] Here I aim to expose some of the hidden dimensions and consequences of the legislation (Walker 1981), to show how the legislation shapes a redundancy process, and to demonstrate the way in which it of itself is one of the 'ideologies and institutional arrangements which legitimise and guarantee the occurrence of redundancies' (Wood and Cohen 1977, 26). I will argue that the legislation is part of the social production of redundancy (Wood and Cohen 1977), structuring both the redundancy process and experiences of redundancy. The legislation is used as a form of social control to regulate the class conflict inherent in any redundancy situation. Ultimately, it lessens the ability of workers and unions to resist redundancies. Thus it is important to study redundancy processes, to include women in these studies, and specifically to examine the impact of redundancy upon women within the context of the issues outlined. We now turn to one particular case study of women clothing workers who lost their jobs in Wales.

THE CONTEXT

To understand the redundancy process we need to place redundancies within the context of (a) the factory, (b) the work situation and workplace experience, (c) the workers' pre-redundancy orientations and attitudes to work, and (d) the relationship of the above to the social structure (Martin and Fryer 1973). These factors are important both as a background to events and as key mechanisms in explaining the redundancy (Wood and Cohen 1977).

The redundancies studied here took place in a clothing factory located in a South Wales Valley, in a sub-region where both male and female official unemployment rates are well above national average. The factory, which opened in 1939, is part of a multinational company and until recently was the major employer of women in an area where the economic activity rates of women have traditionally been low (McNabb 1980). The factory primarily manufactures men's formal clothing with direct outlets through the parent company. However, in more recent years the emphasis has been towards more high fashion casual wear. The factory was divided into about twenty sections of varying size. Each section either produced different articles of clothing from start to finish or was involved in a series of processes in the production of a garment. The exceptions were the cutting room and the pressing section which were solely concerned with that specific task.

145

Typical of the clothing industry as a whole, there was in this factory a strong and distinctive sexual division of labour both on the shopfloor and in the management structure which was rigidly hierarchical and male-dominated.[7] Coyle (1982) has charted the way in which, through a process of rationalisation and deskilling, the sexual division of labour evolved in the garment manufacturing industry. In the factory studied, 85% of the workforce were women. Male and female shopfloor workers were physically separated and engaged in very different tasks within the production process. The women were primarily involved in assembly processes, undertaking repetitive tasks which demanded a high level of manual dexterity, hand/eye co-ordination, concentration, accuracy and speed. The men, on the other hand, were concentrated in the cutting and pressing sections working with heavy machinery. Significantly, their work was classified as skilled while the women's was deemed unskilled. The two groups thus attracted different pay rates and bonus schemes.[8] Differing skill classifications were just one of the many ways in which the sexual division of labour was perpetuated on the shopfloor. As Game and Pringle (1984, 28-9) have suggested, such a division

is based on a series of polarities which are broadly equated with masculinity and femininity. The most obvious distinction is between skilled and unskilled work. The other main ones are: heavy/light, dangerous/less dangerous, dirty/clean, interesting/boring, mobile/immobile. The first of each of these pairs is held to be appropriate for men, or men are assumed to be better at it. The second is seen as appropriately female. In the second case, nature is much more frequently invoked: women 'by nature' are good at boring, fiddly and sedentary work:

What was significant and by no means atypical about the organisation of the production process in this Welsh factory and its sexual division of labour was that first, since the workforce was structurally divided, it was easier for the management to control and manipulate it, and secondly, the sexual division of labour differentially affected the likelihood of layoff (Cornfield 1983).[9] Divisions within the workforce also affected responses and resistance to redundancies.

Allied to the sexual division of labour, and crucial to any discussion of male/female redundancy differentials, is the system of payments. To take the female workers first, women at the factory were paid a basic wage which was supplemented by a piece-rate bonus system, with the bonus varying according to the complexity of the task. Although these bonuses formed a large part of the women's take home pay, their pay remained low.[10] Four significant points emerge from this. Firstly, the wage system structured the women's experience of paid work. Secondly, it caused friction, conflict and competition between the women. As Wajcman has commented, piecework 'imposes a competitive self discipline rather than providing the basis for collective self management' (Wajcman 1983, 122). In other words, the wage system both united and divided the women and helped to militate against a united workforce, a prerequisite for collective resistance to redundancies. Thirdly, the ability to earn bonuses was governed by the availability of work in the factory, something which became a significant problem as the volume of work declined in the period leading up to the redundancies. Fourthly, the women's level of pay dictated their subsequent pay expectations once they had been made redundant and were looking for another job (Callender 1986). By contrast, the men in the factory were paid a higher basic wage than the women, and this was supplemented by a group bonus as opposed to the individual bonuses accorded the women. This group-based bonus had the advantage of overcoming the pressures and the inequitable distribution characteristic of the women's system of pay. In this way, it may have added to a sense of unity among the men. In addition, the male workers received a guaranteed bonus which was paid irrespective of their output.[11]

For the women whom I interviewed, the prime motivation for waged work was financial. Few of them had any choice about working - it was considered a necessity. Although the financial independence and the friendships gained from paid employment were important, their major orientation towards paid work was instrumental, with an emphasis upon extrinsic rewards. Their employment histories and attitudes to paid work were affected by familial ideology and the sexual division of labour between the home and the workplace. However, they did not view their family responsibilites and dual role as limiting because they were an accepted part of their lives. Both caring for the family and paid work were an integral part of these women's lives. The women's attitudes to waged work were also affected by their experiences of employment, their primary and secondary socialisation, and their economic, social, and psychological needs. Prior to the redundancies none of them had intended stopping paid work and several had anticipated working at the factory until their retirement. Once made redundant all of them wanted paid work again. Inevitably these attitudes and orientations had an impact on the women's responses and reactions to the redundancies and were in turn affected by the redundancies.

Although many of the women interviewed found the tasks at the factory boring and uninspiring, they enjoyed their workplace and their workmates. The atmosphere at the factory was friendly and they had devised ways of coping with the formal and informal control and regulation of the labour process. Over the years an 'implicit contract' (Watson 1980) had evolved between the women and the various echelons of management which was rooted in the idea of "a fair day's work for a fair day's wage". This 'contract' was based upon an unwritten code that if the women got on with their work and met their production targets then the staff and management would leave them to their own devices. This implicit contract aided the smooth operation and ordering of the factory by giving the women a (false) sense of security. It influenced their expectations, their behaviour, and the boundaries of responsibility between them and the management. It was precisely this 'contract' which was shattered by the redundancies.

THE REDUNDANCY PROCESS

Stage 1 - The Decline

The factory had expanded steadily until 1970 when the first signs of economic difficulties arose and the workforce of 1500 was put on short time to prevent an estimated 300 redundancies. By the end of 1970, 116 part-time women workers had been made redundant, although the eleven full time jobs, which had also been threatened were reprieved . Production continued at a fairly stable level until the late 1970's by which time the workforce had again risen to 1500. However, by 1978 the impact of

148

the recession and import penetration had begun to hit the clothing industry. To some extent the factory had, in earlier years, escaped these pressures by virtue of one particular profitable and stable contract for a 'classical' high quality product. However, the decision in 1979 to transfer this contract to another subsidiary of the parent company forced the factory into the more fashion orientated but infinitely more competitive market of casual wear. As a result the factory became vulnerable to rapid changes in fashion styles and to declines in consumer demands for their products.

The local management responded in a variety of ways to meet the overall decline in orders and to reduce labour input, with the redundancies being a final step in a sequence of strategies adopted. Although actual layoffs only came at the end of the story, the prior adjustment measures adopted by the management must be seen as the first stage in the redundancy process. In other words, the different stages in the redundancy process, although analytically separate, must be viewed together and understood as part of a total process.

Martin (1982) has pointed out that measures introduced in response to a decline in product markets can be influenced by (a) the quality, adaptability, and pliability of local labour, (b) the nature of trade union reactions, (c) trends in labour costs, (d) established traditions of labour hoarding, and (e) state policies, regional policies and national economic policies. At the garment factory studied, the first strategy of the management was to reduce the intensity of the utilisation of the employed workforce by introducing short-time work and work-sharing.[12] (A strategy also supported by the trade union). This led to the bonus payment systems being altered which had a direct impact on the worker's output. In other words, this measure shifted the costs of economic decline from the employer to the employee. The second strategy adopted by the management was to reduce the size of the workforce by suspending the annual recruitment of school leavers, closing down the training school, instituting a policy of natural wastage (which accounted for a considerable job loss because of the factory's high labour turnover), and cutting facilities within the factory such as the canteen services.

An appreciation of the import of these strategies is essential to our analysis of the eventual redundancies on three counts. Firstly, they had consequences for the characteristics of the redundant population in terms of for example, the age and sex of those made redundant (a factor which could affect their subsequent labour market experiences). Secondly, workers who remained after a partial closure were unlikely to be left unscathed by the redundancies. Thirdly, the measures demonstrated that a redundancy process may start well before there is any official announcement of redundancies.

During this lead-up period (and throughout the redundancy process), the management and union consistently witheld information from the women, with the result that the factory abounded with rumours. Although the veracity of the rumours was constantly denied, they may have been used by management to disseminate information informally, to establish the inevitability of redundancies, and thus to quell potential resistance.[13] The rumours created considerable instability in the workplace and uncertainty amongst the women and their substance was a major source of conversation and speculation. Many women, especially those who were chief breadwinners, were reluctant to accept the rumours' veracity while others were convinced of their authenticity. It is possible that the rumours may have provided a form of anticipatory socialisation (Merton 1968) which affected workers' behaviour and their capacity for collective mobilisation.

The force of the rumours was strengthened by a range of signs pointing to the factory's financial problems. The managerial strategies to avert the redundancies were one such set of signs. Another was the volume of work especially in the cutting room, which was considered indicative of orders coming into the factory. The weight the women attached to these signs varied, like their responses to the rumours. On the one hand, some women either with saleable skills and/or who were ineligible for redundancy pay found new jobs well before the announcement of any redundancies, whilst others believed that the factory, with its long established history was somehow immune from misfortune. Daniel (1970) has commented that it is a nice paradox that as an industry declines so the identification of its employees with the industry rises: they seem unable to extricate their own fate from its fortunes. It is questionable if these women were unable to make such judgements for the signs were ambiguous. Firstly, the volume of work often fluctuated and so was not a very reliable gauge. Secondly, the imposition of short time working could be interpreted as a preventive measure which would save the women's jobs. However, that was not the case and the redundancies were eventually announced.

The redundancies were introduced in stages for ease of implementation. The first group of workers to be laid off were part-timers and those working on the 'twilight shift'. Full timers were made redundant about two years later in July and December 1980 and May 1981. By July 1981, 400 people had been made redundant and the workforce had been reduced to 530 (123 men and 407 women) from the 1978 figure of 1500.

Stage 2 - The Selection of Redundants

The choice of the first set of redundancies disadvantaged women in the factory and indirectly discriminated against them. All the part-timers and the workers on the 'twilight shift' were women and all were made redundant irrespective of their age, length of service or any such criteria.[14] Some of the 'better' workers were later re-employed on a full time basis because the management used these redundancies as a kind of filtering process. But the same women became especially vulnerable to redundancy at the second stage because they were not covered by the 1978 Employment Protection (Consolidation) Act and so were one of the first group of full time workers to be selected for redundancy. The analysis of the selection procedures applied to full time workers will, for the sake of exposition, be divided into three sections: methods, principles and criteria. The implementation and notification process will be discussed later.

Methods of Selection

There were two kinds of redundancy at the factory - voluntary and compulsory - with the former being more common at the beginning of the process. Voluntary redundancies were attractive from the company's viewpoint because they incorporated an element of consent by the employee and because they absolved management from the responsibility of selecting redundants. Similarly, management could call for voluntary redundancies irrespective of what the trade union felt because it was likely that at least some workers would accept. However,

the boundaries between voluntary and enforced
redundancies are not clear and the former cannot
necessarily be regarded as a genuine alternative to
the latter as is commonly assumed (Daniel 1970).
Voluntary redundancies do extend some freedom of
choice to the worker but only within a context
defined by management. As Wood (1977, 66-7) has
commented.

> In voluntary redundancy situations, management
> generally not only maintain control over the
> timing of the redundancies, the actual date of
> dismissal of individuals, the severance terms,
> but also in fact the selection of redundants,
> through for example, having the right to veto
> the decision of an individual to 'volunteer'
> for redundancy.

Indeed at the factory under discussion, management
exercised their prerogatives within all these
spheres. They vetoed requests from older women
verging on retirement and from those they
considered to be 'key' workers, while at the same
time they were encouraging others to take voluntary
redundancy.

The women who were attracted to voluntary
redundancy tended to be older and in poor health
(c.f. Walker, Noble, and Westergaard 1985). Some
felt that they should give way to younger women who
were at the beginning of their working life (c.f.
Bytheway, this volume). Indeed, an interesting form
of self-policing emerged, with age becoming one of
the chief normative criteria by which the women
decided how the redundancies ought to be organised.
As a result pressures were brought to bear on some
women by both management and by peers. Women began
to sanction, informally, the designation of some
redundants although their power was not a property
but was an effect of their strategic position.[15]
Pressures of this kind threatened workers and added
to an already unstable situation. Within the
context of the whole redundancy process, voluntary
selection legitimated the redundancies and divided
the workforce. It helped reduce resistance and
opposition to collective dismissal by fragmenting
shop floor opposition, nurturing conflicts of
interest among workers (Fryer 1981, Wood and Dey
1983).

Principles of Selection

Compulsory redundancies were instituted simultaneously with voluntary redundancies. The selection of compulsory redundants was based upon the principle of last-in-first-out (LIFO). The women were informed that all workers who had joined the firm after a specific date were to lose their jobs. Certain groups of workers were thus in a particularly vulnerable position, especially younger women and mothers who had recently returned to waged work. The principle of LIFO is based upon the notion that continuous employment and loyalty to a firm should be rewarded by protection against job loss but continuous service as a principle of selection for redundancy disadvantages women more than men because women frequently have discontinuous employment patterns (Martin and Roberts 1984: c.f. Cornfield, this volume). So, characteristically women had joined this company on leaving school and had worked there until the birth of their first child; once their domestic commitments had decreased they had returned to their old employer. Other women were temporarily drawn out of the labour market to look after sick or elderly relatives but subsequently returned. Some women who had worked part-time for the company and who earlier had been made redundant later returned on a full time basis. Indeed, an important part of the factory's recruitment policy was to re-engage its ex-employees since they were acquainted with the work and already trained in the company's ways. Yet, when women were being selected for redundancy this earlier period of service and loyalty was discounted.

A significant factor in the discrimination produced by LIFO is that the dismissal system is based upon typically male patterns of employment and employment behaviour. There is no comparable vulnerable group of 'returners' among men. Indeed one of the major attractions of LIFO has been that it protects prime-age male workers from redundancy. Consequently, LIFO indirectly discriminates against women workers.[16] LIFO's inherent bias is related to its origins in trade union custom and practice. The adoption, therefore, of this trade union inspired selection principle helps to highlight women's political exclusion from policy making within trade unions and how trade unions use women workers as buffers in such situations.

LIFO was attractive to the management because it was an established convention for selecting redundants and unlikely to cause controversy amongst the workforce or the union. It was a principle which could be readily comprehended and one which carried an element of 'rough justice', both being factors which were important for the smooth implementation of the redundancy programme. Perhaps more significantly, it was one of the cheapest ways to implement redundancies. The way in which redundancy payments are calculated in the legislation makes young women workers with the shortest service the cheapest to dismiss (Callender 1985a). Thus it can clearly be seen how the ostensibly protective legislation in practice has a direct and divisive impact on the redundancy process, on management's decision making, and on the designation of redundants. The original intentions of the legislation have changed and its perversion as an instrument of industrial relations and the use of labour are clear (Callender 1985a).

On the other side of the coin, LIFO also carries a major disadvantage for the employer in that, organisationally, the principle cannot be used in an absolute unadulterated form without potentially harming management interests. Unless workers are highly homogeneous and interchangeable LIFO is likely to affect different groups unequally, leaving the management without certain types of workers. Retraining would be one way of dealing with this situation but management at the factory studied were unwilling to retrain. Instead management opted for additional selection principles to gain a greater flexibility. The second major selection principle was one of 'the job finishing' i.e. whether the production lines on which the women were working were to be phased out or scaled down. In some cases whole sections were closed down with consequent wholesale redundancy, in others, simply, specific jobs on a section were abandoned. This principle therefore gave the management considerable scope and discretion for dismissing those workers no longer required.

The way in which this particular mode of selection operated made it difficult for challenges to be mounted either by individuals or by the union because there were clear imbalances in access to knowledge and information. There was no concept of 'due process' in this selection rather it was dictated by the management's production plans and the sexual division of labour on the shopfloor. As Walby (1985, 272) has commented:

> The sex segregation of employment makes the unit of selection for ... compulsory redundancy of overriding importance. Very often the selection of particular departments for reduction (in the firms studied) ... led to the pool of potential redundants being almost of one sex or the other.

The sections most severely hit in this factory were female dominated; the male preserves of cutting and pressing were only slightly pruned.

Criteria for Selection

In addition to the stated principles of selection, there is considerable evidence that management also introduced a range of highly discretionary, particularistic and individualistic criteria which were a vehicle for either victimization or privilege. The company rid itself of its more troublesome workers and those with poor work performances. Another criterion for selection was the worker's personality and the extent to which she fitted into the ethos of the factory. This was clearly picked up by the women interviewed who spoke of 'troublemakers', those 'whose face didn't fit', or of one worker who 'wasn't no blue eyes', finding themselves vulnerable. From the women's viewpoint additional factors operated which related to the workers' position in the factory hierarchy; who they knew within that hierarchy; and their relationship to the union. These connections were manipulated by both management and individual workers to save some jobs. Male workers particularly benefitted from their close relations with the union. They were able to preserve their jobs or, at least, moderate the impact of the redundancies apparently in collusion with the union and management. As one of the women interviewed commented,

> The men that were working in the cutting room, they've had them painting the factory - haven't been doing any of their own work 'coz there's no work there for them ... they've got a stronger union I think ... its the same union as us but it's different for the men. The men keep together, they'll fight for what they want.

The special relationship of the men with the

155

union was apparent in several areas. Firstly, despite the predominantly female workforce most union officials were men. (The women's lack of participation in trade union activities will be examined in more depth below). These officials worked in either the cutting room or pressing section and thus automatically had a deeper understanding of the men's work situation and probably had more sympathy for them. Secondly, the union protected their male workers' interests by adhering to the notion of a 'family wage' (Barrett and McIntosh 1980) which ensured that the men consistently earned higher wages and bonuses than the women. These differentials could be explained away by differences in the production process but the men's better holiday pay which was calculated on a more favourable basis could not. When the women went on strike to get parity their efforts were supported neither by the male workers nor fully by the union. When in the 1970's equal pay legislation was implemented in the factory, jobs were reclassified and workers moved around so that men and women were not doing the same or broadly similar work. Thus differentials in men and women's pay were maintained and the trade union played an important role in perpetuating these inequalities (Rubery 1978). These differences were an expression of the sexual division of labour and the way in which both the management and the trade union manipulated it to their respective advantage.

In the context of the redundancies, the issue of unequal pay was important because it affected the size of redundancy pay and thus the relative costs of dismissal. More significantly, the union certainly protected male workers from job loss by agreeing to part-timers being made redundant before full timers. Underpinning such a policy is a familial ideology and a male-stream notion of employment. Such collective redundancy agreements perpetuate and are legitimated by the myth that part-timers work for pin money, that their paid work is of secondary importance, and that they are less committed to paid employment. Additionally, as has already been suggested, the union unquestionably agreed to LIFO as a selection principle despite the fact that LIFO disadvantages women. This highlights the trade union's ineffectiveness for women workers, its insensitivity to the specificity of women's employment, and its ingrained acceptance of patriarchal ideology and values. It is likely that two further factors helped protect men's jobs.

First of all, the men were skilled workers and so more difficult to replace and more expensive to dismiss. Secondly, the dominant ideology of placing greater value and emphasis on men's employment than women's (Callender 1985b) would probably have also affected management thinking.

The discretionary features of the selection process were institutionalised in a 'hardship list' drawn up by the union and submitted to the management. Introduced only for the early redundancies, it listed workers who, due to personal circumstances, would be particularly badly affected by redundancy. However, the criteria for inclusion were never publicly articulated. For the management the list represented selectivity clouded in beneficence: for certain women, a placatory jesture comprising a reprieve from redundancy. However, it was a divisive instrument because it created conflict amongst the women and fragmented the workforce. Many women thought the list was poorly administered and that management were just 'playing' with them by making them believe management were genuinely trying to save jobs. It added to the women's sense of insecurity as they compared themselves with other women and waited to hear if it was their job which had been saved. Significantly, their resentment over the list tended to be directed at other women rather than either the management or the union. As with the voluntary redundancies, an apparently benign measure reduced the possibility of collective, unified opposition to the redundancies.

Given the selection methods, principles and criteria adopted at this factory, it can be seen that the redundancy process, in this partial closure, was an 'an assortative one - that is, some groups or categories of workers were more vulnerable than others to selection or self-selection' (Lee and Harris 1984 p. 24). The 'assortative' nature of the process structured the population of those entering the labour market and that population was likely to comprise those whose labour market chances were relatively poor (Harris, Lee, and Morris 1985). Moreover, the population was predominantely female - an outcome of the structured nature of the labour market, the sexual division of labour on the shopfloor, women's employment patterns, negotiations between the union and management, and patriarchal ideology. As Walby (1985, 275) has observed,

Most of the forms of job loss which disadvantage women <u>vis à vis</u> men stemmed (<u>sic</u>) from the prioritising the claims to employment of those who have been in specific jobs longest, a category of worker which is also the best represented in work place discussions and negotiations. Women's disadvantaged position in society is thus reflected in the work place processes of job loss.

Women's Reactions to the Selection Process

Reactions to the selection were partly dictated by what redundancy meant to the women. Firstly it challenged their common sense beliefs about the type of workers who lost jobs and about notions of 'good' and 'bad' workers. It was difficult for some women to conceptualise the universalism of redundancy, and to disassociate it from the idea of being sacked, with its incumbent negative connotations for the individual. Similarly the redundancies broke the 'implicit contract' established between management and workers. Not surprisingly, it then took time for the women to assimilate their new experiences and to reformulate their attitudes towards work. As some became more accustomed to the idea of redundancy, they developed their own criteria for assessing who should be made redundant and they evaluated the formal selection process in accordance with their own notions of justice. Their attitudes were encapsulated in the queueing principle (Martin and Wallace 1984), namely, that in times of high unemployment certain social groups have greater claims to paid employment. As already noted, one criterion used by the women was age. There was a feeling that older women should give way to younger women - yet, as we have seen, those most affected by the LIFO principle were younger workers, many of whom felt aggrieved. The result was friction between the different age groups. Another criterion was related to the extent to which employment was 'needed' in terms of household finance. Some women resented the fact that despite the 'hardship list' their personal circumstances were not taken into consideration and they begrudged women who were able to retain their jobs although not 'needing' to work.

Despite the fact that some women developed their own normative criteria for the selection of redundants, all the women 'accepted' the primacy of the management's stated principles. There remained a hidden agenda as only the LIFO principle was fully articulated to them. Consequently, a great deal of confusion and hostility developed when this one known principle was not adhered to strictly. The women strongly objected to the unfairness exhibited by the discretionary elements of the selection. They became embittered and this in turn created animosity within the workforce. One woman summed up the situation as follows:

> It was ... why should I be put out? I've been here longer than her. Dog eat dog. They'd cut your throat for a pence there ... people who had been friends and worked for years together. You could feel the attitude to each other change.

The friendly trusting atmosphere in the factory had been shattered because of the selection process. Understandably, the redundant women who reacted most strongly to the selection were those who started working for the company before the stated cut-off date but who were still made redundant. Not only were they acutely aware of the injustice but they also felt their loyalty should have been rewarded.

The factionalization inherent in the selection process partly explains why many women individualised their redundancy and blamed themselves for it, a tendency also encouraged by the women's sense of powerlessness. (The fact that a few women were able to place their redundancy within a wider structural context will be discussed below). In general, however, emotions were channelled into fighting other women and complaining about the ineffectiveness of the union. Since management tended to keep a low profile, little aggression could be directed at them. And the union failed to capitalise on the women's anger and bitterness and direct it to a more appropriate target - the management.

Stage 3 - The Notification Procedure

The timing of notification for redundancy was partially dictated by the redundancy legislation which stipulates the minimum periods of consultation between the employer and the union, depending upon the number of workers to be made redundant. At the time of the redundancies studied (1980-81), the minimum period was 90 days if 100 or more employees

were to be dismissed. The rationale behind the
lengthy advance notice and consultation according
to Booth (the Minister of State for Employment when
these measures were introduced), was to ensure
'good employment practices ... already accepted as
such by many employers' (Booth 1975). In other
words, the provisions were in line with the
industrial relations school of thought which
emphasizes the resolution of industrial conflict
through the rational application of agreed rules
and procedures. In theory, lengthy notification
would reduce the possibility of souring and
deteriorating shopfloor industrial relations.
Furthermore, Kahn (1964) suggested that a long
period of notification would reduce bitterness
among workers. Daniel's recommendations in 'Strategies
for Displaced Employees' (1970) typifies this
industrial relations approach. He suggests that
lengthy notification is important because it allows
employees time to adjust to the idea of redundancy
and to reorientate themselves, giving them time to
evaluate alternatives and plan their future, while
a long notice gave employers time to consult with
employees, to explain the reasons for redundancies,
and to develop programmes to aid displaced workers.
Moreover, maximum notice gave workers opportunities
to find alternative employment, encouraged early
job search, and potentially shortened the duration
of unemployment. In the factory studied, it is
highly questionable whether the long notification
gave either the management or the employees any of
these purported advantages. Rather, the redundancy
process highlighted the weakness of the legislative
procedural rules, showing how they can be
manipulated to the management's advantage and the
way in which the legislation is based upon
misplaced and outmoded assumptions. Certainly, in
this redundancy situation the resolution of
conflict was not realised through rules and
procedures but through the disparity of power, both
between management and the workforce, and between
different sections of the workforce.

Contrary to the spirit of the legislation, the
most distinctive feature of the women's notification
was the lack of a standardised procedure. The first
step was a meeting held by the union which occurred
at the start of the 90 day consultation period. At
the meeting the union announced that redundancies
were to occur, that the women were to be selected
on the basis of LIFO according to a specified cut
off date, and that lists of redundants had been

drawn up. Not all the women attended the meeting but the news spread and calculations were quickly made as to who was on the 'hit list'. It was at this stage that the divisions between the redundants and the non-redundants began to appear.

The second step was the personal notification of those actually selected for redundancy. Those who were chosen were informed by different people in the factory hierarchy, ranging from a floor manager to another worker, and in a variety of ways. Some were told individually in a highly personal way, whilst others were informed imperson- ally, as, for example, by having their name read off a list in the presence of a group of workers. Other women were not told and some had to find out for themselves.

The ways in which the women were informed had some impact on their reactions, with those being told personally feeling the least rejected ·by the experience. But in the main, the feeling was that their world and security had collapsed - 'it hit me for six', 'it gave me a shock, ... it really did hurt like, it sunk to the bottom of your stomach',

> Terrible, it was awful ... they came on the section with this list, oh yes, your name's on the list. Well, I could have gone through the floor ... I thought Oh God that's it now. It was as if somebody had dropped a brick on my head, if the floor could have opened up I'd have gone.

The degree of shock at hearing the news was also related to the woman's earning status within their household. Older women in particular were crushed. Other women expressed a sense of doom over their future prospects and some were 'heartbroken'. For a few women the earlier announcement of a cut-off date had acted as a buffer and prepared them for the news, but for others, especially those who had joined the company after the specified date, it had the opposite effect. Whatever their initial reaction, though, none of the women viewed their redundancy in positive terms: at best they accepted it and were resigned to it.

The final step in the notification process for some of the women was an individual interview with the management. Indeed for some, this was the first time they knew definitely that they were to lose their jobs. These interviews can be seen as a tactic by management to diffuse resistance and 'cool out' (Goffman 1952) the women. But, many women disliked their floor manager and doubted the sentiments expressed so they used the interviews to lash out at management. Although for some women, the interviews did act as an effective form of consolation, others felt humiliated by them and these feelings of humiliation fed into their feelings of shame at being made redundant.

Overall, the insensitive notification procedure left a bitter taste which affected the attitudes of the women to the management's handling of the redundancies.[18] Delays in the notification caused great uncertainty. Some women took this stalling strategy as a sign that perhaps they had been 'saved'. Others would not, and acted in a more assertive fashion by making demands on the management and walking out until their situation was clarified. As one woman explained

> We didn't know until about four weeks before we were finishing whose names were actually down on paper ... The management didn't release the list ... If you started from 1978 onwards you would be finishing. So you had to try and work out whether you'd raced it by one or two weeks ... They wasn't telling us, all the ones that were being finished, so we got up and walked out ... the only way we could have a meeting was to walk out. Just the ones that were finishing walked out ... The other girls didn't really want to know ...

Stage 4 - Working Out Notice

This stage in the redundancy process embraces the 90 days from the official announcement until the redundant's final day at the factory. The duration of this period was again influenced by the procedural rules of the employment protection legislation. In terms of its social dynamics, it was a very complex time and these complexities demonstrate some of the hidden dimensions and consequences of the governing legislation. For the sake of exposition, the women's interpretation of the behaviour of management, the union, and the women will be analysed separately.

Managerial Strategies

The way in which the redundancies were managed was

decisive in structuring the problems and issues which the women faced and perceived (Wood 1981). Management had decided that all the redundants were to leave together on a specified date. Although there are statutory regulations governing notification periods, management still retained considerable control and choice over the women's actual dismissal date and thus the length of time the women spent 'working out their notice'. During this stage the atmosphere in the factory and the relationship between the women and management was one of bitterness, insecurity and tension in contrast to the friendly, congenial ambiance which had prevailed prior to the redundancies. Hence one task faced by management at this point, was to try to normalise the situation and heal some of the fissures created by the broken 'implicit contract' in order that the redundancies could be implemented with minimum disruption to production. Their efforts had to be directed at both those who were to be made redundant and those who were staying on, although the strategies adopted needed to be different for the two groups.

With the breakdown of informal mechanisms of managerial control, management endeavoured to reassert its authority in various subtle ways. At the same time they also played the game of adopting a softer approach, for instance, by being less demanding over production standards. Control over output was also attempted by increasing bonuses for some workers while decreasing them for others. A further tactic was the adoption of a 'business as usual' approach. A second task which faced the management was to encourage the women to 'share' their practical concerns, i.e. to establish in the women's minds the necessity of the redundancies and then to help the women to come to terms with the situation. In other words, management strove to manufacture some form of consent through an insistence on the inevitability of the lay-offs. The management, by demonstrating the necessity of redundancies hoped to indicate that resistance was futile and by so doing to dispel any recalcitrance.

Management also directly tried to reduce the possibility of resistance amongst the women. Not all the tactics utilised for averting intransigence were explicit or premeditated, but they can nevertheless be construed as intending to disperse or forestall resistance (c.f. Hardy 1985). Firstly, as already noted, management fuelled the women's uncertainty and delayed the final notification of some redundancies by withholding information as for example, with the discretionary hardship list. Secondly, the lure of redundancy payments was used to weaken resistance. Under the provisions of the 1978 Employment Protection (Consolidation) Act, employers are able to threaten workers contemplating taking action against closure with the loss of their redundancy rights (Levie, Gregory, and Callender 1984). Moreover, the appeal of redundancy payments has been exacerbated by myths about the size of settlements and stories of 'golden handshakes'. Management did nothing to dispel the women's false expectations and did not tell them about the amount they would receive until very late in the redundancy process. The promise of payments, therefore, acted as a bribe to make the women go quietly, and ensured that the women continued working after receiving their notification, thus sustaining production. Again, this illustrates well the way in which the redundancy legislation was used as a form of social control structuring the redundancy process.

Thirdly, the management continued to nurture existing divisions within the workforce by implementing various divide-and-rule tactics. Rivalries were fostered between redundants and non-redundants, voluntary and enforced redundants, old and young, men and women, workers eligible and ineligible for redundancy payments, and workers in different sections of the factory. All were treated differently and exploited according to their disparate interests. In other words, the redundancies were implemented in a way which had a differential impact on each group, making collective unified resistance very difficult to organise. In particular, the management manipulated the sexual division of labour and the earlier harmonious relations with the union. Finally, after the announcement of one batch of redundancies, non-redundants were put on short time, while the redundants worked full time. Although this strategy was part of the company's recovery plan, nonetheless the organisation of collective resistance was inhibited simply because the majority of the workforce was absent for most of the week.

Trade Union Response
Both the strategies adopted by the management during this stage of the redundancy process and the women's reactions to the redundancies were to some

extent affected by the union. Redundancies 'exemplify labour weakness, whether male or female, unionized or non-unionized' (Martin and Wallace 1985 p. 6). In fact, there is evidence of considerable co-operation between the union and management over the redundancies as there had been on other issues prior to the redundancies. Certainly some women felt that the union was 'hand in glove with management' or '80% management, 20% workers'. Consequently the redundancies did not precipitate any fundamental conflict of interests between the union and management (Wood and Dey 1983 p. 47). The management's prerogatives to manage, monopolise information and declare redundancies were not questioned by the union. As a result, management were able to impose their definition on the situation and define the parameters of discussion. Collective bargaining and procedural rules <u>did not</u> dictate the outcome of the redundancies as has been suggested by industrial relations commentators (Wood and Dey 1983). Rather the outcome was directed by the differential power between the workers and management, and the special relationship between management, the union, and the male workers which had built up over the years. This special relationship meant that the union did not place the women's interests at the forefront of their activities (Hunt 1982). This fact which was largely a result of an unrecognised ongoing social process of patriarchal exclusion and sectionalism within the union rather than an example of explicit collusion and conspiratorial decision making.[19]

Given the existing social relations and the distribution of power and control, it could be argued that the union was powerless (Fryer 1973). In other words, that it had little choice but to accept management's definition of the redundancy situation for a rejection of it may have been counter-productive. This indeed would seem to have been the case for the union was weak despite its size and the existence of the closed shop.[20] It may have been, therefore, that the union's best strategy was to cooperate fully with the management.

For the women, the union was the more visible party in the redundancy process rather than the management. In fact, the union's actions fed into the effectiveness of those management strategies described above. Union officials reiterated management's statements on the inevitability of the redundancies and advised the women against any form of resistance. Without an effective and supportive union leadership collective action was doomed. Additionally, the union negotiated over redundancy payments and some individual redundancies in an attempt to save a few women's jobs. They did not, however, take on board the discriminatory nature of the redundancy payments legislation or pay attention to the specificity of women's employment histories and patterns. Nor did they seek alternative strategies to the redundancies.

The Women's Responses

The women's responses during this final stage of the redundancy process, some of which have been mentioned above, were very complex. Their emotional reactions can not easily be categorised. Neither can they be understood solely in terms of a dichotomy between acquiescence and resistance (Wood and Dey 1983). To do so is to obscure the complexity of their reactions and the range of their responses. The objective of the following discussion will be threefold: firstly, to give a flavour of those responses rather than a comprehensive list of all reactions, secondly, to highlight the way in which existing studies in this area present a simplistic treatment of 'worker reactions' to redundancy, and thirdly, to challenge the stereo-typical images of women workers as passive, docile and fatalistic when faced with redundancy. The women's reactions must be placed within the context of their social situation, their work experiences and the way management structured the redundancy process, because their responses were mediated by social and institutional factors (Wood and Dey 1983, 111).

This period saw the women's initial shock and dismay at the news of their redundancy transformed into bitterness, anger, uncertainty and a sense of betrayal by the management and the union. The atmosphere in the factory had deteriorated still further and, as one woman commented 'it was terrible, everybody was so nasty and bitter. They couldn't get over how people had to go'. Some of the factors responsible for this sense of bitterness have already been mentioned but a major additional factor during this stage was the resentment many women felt at being at the factory and having to work. They had to continue turning up for work simply because they could not afford to lose pay or their redundancy payment. They had lost their earlier motivation and sense of purpose and belonging. The pleasures of working and the camaraderie of the workplace had disappeared. Moreover, there was often insufficient work at the factory so the women got bored or fought over what work was available to ensure that they still received bonuses. Coupled with the bitterness was a sense of insecurity: they felt powerless to avert the redundancies and this powerlessness was exacerbated by their fear of the future - most women had an acute awareness of the state of the local labour market and the scarcity of jobs. The strain on the women was considerable and emotionally the whole period was very draining.[21]

Additionally, there was bitterness over the betrayal of the union. A majority of women believed that the union could have done more to avert or prevent the redundancies. In their eyes the union should have tried harder to save jobs, fight the redundancies, ensure that the principle of LIFO was adhered to, negotiate better redundancy payments, and support those women who actively challenged their redundancy. The women accused the union of being deceitful, dishonest, withholding information, not fulfilling its promises, favouring its male members, and siding with management.

During this period, the women who were to be made redundant developed a range of adaptations and responses to their situation which were a mixture of defence mechanisms, rationalisations and resistance. A distinct change in some women's attitude to their work at the factory could be traced. Many adopted a non-caring attitude and did the minimal amount of work necessary in a desultory fashion, in marked contrast to their work performance before the redundancies. The actual work content became meaningless, making it easier for the women to cut themselves off from the factory and encouraging a desire to leave. A more extreme version of this withdrawal was absenteeism or becoming ill. Illness played a variety of roles. For some women it was a reaction to the strain and stresses of the situation, whilst for others it was an excuse for absenteeism or it formed a compensatory role to the lost work-role or it was combination of these.

Some women called upon their pride and refused to 'give in' or consider themselves 'beaten' by the redundancies or by the management, in a variation on what Goffman (1952) has described as an I'll show them attitude. Such an attitude could lead to either active resistance or resignation. Other women tried to underplay the significance of their job (a mitigation of their worker role), or simply became resigned to their fate. Although none of the women were looking forward to their redundancy, some did see it as a means by which they could potentially increase their personal freedom, lift some of the burdens of their dual role, and free themselves from the authority and discipline of the workplace.

In general though, there seems to have been a tendency for the women to oscillate back and forth between seeing their redundancy in highly personal, individualistic terms and in more universalistic structural terms. The former was a reflection of their feelings of rejection and shame, the latter a reassertion of their self esteem and image as 'good' workers. Interestingly, when the women were asked 'Do you think it was your fault you were made redundant?' most thought it was not. They placed the fault with (a) the management for failing to attract contracts and having cut the workforce, (b) the government and its policies, and (c) general economic decline. However, when the women were asked 'Why do you think you were made redundant?' there was a tendency for them to blame themselves. The defensive replies to the first question contrasts with the responses to the second. The different replies are difficult to explain but they do highlight the subtleties involved in coming to terms with job loss. The answers may possibly be an artifact of the question which may explain the variety of responses recorded in other studies on redundancy which use similar questions. Additionally, the responses do point to the pain involved in a process of self-incrimination, the privatised nature of the experience, and the dynamics involved in blaming the victim (Ryan 1971).

In other cases, though, it was recognised that the workforce was relatively powerless to avert the redundancies and that simply hoping that jobs would somehow be reprieved was actually unrealistic. Moreover, some women were justifiably concerned that if they resisted the redundancies they would lose their redundancy pay. Indeed, it could be argued that there was nothing fatalistic about the women's resignation, but rather that their acceptance of the redundancies was a form of passive resistance. Many women were only too aware of the way they had been manipulated and rendered powerless.

There is now a well established literature on

the determinants of workplace militancy and collective action against redundancies (Hyman 1977). However, rarely does this research recognise responses of <u>individual</u> workers as legitimate and significant compared with collective resistance. Nor are women considered as central in work-place politics. Women are portrayed as both less likely than men to participate in worker resistance and to initiate militant action in support of their claims (Barron and Norris 1976). The nature of women's claims are characterised as being different and inferior to men's. This characterisation 'is a product of male-stream analysis - that is, it derives from traditions of thought which are, in both their theoretical and empirical dimensions, rooted in masculine experience'. (Siltanen and Stanworth 1984 14).

The women at the factory did not resist the redundancies collectively and the factors which militated against such action have already been highlighted. According to the interviews, however, the majority of the women would have taken part in industrial action if asked to do so. But, they did resist in highly individualistic ways which were often invisible and sometimes passive, sometimes active (Purcell 1979). Their resistance can be classified as acts of grievance or acts to try and save their jobs. Some of these acts of protest included the above mentioned characteristics of a non-caring attitude to work, or not working properly, absenteeism, and sickness. Some women manipulated for their own ends the time-off which they were legally entitled to for seeking alternative employment.[22] The factory required that the women provide evidence (e.g. an employer's card or letter) that their time off had been spent in actually looking for work. So some women called upon friends in employment to supply the proof, while others collected a batch of letters on one day which they subsequently submitted for different days off. One woman intentionally chose to take off those days which would be most disruptive to her section. As a form of defiance other women refused to attend the farewell parties which had been organised which demonstrated a refusal to be 'cooled out'. Similar gestures of defiance were exhibited on the women's last day at the factory. On their last day they did no work, held their own parties, and left early. A group of women had a very abusive showdown with the floor manager after he told one of the women to 'get out ... and don't

go through the front doors, use the side doors
through the canteen'.
      The second form of active resistance was aimed
at trying to save their jobs. They challenged their
redundancy through the union and badgered both
union officials and the floor manager. One woman
took her case to an industrial relations tribunal
because she believed that, on the principle of
LIFO, she had been unfairly dismissed. Her case
failed partly because of the lack of trade union
support and partly because of the shortcomings of
the legislation (McMullen 1981). Sometimes the
women's efforts were aimed at getting 'rid' of
another woman at the factory who had a shorter
length of service. One woman reported another
workmate to the management for 'pinching stuff from
work ... because she had lost her job she split on
somebody else, ... she wanted to save her job'.
However, the individualism and infighting reached
its heights when the hardship list was drawn up and
speculation was rife.
      What all of the above illustrates is that the
women at this factory were prepared to resist
redundancies just as many women before them.[23] They
were not passive or fatalistic. There was no
evidence to suggest, as Wood (1981) has done, that
the women were more passive or less committed to
opposing their redundancies because they were less
committed to their specific employer or more
ambivalent about their job loss, because their
lives straddled paid employment and the home, or
because they believed they could get another good
job. For these women the opposite was true. They
were very committed to their employer and paid
employment and were very pessimistic about their
job prospects. Martin and Wallace's conclusions
about the redundant women they studied were also
applicable to the women in this factory. 'The women
... were no more and no less acquiescent in the
redundancies in their plants than men similarly
employed'. Martin and Wallace 1985, 284).

SUMMARY

In this chapter I have tried to address some of the
large gaps in our knowledge about women and
redundancy - an area which has been largely ignored
in male-stream literature. Moreover, I have
concentrated upon the women workers' perception of
events - perceptions which tend to be hidden,

undervalued and left unspoken. Through my analysis
of a particular closure and the women worker's
experiences, I have attempted to highlight the
weave of complex and ambiguous conceptual and
empirical issues which must constitute any study of
redundancy. I considered the impact of redundancy
legislation upon these complexities and demonstrated
how that legislation shaped the redundancy process,
the experience of redundancy, management decision
making, the redundant population, and responses to
redundancy. It was suggested that the procedures
introduced for selecting redundants render women
workers especially vulnerable to redundancy in
comparison to men. This was because the major
selection principle of LIFO, which reflects trade
union custom and practice, is based upon assumptions
about male employment patterns and upon a male
dominated conception of work and so fails to
consider the position of women in the labour market
- a market which by its very nature leads to gender
inequalities. Moreover, the additional particularistic
criteria used to select redundants embody traditional
patriarchal criteria, to the women's disadvantage.
       Finally the chapter challenged the notion that
women workers are more acquiescent than men in
redundancy situations. Divisions existed in the
workforce examined prior to the redundancy and new
schisms emerged during the redundancy process. This
fragmentation was divisive and was manipulated in
the redundancy situation to militate against a
united workforce - a prerequisite for collective
action. Other factors which militated against such
action at this factory included the management of
the redundancy process, the structural divisions
among the workforce, especially the sexual division
of labour, the lack of trade union support; the
redundancy payments legislation, the women's
defence mechanisms and rationalisations, and the
individualistic way in which the women interpreted
the redundancies. So although the women did not
resist collectively, they did resist on an
individual basis. Such actions are often invisible
and thus tend to be ignored by researchers. This
does not mean that they are any the less
significant than collective action. Also contrary
to the male-stream literature on workplace
politics, there was no evidence that the women were
more acquiescent or fatalistic than men would have
been in a similar situation. Nevertheless, it
remained the case that all the women's attempts at
resistance were fruitless, the management maintained

171

control and the women were powerless. Ultimately, it was the inequality in the distribution of power that governed the redundancy process and determined the effectiveness of the workers' reactions to redundancy. The women were a commodity that could be bought and sold in the market place. The final words must be left with one of the women

> ... there was nothing in your pay or nothing when you left. No "thank you". There was no manager or foreperson or anything outside saying "Well thank you for your service and all that you've done, we'll consider you to come back". Nothing at all. I think it was done awful.

NOTES

1. My thanks to Kirk Mann and Leonie Archer for their helpful comments on the first draft of this paper.

2. The empirical work entailed interviewing in depth a small group of women who had been made redundant in the partial closure of a clothing factory. All the women interviewed were or had been married, were aged between 20-59, had been made redundant involuntarily, and had worked full time in low paid manual jobs on the shop floor - jobs which were classified as unskilled. The interviews, which were unstructured and tape recorded, were conducted at the end of 1981 and beginning of 1982 - nine to twelve months after the women's redundancy.

3. Defining women's work is also problematic compared to men. The blurring of the boundaries for women between employment and economic inactivity and between employment and economic activity renders their classification within the labour market problematic. For a full discussion of this and associated issues see Callender 1985b. The term 'work' in this paper has been used to imply paid employment.

4. For a brief review of the conflicting debates over women's vulnerability to unemployment as compared to men see Callender 1985b.

5. Employers are required to consult (not negotiate) with trade unions about proposed redundancies and before the redundancies are announced. Minimum periods of consultation are stipulated depending upon the number of employees to be made redundant. The employer is required to give the union a range of information about the reasons for the redundancies, the numbers and descriptions of workers affected, how they are to be selected and the methods of executing the dismissals.

6. The relationship between this legislation and the redundancy process has been examined by other commentators but primarily from an industrial relations perspective. They have been concerned with the effectiveness of collective bargaining for regulating industrial conflict and with the development of 'strategies for displaced workers'. From this perspective redundancy is seen as a challenge to industrial order amenable to regulation through mutually accepted rules of conduct. Thus the impact of the legislation is interpreted in a

rather narrow sense and is based upon a range of assumptions.

7. This theme of the sexual division of labour is central to an understanding of women in the labour market and gender relations generally, and the redundancy process in particular. The sexual division of labour is a defining feature of capitalism, a basic dynamic in capitalist societies, and under capitalism takes highly specific forms (Game and Pringle 1984). As a concept it relates to the allocation of work on the basis of sex, within the home and the workplace, as well as the divide between home and workplace which is characteristic of capitalism.

8. It is questionable whether the tasks involved in the men's work demanded more skill than the women's. It is suggested that both required skills of equal value but of a different nature. For a full discussion on the way in which notions of skill are socially constructed whereby women's skills are valued less highly than men's see Cockburn 1983, Phillips and Taylor 1980.

9. Where women are engaged directly upon production tasks they are disproportionately likely to suffer job loss compared to men (Martin and Wallace 1984).

10. See Byrne et. al. 1983 and Hakim and Dennis 1982 for discussions on the problems involved in defining and measuring low pay and especially for women workers.

11. The payment system was both a product and an explanation of the situation of the majority of its workforce: women (Pollert 1981). It was a manifestation of both class and gender relations within capitalist society.

12. This was aided by the government sponsored short-time working schemes which were initiated especially to encourage firms to defer redundancies. Eligibility for compensation through such schemes is limited and so short-time is a rather inflexible and temporary expedient for management to avert redundancies. It was during this period that the EEC put pressure upon the British Government not to support declining industries, in particular the clothing industry

13. This time could also have been used to plan a strategy for resisting the redundancies.

14. Part-timers' vulnerability to redundancy has been well documented (Walby 1983) and their vulnerability is reinforced by some trade unions and the state. Some redundancy agreements stipulate

that part-timers should be selected for redundancy before full time workers. In September 1982, an Employment Appeal Tribunal declared that such provisions discriminated unlawfully against women (Equal Opportunities Commission, 1982, 1983)

15. This notion of power as a strategy rather than a property which is exerted over others is well developed by Foucault (1978).

16. Furthermore, within that disadvantaged group, LIFO is neither equitable nor does it incorporate a concept of need.

17. See Lee (1985) for the distinction between 'excision' and 'depletion' as methods for slimming down the workforce.

18. Martin (1985) has discussed why it is important for a company to maintain good relations with staff despite redundancies. However, at the factory under discussion the company made few attempts to ensure that employees maintained a positive evaluation of the company and the women were highly critical of the management's handling of the redundancies.

19. There is evidence of trade unions' explicit collusion and conspiratorial decision making but these tend to be less common. One such recent example is an incident at Hoover's, Merthyr Tydfil. It illustrates well that where there is a direct conflict of interests between men and women workers, trade unionists discriminated against the women in the selection of redundants. The men tried to save their jobs at the expense of the women's, and refused to represent the women's interests. Many women had seniority over men but despite this were selected for redundancy. What was at issue was women's right to paid employment and the patriarchal forces that undermine that right and restrict women's access to paid employment (Walby, 1983).

20. Martin (1985) has discussed more general problems facing unions during a recession which weakens their effectiveness. The weakness of the local union at the factory reflected the weakness of the union nationally which was related to the nature of the industry it represented, the unstable product market conditions of the clothing industry, and lack of traditional solidarity which was characteristic of the industry. However, in the factory's past there had been industrial action over issues of pay though the union had played a rather hesitant role.

21. It is likely that men react to redundancy as emotionally as the women described in this study

but the emotional effect for men is either omitted in many studies or disguised by the discourse on male redundancy.

22. Under the 1978 Employment Protection (Consolidation) Act as amended by the 1982 Employment Act, an employee who is given notice of dismissal because of redundancy is entitled to reasonable time off with pay during working hours to look for another job or make arrangements for training for future employment.

23. The women's sit in at Lee Jeans in Greenock is a well known case (Lorentzen 1984). Wacjman (1983) reported how women took active steps to retain their jobs by setting up a co-operative while Coyle (1984) demonstrated how the women in her study were prepared to strike but the union would not let them.

REFERENCES

Barrett, M. and N. McIntosh, (1980) 'The "Family Wage": Some Problems for Socialists and Feminists', Capital and Class, 11, 51-72

Barron, R.D. and G.M. Norris, (1976) 'Sexual Division and the Dual Labour Market', in D. Barker and S. Allen (eds.), Dependence and Exploitation in Work and Marriage, Longman, London, pp. 47-69

Beechey, V. (1982) 'What does Unemployment Mean?', Critical Social Policy, 1, 71-8

Booth, A. (1975) Hansard Vol. 891, col. 43, 28 April, 1975, H.M.S.O., London

Byrne, D., C. Pond, and R. Smail, (1983) Low Wages in Britain, Low Pay Review, Low Pay Unit, London

Callender, C. (1985a) 'Gender Inequality and Social Policy: Women and the Redundancy Payments Act', Journal of Social Policy, 14, 189-213

Callender, C. (1985b) 'Unemployment: The Case for Women', in C. Jones and M. Brenton (eds.), Year Book of Social Policy in Britain 1984, Routledge and Kegan Paul, London, pp. 47-73

Callender, C. (1986) 'Women Seeking Work', in S. Fineman (ed), Unemployment: Personal and Social Consequences, Tavistock, London, (forthcoming)

Cockburn, C. (1983) Brothers: Male Dominance and Technological Change, Pluto Press, London

Cornfield, D. (1983) 'Chances of Layoff in a Corporation: A Case Study', Administrative Science Quarterly, 28, 593-620

Coyle, A. (1982) 'Sex and Skill in the Clothing Industry', in J. West (ed), Work, Women and the Labour Market, Routledge and Kegan Paul, London, pp. 10-26

Coyle, A. (1984) Redundant Women, The Women's Press, London

Daniel, W.W. (1970) Strategies for Displaced Employees, Political and Economic Planning, Broadsheet 517, London

Daniel, W.W. (1972) Whatever Happended to the Workers at Woolwich?, Political and Economic Planning, Broadsheet 537, London

David, M. (1983) 'The Right in the USA and Britain: A New Anti-Feminist Moral Economy', Critical Social Policy, 2, 31-45

Equal Opportunities Commission (1982) Sex Discrimination Decisions, No. 2 - Selection for

Redundancy, E.O.C., Manchester
Equal Opportunities Commission (1983) <u>Sex Discrim-
    ination Decisions</u>, No. 4 - Selection for
    Redundancy (Part-time Workers), E.O.C.,
    Manchester
Foucault, M. (1977) <u>Discipline and Punish: The
    Birth of the Prison</u>, Allen Lane the Penguin
    Press, London
Fryer, B. (1973) 'Appendix' in R. Martin and R.
    Fryer, <u>Redundancy and Paternalist Capitalism</u>,
    Allen and Unwin, London, pp. 216-60
Fryer, B. (1981) 'State, Redundancy and the Law',
    in R. Fryer (ed.), <u>Law, State and Society</u>,
    Routledge and Kegan Paul, London, pp. 136-59
Game, A. and R. Pringle, (1984) <u>Gender at Work</u>,
    Pluto Press, London
Goffman, E. (1952) 'On Cooling the Mark Out',
    <u>Psychiatry</u>, <u>15</u>, 451-63
Hakim, C. and R. Dennis, (1982) <u>Homeworking in
    Wages Council Industries</u>, Research Paper 37,
    Department of Employment, London
Hardy, C. (1985) <u>Managing Organisational Closure</u>,
    Gower, Aldershot.
Harris, C.C., R.M. Lee, and L.D. Morris, (1985)
    'Redundancy in Steel: Labour Market Behaviour,
    Local Social Networks and Domestic Organis-
    ation', in B. Roberts, R. Finnegan, and D.
    Gallie (eds.), <u>New Approaches to Economic
    Life</u>, Manchester University Press, Manchester,
    pp. 154-66
Hunt, J. (1982) 'A Woman's Place is in Her Union',
    in J. West (ed.), <u>Work, Women, and the Labour
    Market</u>, Routledge and Kegan Paul, London,
    pp. 154-71
Hyman, R. (1977) <u>Strikes</u>, Fontana, London
Kahn, H. (1964) <u>Repercussions of Redundancy</u>, Allen
    and Unwin, London
Lee, R.M. (1985) Redundancy, Labour Markets and
    Informal Relations. <u>Sociological Review</u>, <u>33</u>,
    469-94
Lee, R.M. and C.C. Harris, (1984) 'Redundancy
    Studies: Port Talbot and the Future',
    <u>Quarterly Journal of Social Affairs</u>, <u>1</u>, 19-27
Levie, H., D. Gregory, and C. Callender, (1984)
    'Redundancy Pay: Trick or Treat', in H. Levie,
    D. Gregory, and N. Lorentzen (eds.), <u>Fighting
    Closures: De-industrialization and the Trade
    Unions 1979-1983</u>, Spokesman, Nottingham
Lorentzen, N. (1984) '"You Can't Fight for Jobs and
    Just Sit There": the Lee Jeans Sit-in' in
    H. Levie, D. Gregory and N. Lorentzen,

Fighting Closures: De-industrialization and the Trade Unions: 1979-83 Spokesman, Nottingham, pp. 193-208

McMullen, J. (1979) Rights at Work, Pluto Press, London

McNabb, R. (1980) 'Segmented Labour Markets, Female Employment and Poverty in Wales', in G. Rees and T. Rees (eds.), Poverty and Social Inequality in Wales, Croom Helm, London, pp. 156-67

Martin, J. and C. Roberts, (1984) Women and Employment a Lifetime Perspective: The Report of the 1980 DE/OPCS Women and Employment Survey, H.M.S.O., London

Martin, R. (1985) 'Women and Redundancy: Some Case Studies in Manufacturing Industry', Employment Gazette, pp. 59-63

Martin, R.L. (1982) 'Job Loss and the Regional Incidence of Redundancies in the Current Recession', Cambridge Journal of Economics, 6, 375-95

Martin R. and R.H. Fryer, (1973) Redundancy and Paternalist Capitalism, Allen and Unwin, London

Martin, R. and J. Wallace, (1984) Working Women in Recession: Employment, Redundancy and Unemployment, Oxford University Press, Oxford

Merton, R. (1968) Social Theory and Social Structure, The Free Press, New York

Phillips, A. and B. Taylor, (1980) 'Sex and Skills: Notes Towards a Feminist Economics', Feminist Review, 6, 79-88

Pollert, A. (1981) Girls, Wives, Factory Lives, Macmillan, London

Purcell, K. (1979) 'Militancy and Acquiescence among Women Workers', in S. Burman (ed.) Fit Work for Women, Croom Helm, London, pp. 112-33

Rubery, J. (1978) 'Structured Labour Markets, Worker Organisation and Low Pay', Cambridge Journal of Economics, 2, 17-36

Ryan, W. (1971) Blaming the Victim, Vintage Books, New York

Siltanen, J. and M. Stanworth, (1984) Women and the Public Sphere: A Critique of Sociology and Politics, Hutchinson, London.

Wajcman, J. (1983) Women in Control, Open University Press, Milton Keynes

Walby, S. (1983) 'Women's Unemployment: Some Spatial and Historical Variations', Paper presented to the 4th SSRC Urban Change and Conflict Conference, Clacton, Essex

Walby, S. (1985) 'Approaches to the Study of Gender Relations in Unemployment and Employment', in B. Roberts et. al., New Approaches to Economic Life, Manchester University Press, Manchester, pp. 264-79

Walker, A. (1981) 'Social Policy, Social Administration and the Social Construction of Welfare', Sociology, 15, 225-50

Walker, A., I. Noble, J. Westergaard, (1985) 'From Secure Employment to Labour Market Insecurity: The Impact of Redundancy on Older Workers in the Steel Industry', in B. Roberts et. al. New Approaches to Economic Life, Manchester University Press, Manchester, pp.319-37

Watson, T. (1980) Sociology, Work and Industry, Routledge and Kegan Paul, London

Wood, S. (1977) 'A consideration of the Study of Redundancy', Scottish Journal of Sociology, 2, 51-70

Wood, S. (1981) 'Redundancy and Female Employment', Sociological Review, 29, 249-83

Wood, S. and J. Cohen, (1977) 'Approaches to the Study of Redundancy', Industrial Relations Journal, 8, 19-27

Wood, S. and I. Dey, (1983) Redundancy: Case Studies in Cooperation and Conflict, Gower Aldershot

Chapter Eight

PLANT CLOSING: A COMPARISON OF EFFECTS ON WOMEN AND
MEN WORKERS

Carolyn C. Perrucci, Dena B. Targ, Robert Perrucci
and Harry R. Targ

During the past decade there has been a plethora of
social science research on gender inequality which
has commonly compared women to men in terms of the
nature and extent of occupational and income
attainment (cf. Perrucci, 1978; 1980). Gender
differences in familial influences on work
commitment and rewards have been documented
(Perrucci and Targ, 1978; Perrucci, 1978); at the
same time, gender differences in work-related
attitudes and behaviour have been noted to be
minimized under conditions of equal opportunity
(Kanter, 1977).

In marked contrast to the voluminous research
on men and women in employment is the paucity of
attention to a complementary way of analyzing
gender inequality - through research on the nature
and consequences of unemployment (cf. Schlozman,
1979; Targ, 1983). Gender differences in familial
influences on job leaving (Barrett, 1979) and on
job search have been documented (Sheppard and
Belitsky, 1966), and women's reactions as wives of
unemployed men have received some attention (Buss
and Redburn, 1983; Larson, 1984; Morris, 1983a,b).
Although there has been a recent increase in
research on effects of unemployment, it has
concentrated on male workers and their families
(Targ, 1983). Systematic comparisons of women and
men workers' reactions to the involuntary loss of a
paid role in the formal economy are sparse indeed
(for notable exceptions see Callender, 1985; Nowak
and Snyder, 1983; Perrucci et. al., 1985; Wood,
1981). Perhaps this gap in the literature both
reflects and contributes to traditional assumptions
about the proper role of women in society. Because
it is commonly assumed that women can depend on men
for financial support, women's unemployment is not

181

thought to be a major social problem. This precludes attention to women's needs, both psychological and economic, and contributes to an ambivalent attitude towards high unemployment generally and possible national remedies (Barrett, 1979). Yet, all available evidence indicates that unemployment from plant closings is an increasingly important phenomenon in the United States and one which impacts on both men and women (Bluestone and Harrison, 1982; Illinois Advisory Committee, 1981).

In the survey research which we report here, both the men and women respondents have recently experienced job loss due to this common cause: the closing of the RCA television cabinet-making plant in which they had been employed as blue-collar workers for some time. Moreover, the demographic characteristics of these displaced[1] workers permit a comparison of the women and men by marital status. Data obtained from blue-collar workers at an ongoing plant which had been producing roller bearings for eight years in the same small community provide numerous comparisons with the displaced RCA workers. Economic, social and psychological effects of the plant closing are examined. Men's and women's reactions are expected to be similar to the extent that their prior and future constraints and opportunities are similar (Marshall, 1984).

METHODOLOGY

This chapter is part of a larger study of the impact of a plant closing on displaced workers and the community in which they lived[2]. In December of 1982 an RCA cabinet-making plant that had been in operation since 1945 was closed. The plant was in an Indiana city with a population of 5100 and a county of 24,000. On closing day, 450 workers lost their jobs and another 378 workers, who were laid off in several stages within thirty-five months prior to the closing, were also part of the closing contract. Late leavers, those with the most seniority (years of service with the company), were more likely to be men, older and less-educated than the early leavers. Intensive discussion between the union and management took place for several months prior to the closing. The union had presented three wage concession packages to management in order to try to keep the plant open. The final offer was for a 36 per cent wage cut and the termination of a dental insurance plan. All three offers were rejected by management, who claimed that the cuts would not offset projected losses stemming from decreased consumer demand for console TV's, excessive maintenance costs for an old plant, and increased foreign competition. Union representatives rejected these claims, pointing out that RCA had constructed a new cabinet-making plant in the South and was transferring its operation to a non-union wage area.

It was in this context that we were given access to the list of union members from the President of the union local. With his assistance we identified and excluded from further consideration those who were deceased, retired or no longer living in the community, leaving 686 for study. In August of 1983 we distributed a mail questionnaire to this group of former RCA workers. The questionnaire concerned their work history, union activities, political/social beliefs, and the impact of the closing on family, health, and financial situation. A total of 328 usable questionnaires was received for a return rate of 48 per cent. See the appendix for measures of the variables used in this study.

DEMOGRAPHIC CHARACTERISTICS OF THE SAMPLE

In order to provide a background for understanding the data and results to be presented later, we present an overview of the demographic characteristics of our 328 respondents, with comparisons to the population of 828 covered by the RCA closing contract (Bonney and Richert, 1983), the control group of 42 continuously employed workers from the ongoing plant, and between men and women, both single and married (see Table 8.1).

Regarding gender, a little over half of our respondents and of the RCA population were women (55 vs. 53 per cent, respectively). Only 31 per cent of the continuously employed workers (control group) were women. As to marital status, over 70 per cent of both the displaced workers and the employed workers were married. Among the displaced workers, marital status was similar for women and men (data not shown).

Household size consisted of three individuals, on the average, for both the displaced and continuing workers (i.e., control group). Among the displaced, household size was similar for both men and women. Married men had an average of four people in their households; married women an average of three. Single women had an average of 2.6; compared to 1.6 for single men (data not shown).

Table 8.1: Demographic Characteristics of RCA Population, RCA Respondents and Continuously Employed McGill Respondents

Characteristics	RCA Population (N=828)	RCA Respondents (N=328)	McGill Respondents (N=42)
Per cent Female	53.0	55.0	31.0
Per cent Married	NK	76.0	71.4
Average Number in Household	NK	3.0	3.0
Average Years of Age	42.0	44.0	32.0
Average Years of Education	NK	11.0	12.0
Per cent Born in Indiana	NK	81.0	85.7
Per cent Born in White Co.	NK	40.0	32.4
Average Number of Years Work at Plant	13.9	15.0	4.7
Average Number of Months Laid Off	13.5	13.0	NA
Per cent Still Unemployed in Summer 1983	51.0 (Sept '83)	70.6 (Aug '83)	NA

The average age of the RCA population, our respondents, and women and men within our sample was essentially the same; that is, early forties. This was greater than the average age, 32 years, of the control group.

On average, the educational attainment of the displaced workers fell a year short of high school graduation whereas that of the still-employed control group was twelve years. Among the displaced workers, there was no educational difference between men and women (data not shown).

Over 80 per cent of the workers, displaced and continuing, were born in Indiana. Among the unemployed, local roots applied to both men and women. Moreover, 40 per cent of the displaced and

32 per cent of the still-employed workers were born in the county in which they were formerly or currently employed.

In addition to lifetimes invested in the state and county, the displaced workers had a monetary investment in homes. Thirty per cent had paid up mortgages; and another 53 per cent were still paying on mortgages. Home ownership percentages were similar for men and women, whether married or single (data not shown).

As to employment and unemployment histories, the RCA population and our respondents were similar in the average number of years of service at RCA. The displaced workers had longer average work histories as of when the RCA plant shut down (15 years) than did the control group of continuing workers (5 years).

The average number of months unemployed for the RCA population and our survey respondents was similar (14 vs. 13 months). The per cent still unemployed was lower among the RCA population (51 per cent in September) than among our respondents (71 per cent in August).

Overall, then, it appears that our respondents are representative of the population of workers dislocated by the RCA closure but differ in age and sex composition from the continuously employed comparison group.

In the remainder of the chapter we first examine three categories of effects of plant closures on dislocated workers. For each category we review the related literature and then present our own findings. These three categories are economic effects, psychological effects, and family effects. Secondly, we examine three factors which may moderate the effects of job loss - a sense of mastery over one's fate, perceived social support, and optimism about one's economic future. Thirdly, we assess the combined impact of several economic, social and psychological variables on the depression level of dislocated workers. The chapter ends with a summary and conclusions.

ECONOMIC EFFECTS OF PLANT CLOSINGS

Studies which compare economic effects of plant closings for blue-collar women as well as men are relatively few in number. They are, however, consistent in finding two negative impacts which are greater for women than men. The period of

185

unemployment following job loss from a shutdown is longer for women than men (Aronson and McKersie, 1980; Lipsky, 1979; Nowak and Snyder, 1983). Additionally, for women more than men, re-employment, when it occurs, tends to be in part-time and lower-paying sales and service jobs, rather than production work (Bluestone and Harrison, 1982; Liem and Rayman, 1982; Nowak and Snyder, 1983).

For women, being married is often considered to be a buffer from the economic stress of job loss. However, findings on the effect of marital status on duration of unemployment and nature of re-employment do not entirely support this view. A study by Rosen (1983) which focused on women only, examined effects of displacement, both permanent and temporary. Among the displaced workers, married women were as likely as the single women to look for work and to become re-employed (60 per cent re-employed between 5-9 months after job loss). Most of those who were re-employed, 61 per cent, were recalled to their former companies and jobs. More generally, Lipsky (1979) found longer unemployment for single workers; Aronson and McKersie (1980) found longer unemployment for those who had another wage earner in the household, who was most often the spouse.

Another economic variable, perception of economic distress, was found to be greater among unemployed than employed men and women (Schlozman, 1979). Schlozman found that among the unemployed in general, women were less likely than men (73 per cent vs. 82 per cent) to be dissatisfied with their income. However, among the unemployed who were main wage earners with dependent children, women were more likely than men (92 per cent vs. 81 per cent) to be dissatisfied with their income.

In response to unemployment, women make a variety of cutbacks in economic expenditures for both essential as well as luxury items. Rosen's (1983:21) study of women only found that job losers cut back more than the employed on 9 of 21 items and reported cutting back most frequently on groceries and clothing, followed by recreation, vacations, gifts and household maintenance. These unemployed women also reported more cut backs than the employed on insurance and medical care. A study by Rayman (1982) which compared unemployed men and women on expenditures for luxury items only, found men more likely than women to make cutbacks (70 per cent vs. 54 per cent) (Rayman, p. 328). The author suggested that men could afford more luxuries before job loss and/or were more likely to be the main wage earner.

In addition, there is some evidence that temporarily unemployed workers use a variety of strategies to extend household income. For example, Young and Newton (Weeks and Drengacz, 1982:310-11) reported that workers who were laid off from the wood products industry planted vegetable gardens, hunted and fished, and shared household resources, repair tools and labour with neighbours.

Our own RCA plant closing study systematically compared displaced men and women workers on all the economic factors mentioned; namely, length of unemployment, re-employment status, income loss, perceived economic distress, cutbacks in consumer expenditures and increased engagement in money-saving activities.[3]

RCA FINDINGS

Length of Unemployment

Seventy-one per cent of all displaced workers were still unemployed eight months after the plant closed: 66 per cent of the men and 74 per cent of the women. Overall, 17 per cent were re-employed full-time, 12 per cent part-time. A larger percentage of the men (25 per cent) than of the women (11 per cent) were working full-time. Among those displaced early (between 20 and 32 months when contacted), 54 per cent were still unemployed. Twenty-eight per cent were re-employed on a full-time basis; 18 per cent on a part-time basis. These patterns were similar for women and for men. Among those displaced last (between 8 and 9 months when contacted), 75 per cent were still unemployed. Sixteen per cent were re-employed as full-time workers; ten per cent as part-time workers. Again, these patterns were similar for women and for men.

Income

Prior to the closure, men's 1982 income exceeded women's, on the average ($15 vs. $11 thousand). For those who were able to work for most of the year in which the plant closed, those with greatest seniority, men's average income still exceeded women's ($18 vs. $15 thousand). All workers contributed substantially to their family's 1982 income, although male workers contributed a larger proportion than did women (81 per cent vs. 63 per cent of family's 1982 income). For married workers, the men earned 78 per cent of the family income; the women earned 49 per cent.

Displaced workers reported having a variety of alternative sources of income at the time of our survey. The only alternative source available to a majority (71 per cent) was unemployment compensation, paid to those who were still unemployed at the time of our survey. In addition, 44 per cent of the workers reported that they still had some severance pay available to them.

For those displaced workers who were re-employed, one estimate of whether or not they had recovered financially was made by comparing their 1983 with their 1982 weekly salaries. Among those who worked nearly all of 1982, men were earning 67 per cent of their former weekly salaries; women were earning 59 per cent during the following year. These workers had been on their jobs an average of 4.3 and 1.7 months, respectively.

Perceived Economic Distress
As to perceived economic distress, as measured by the number of categories of consumer items a displaced worker indicated s/he could not afford (for example, the kind of food they/their family should have), displaced workers noted they could not afford an average of five of the eight categories listed. The items that over 50 per cent of the sample were unable to afford were leisure activities, replacement of worn-out furniture or household equipment, clothing and car. Men and women were the same in the number and pattern of categories they were unable to afford. The comparison sample of continuously employed workers reported they were unable to afford an average of 2.5 of the eight consumer categories. For only one category, leisure activities, did a majority of the comparison sample report inadequate resources.

The increased economic distress because of unemployment obtained for women as well as men. Among the women, the unemployed were unable to afford an average of five categories; the continuously employed, an average of three. Among the men, the unemployed were unable to afford an average of five categories; the employed, an average of two.

Cutbacks

The economic effects of unemployment can be reflected in expense adjustments made by individuals and families. From a 20-item list of a variety of living expenses, including insurance, health care, and entertainment, the overall average number of adjustments was nine. The expenses cut back or eliminated by more than 50 per cent of the sample were gifts, charitable contributions, entertainment, children's expenses (other than schooling), food, home upkeep and repair, dental care, magazines or newspapers, auto upkeep and repair, and respondents' education and/or training. Forty-nine per cent had cut back or eliminated health care.[4] There was no difference between men and women as to the number or kinds of adjustments made.

Home Production

A related area indicating response to financial difficulties is increased home production. From a nine-item list of money-saving activities (i.e., shopping for food bargains and do-it-yourself home repairs), all respondents reported increased engagement in an average of six such activities. The majority were spending more time on seven of the nine activities listed: shopping for food bargains; shopping for clothing bargains; gardening; preparing meals; canning; home repairs; auto repairs. Women and men reported increased participation in the same number of money-saving activities. The types of activities women and men were likely to engage in followed a traditional division of labour (Duncan et. al., 1973). More specifically, women were more likely than men to be shopping more for bargains, both food and clothing ($X^2 = 10.01$, df = 1, p < .01; $X^2 = 6.90$; df = 1, p < .01). Women were also more likely than men to be spending more time on preparing meals and canning ($X^2 = 12.08$, df = 1, p < .001; $X^2 = 6.02$, df = 1, p < .05). In addition, the women were spending more time on sewing ($X^2 = 11.30$, df = 1, p < .001). Men were more likely than women to be spending more time on both home and auto repairs ($X^2 = 4.59$, df = 1, p < .05; $X^2 = 8.73$, df = 1, p < .01).

PSYCHOLOGICAL EFFECTS

Social research on the impact of economic changes on physical and mental health is multilevel in nature, ranging from work which relates downturns in the economy to aggregate indicators of mental illness (Brenner, 1973) to work which emphasizes how different individuals cope with stress, economic or otherwise (Caplan, 1979). An apparent discrepancy in findings about the health effects of unemployment in aggregate versus individual-level research underscores the importance of determining the multiple structures and processes through which unemployment affects individual well-being (Kahn, 1979).

A longitudinal study of two plant closings (one rural and one urban) examined both physical and mental health effects for displaced blue-collar men (Kasl, Gore and Cobb, 1975; Gore, 1978; Kasl and Cobb, 1979). The authors did not find either number of physical symptoms, or number of days that a respondent did not feel well, or depression to be related to periods of unemployment. Days respondent did not feel well was higher, on the average, for men who subjectively rated the job loss experience as more severe (i.e., said that it took longer 'before things got pretty well back to normal') (p.112). Interestingly, subjective severity rating was higher for men who scored low on a general adjustment scale, but was related to objective severity of the event (i.e., length of employment) only for men in the urban (but not the rural) plant shutdown.

A subsequent analysis of these plant closing data indicated that perceived economic deprivation from unemployment was not correlated with number of illness symptoms, cholesterol, or depression (Gore, 1978). Yet other analyses (Kasl and Cobb, 1979) indicated that for four physiological variables (pulse rate, diastolic blood pressure, serum uric acid, and serum cholesterol), scores were higher for men who went from a period of anticipation of the plant closing to unemployment than for men who went from anticipation of the plant closing to immediate re-employment at some other workplace. For three of four mental health indicators (depression, anxiety-tension, suspicion, but not psycho-physiological symptoms) the change in scores was primarily a 'decline from an anticipation effect among the promptly re-employed rather than a rise among those going on to unemployment at Phase 2' (p. 289). For neither the physiological nor mental health indicators were there reliable trends in scores associated with longer periods of unemployment (i.e., up to two years). The authors concluded that job loss and unemployment had effects which were limited in both magnitude and in duration on middle-aged blue-collar men's mental health.

Similarly, another longitudinal study of the effects of a plant closing on blue-collar men found relatively mild long-term psychological impact (Buss and Redburn, 1983). Specifically, on each of twelve mental health scales, unemployed steel workers 'showed more stress symptoms than those who had found new jobs, were retired, or were continuously employed' (Buss and Redburn, 1983:71). However, one year after the closing, for only four scales - increased alcohol consumption, experience of family problems, felt victimization and felt anxiousness - were scores significantly different. By the time of the second wave of the study at two years after the closing, these scale scores were not significantly different.

In contrast to findings of the two plant closing studies just mentioned were two studies by Liem and Liem, and Rayman and Bluestone of blue-collar workers whose unemployment was due largely to layoffs from cutbacks rather than from plant shutdowns. Liem and Liem (1979) found that among married men, the unemployed had higher levels of psychiatric symptoms than a control group of employed men, at one month and especially at four months after job loss. Men re-employed by the fourth month after initial job loss showed lower levels of psychiatric symptoms than controls for five of nine symptom clusters; namely, depression, anxiety, hostility, paranoia, and somaticism.

Similar to these findings, Rayman and Bluestone (Liem and Rayman, 1982) found that among men and women aircraft industry workers, most of those who had experienced job loss sometime during a ten-year period of time reported 'related periods of serious physical or emotional stress'. More commonly reported forms of strain included high blood pressure, alcoholism, increased smoking, insomnia, neurasthenia, and worry and anxiety.

Another study concerned disruption of worklife for an urban group who had been fired, laid off, downgraded, or disabled due to illness (Pearlin, et al., 1981). Such work disruption was related to increased depression over a four-year period of time. An additive regression model indicated that increased economic strain, and diminished perceptions of mastery over one's fate and conception of self-esteem, which resulted from both job disruption and economic strain, were also related to an increase in depression. Emotional supports and coping strategies had indirect influence on depression by reducing economic strain and by helping to maintain a sense of mastery when changes in job disruption and economic strain were held constant. An interactive regression model indicated that the mediating functions of social supports and coping strategies benefited the job losers more than those who had been stably employed.

In the only prior study to systematically compare blue-collar women and men's mental health effects from a U.S. plant closing, Snyder and Nowak (1983) found that between one and two years after a shutdown, unemployed men were more 'demoralized' than re-employed men. Re-employed men with lower present wages relative to their pre-shutdown wages were more 'demoralized' than re-employed men with higher relative wages. On the other hand, re-employed women were as 'demoralized' as unemployed women and relative wages did not affect the demoralization of women.

In a regression equation to account for demoralization, Nowak and Snyder (1983) reported statistically significant predictors were poor health (in terms of number of reported physical symptoms); severity and extent of expenditure cutbacks; per cent of savings exhausted; and living with children but no spouse or with parents but no spouse. Nonsignificant variables in the equation were gender of workers, number of dependent children under 18 years of age, and absolute level of 1982 income.

Two other studies of general unemployment, not plant closings, found that unemployment was related to mental health. In the Schlozman (1979:307) research, comparable percentages of unemployed men and women reported being 'dissatisfied with life as a whole.' However, among the unemployed who were main wage earners with children, a greater per cent of women than men indicated such dissatisfaction with their lives. In the Warren (1978) study, a larger per cent of unemployed women (33 per cent) indicated symptoms such as headache, tension, depression or trouble falling asleep than employed women (18 per cent) and unemployed men (10 per cent) and employed men (10 per cent).

RCA FINDINGS

Overall, displaced RCA workers had an average score of 17.2 on a depression scale which was adapted from research by Pearlin and associates. This was a nine-item scale, with a possible range of scores from 9-27, in which a higher score indicated higher depression. The comparison group of continuously employed workers evidenced somewhat lower depression, according to their mean score of 13.7 ($F=15.08$, df=1, 315, $p < .001$).

When the comparison group's scores were disaggregated by gender, women indicated greater depression than men (15.8 vs. 12.6, respectively; $F=7.37$; 1,38 df; $p < .01$). This sex difference in depression is consistent with extant data regarding the general American population (Kessler and McRae, 1981; Radloff and Rae, 1981). Interestingly, when the former RCA workers were disaggregated by sex, women's depression was somewhat greater, but comparable, to that for men (17.6 vs. 16.8). For men, depression levels were similar for the singles and the marrieds. For women also, marital status had no effect on depression.

A comparison of each gender for the RCA sample versus the control group suggested that for men, but not for women, job loss from a plant closing increased depression. This finding is consistent with that of Snyder and Nowak (1983) regarding demoralization as a result of a plant closing. It is unclear whether sex differences in the attachment to work or in the social stigma attached to being unemployed or other factors are causing this difference in demoralization.

FAMILY EFFECTS

Although unemployment is usually discussed in individual terms, economic and psychological effects can extend to the whole family. Among unemployed men there was a decrease in family cohesion and an increase in family tension (Liem and Rayman, 1982:1119; Schlozman, 1979:308-9). Comparing men and women, more men reported increased family tension since job loss: 50 per cent vs. 35 per cent (Schlozman, 1979:308-9).

RCA FINDINGS

Overall, most of the former RCA workers reported that financial pressures since the shutdown had caused little change in the quality of their relationships with their spouse, children, other family members or friends. Moreover, for only one category of relationships, those with family other than spouse or children, did effects differ for displaced women versus men. Specifically, men were more likely than women to indicate that their extended family relationships had worsened. Single men were particularly likely to report deterioration of extended family relationships, but sex differences within marital status were not statistically significant.

MODERATING FACTORS

There are several possible mechanisms by which job loss may affect health. Job loss may result in loss of income and fringe benefits that had sustained good nutrition and good medical care, thus impacting unfavorably on health (House, 1979). As already mentioned, our and others' research indicated that many of the unemployed made cutbacks in expenditures for food, dental care, and medical insurance (Rosen, 1983; Schlozman, 1979). Moreover, Nowak and Snyder (1983) and Rosen (1983) found a positive relationship between cutbacks and demoralization. Whether cutbacks affect displaced workers' physical health is unknown at this time.

Alternatively, job loss may affect health through stress from loss of such things as meaningful work, income, self-esteem, social ties, or a routine which structures one's time and activities (House, 1979; Liem and Liem, 1979; Pearlin et al., 1981; Pearlin and Schooler, 1978). Importantly, some research has indicated a moderation effect of social support vis-à-vis unemployment, an effect which is stronger for psychological than for physiological variables (Liem and Liem, 1979:362). Specifically, at low levels of unemployment (i.e., among blue-collar men unemployed about five weeks or less), perceived social support from family and friends had no effect on perceived economic deprivation; whereas at higher levels of unemployment (more than five weeks in first year), 'low social support contributed to a sense of relative economic deprivation' (Kasl and Cobb, 1979:271).

It appears that sources of support differ for women versus men. For example, unemployed women are less likely than men to seek help from their spouses, but are more likely than men to turn to other family members, friends, and neighbours (Rayman, 1982:329; Warren, 1978:96-7). Women may be less likely than men to seek help from their spouses because husbands are not as upset as wives about their spouses' unemployment. The majority of the married women interviewed by Nowak and Snyder (1984) reported that their husbands were not unhappy about their wives' unemployment. Either the husbands were happy to have their wives home although upset over the income loss or they had said nothing. In contrast, the majority of the men reported that their wives had negative reactions to their unemployment. The data are mixed, however, regarding whether women (Rayman, 1982) or men (Warren, 1978) are more likely to maintain ties with former co-workers. Whether social support, from whatever source, has a moderating effect on the health consequences of unemployment for women remains to be examined.

In addition, research by Pearlin and Schooler (1978) indicated that mastery is a personal resource which lessens the relationship between economic strain (i.e., perception of inability to afford important household items) and resultant emotional stress. For their urban sample, men scored higher on mastery than did women. Pearlin and Schooler also found that one coping response to economic strain was having optimistic faith in one's economic future. Women were less likely than men to use this particular coping response.

RCA FINDINGS

Mastery
On the Pearlin et al. (1981) measure of mastery or feeling of control over their own lives, there was a difference between the displaced workers and the comparison sample of employed workers. Summary scores for the former averaged 19, and for the latter, 21. There was a possible range of 7-28, with 7 representing low mastery; 28, high. For the displaced workers, there was no difference in sense of mastery between men and women, single or married.

Social Support
Social support, in the form of love and support from family and friends, varied little between the displaced workers and the comparison group. Fifty-seven per cent of the former and 65 per cent of the latter reported having 'lots of love and support'. For the displaced, there was no difference between men and women in the per cent who received 'lots of love and support'. There were also no sex differences in the level of social support for either single or married displaced workers.

Optimism
Overall, the displaced workers were not optimistic about their economic future. Forty-one per cent agreed with the following statement: 'No matter what I do it will be near impossible to find a job in the months ahead.' An additional 26 per cent were unsure about their economic future. Women were as pessimistic as men, regardless of their marital status.

MULTIPLE REGRESSION FOR DEPRESSION

We concluded our data analysis with an assessment of the collective influence of several economic, social and psychological variables on the mental health of displaced workers. By means of multiple regression, we analysed the impact of nine variables on depression scores for our sample of former RCA workers. These variables were: current employment status, number of expense cutbacks, mastery, social support, optimism about one's economic future, gender, marital status, age and educational attainment of respondent. The first seven variables were discussed earlier in this chapter. In addition, older age and lower educational attainment have been found to be related to poor mental health, e.g., dissatisfaction with life. This is because age and education were associated with difficulty in finding a new job and downward job mobility leading to high economic deprivation which, in turn, caused high feelings of anomie (Aiken, Ferman and Sheppard, 1968).

Three of the nine variables were significantly related to depression. As expected, the economic variable of cutbacks was significantly related to depression. The greater the number of cutbacks, the greater the depression. Interestingly, current employment status, i.e., whether unemployed or re-employed, was not significantly related to depression, once other variables were in the equation. This suggests that there are continuing effects of the plant closing experience which do not end with re-employment. Of three potentially moderating factors, a sense of mastery, perception of social support, and optimism about one's economic future, two influenced depression. One of these, a sense of mastery, was the single most influential variable in the equation. As expected, the higher one's sense of mastery, the less one's depression. Similary, perceived social support from family and friends was negatively related to depression. The effect of optimism may not be apparent because of its positive correlation with mastery $(r=.31)$.

None of the four remaining variables, gender, marital status, age and educational attainment, significantly impacted on depression net of other variables in the equation. None of these impacted on depression either directly or indirectly through relationships with cutbacks, mastery or social support (data not shown). Overall, the amount of variance explained by these variables was 30 per cent.

Table 8.2: Multiple Regression for Depression for Displaced RCA Workers (N=328)

Independent Variable	Unstandardized Coefficient	Standardized Coefficient	Sign
Current Employment Status	.54	.07	NS
Cutbacks	-.23	-.20	.001
Mastery	.58	.37	.001
Social Support	-1.05	-.14	.01
Economic Optimism	-.20	-.03	NS
Gender	-.39	-.03	NS
Age	.03	.06	NS
Marital Status	.11	.01	NS
Education	-.17	-.05	NS
Constant	11.21		
R^2	.30		

SUMMARY AND CONCLUSIONS

Studies of the economic and psychological effects of unemployment on individuals and families during the Great Depression concentrated on the job loss of male breadwinners. This precedent was generally followed until this decade (Targ, 1983). There continues to be a paucity of studies of unemployed women. Our study contributed to this literature by systematically comparing women with men who had been displaced by a single plant closing in a small, Midwestern town in the U.S.A.

Overall, both the men and women had been adversely affected economically by job loss following the plant closing. A large percentage of both women and men were still unemployed. Those who were re-employed had not recovered their former salaries. This loss was important to both women and men because both had contributed substantially to their family's income level before the shutdown. Displaced men and women were also comparable in their perceptions of economic distress, the number of cutbacks on expenditures they had made, and in the number of money-saving activities in which they were increasingly engaged.

The displaced workers had a relatively strong sense of mastery and the majority perceived that they had strong social support from family and friends. They also felt no effects of financial pressure on their relationships with spouse, children, other family members and friends. In contrast, the displaced workers were not optimistic about their own economic future. Displaced women were comparable to men regarding mastery, social support, most relationships, and lack of optimism. It was only for relationships with family (other then spouse or children) that a larger percentage of men than women experienced a deterioration. Judging from a comparison with controls (i.e., continuously employed workers in another plant), it appeared that displacement led to increased depression for men, but not for women. Depression scores were comparable for men and women. Overall, their scores indicated moderate levels of depression.

In our model of economic, social and psychological effects on depression, three of seven variables had statistically significant effects. These were a sense of mastery, number of financial cutbacks, and strength of social support from family and friends. The model accounted for 30 per cent of the variance. The results of this study indicate that it is important for researchers, union officials and local and national policymakers to consider the effect of plant closing on women as well as men. Recent discussions of plant closing legislation emphasize several central issues: (1) early warning to allow the workers and the community time to assess the impact of the closing and take steps to ameliorate it; (2) discussions between managers and workers to establish policies for retraining, transfer within the company or job search assistance; (3) severance pay to cushion the financial blow of unemployment; and (4) the continuation of health insurance coverage which had previously been available through employment-related group policies (Harrison, 1984).

Some of these provisions are available to workers through their collective bargaining agreements. However, overall, only 20 per cent of American workers are currently covered by such union contracts. For men, this figure is 28 per cent and for women 16 per cent (Harris, 1982; Harrison, 1984). Moreover, as women in unionized manufacturing jobs become displaced by plant closings, they are more likely than men to be re-employed in non-unionized service jobs (Liem and Rayman, 1984; Nowak and Snyder, 1983). Our research suggests that unemployment is an important problem for both women and men as well as their families and communities (Perrucci et. al., 1985). Unfortunately, during the 1980's, when there is a great need for services, the social safety net has contracted at national, state and local levels (Liem and Rayman, 1984).

NOTES

1. By displaced workers we mean a total workforce at a particular plant whose jobs have been lost because of the closing of the plant.

2. In the United States there is wide variation among plant closures in the length of advance notification workers are given. For some rare cases, notice is given six months or more prior to the shutdown to allow workers time to plan and search for alternative employment (Harrison, 1984; Perrucci and Targ, 1985). At the other extreme are plants that close with literally no advance notice to the affected workforce. The RCA closure falls somewhere in between the extremes. We expect that the period of management-union negotiation may have provided false hope for the RCA workers, delaying their search for work alternatives.

3. We have chosen to conceptualize cutbacks in expenditures and increases in home production as responses to economic strain following job loss. An alternative conceptualization would focus on these responses as coping strategies. Relatively little U.S. research examines active coping strategies as a response to unemployment (e.g., Perrucci and Targ, 1985).

4. The importance of health care to the displaced workers' overall well-being is indicated by the fact that those who cut back on health care were more depressed than those who did not (19.4 vs. 14.9, F=49.3, df 1,246, p=.001).

REFERENCES

Aiken, M., L.A. Ferman and H.L. Sheppard (1968) Economic Failure, Alienation and Extremism, The University of Michigan Press, Ann Arbor, MI

Aronson, R.L. and R.B. McKersie (1980) Economic Consequences of Plant Shutdowns in New York State, New York State School of Industrial and Labour Relations, Cornell University, Ithaca

Barrett, N.S. (1979) 'Women in the Job Market: Unemployment and Work Schedules' in R.E. Smith (ed.), The Subtle Revolution: Women at Work, The Urban Institute, Washington, D.C., pp.63-98

Bluestone, B. and B. Harrison (1982) The Deindustrialization of America: Plant Closing, Community Abandonment and the Dismantling of Basic Industry, Basic Books, Inc., New York

Bonney, S. and M.K. Richert (1983) Project Care - A Program to Teach Job Search Skills to Dislocated Workers, Lafayette Displaced Workers Assistance Agency, Inc., Lafayette, IN

Brenner, M.H. (1973) Mental Illness and the Economy, Harvard University Press, Cambridge

Buss, T.F. and F.S. Redburn (1983) Mass Unemployment and Community Mental Health, Sage Publications, Beverly Hills, CA

Callender, C. (1985) 'Unemployment: The Case for Women' in C. Jones and M. Brenton (eds.), The Yearbook of Social Policy in Britain 1984, Routledge and Kegan Paul, London

Caplan, R.D. (1979) 'Social Support, Person-Environment Fit, and Coping' in L.A. Ferman and J.P. Gordus (eds.), Mental Health and the Economy, The W.E. Upjohn Institute for Employment Research, Kalamazoo, MI, pp.89-137

Duncan, O.D., H. Schuman and B. Duncan (1973) Social Change in a Metropolitan Community, Russell Sage Foundation, New York, NY

Gore, S. (1978) 'The Effect of Social Support in Moderating the Health Consequences of Unemployment' Journal of Health and Social Behaviour, 19, 157-65

Harris, J. (1982) 'Women Workers', Economic Notes, 50, 5

Harrison, B. (1984) 'Plant Closures: Efforts to Cushion the Blow', Monthly Labour Review, 107, 41-3

House, J.S. (1979) 'Discussion' in L.A. Ferman and
     J.P. Gordus (eds.), Mental Health and the
     Economy, The W.E. Upjohn Institute for
     Employment Research, Kalamazoo, MI, pp.315-20
Illinois Advisory Committee to the United States
     Commission on Civil Rights (1981) Shutdown:
     Economic Dislocation and Equal Opportunity,
     U.S. Commission on Civil Rights, Washington,
     D.C.
Kahn, R.L. (1979) 'Economic Changes and Mental
     Illness: A Commentary' in L.A. Ferman and J.P.
     Gordus (eds.), Mental Health and the Economy,
     The W.E. Upjohn Institute for Employment
     Research, Kalamazoo, MI, pp.225-33
Kanter, R.M. (1977) Men and Women of the
     Corporation, Basic Books, Inc., New York
Kasl, S.V. and S. Cobb (1979) 'Some Mental Health
     Consequences of Plant Closings and Job Loss'
     in L.A. Ferman and J.P. Gordus (eds.), Mental
     Health and the Economy, The W.E. Upjohn
     Institute for Employment Research, Kalamazoo,
     MI, pp.255-99
Kasl, S.V., S. Gore and S. Cobb (1975) 'The
     Experience of Losing a Job: Reported Changes
     in Health, Symptoms and Illness Behaviour',
     Psychosomatic Medicine, 37, 106-22
Kessler, R.C. and J.A. McRae, Jr. (1981) 'Trends in
     the Relationship Between Sex and Psychological
     Distress: 1957-1976', American Sociological
     Review, 46, 443-52
Larson, J.H. (1984) 'The Effect of Husband's
     Unemployment on Marital and Family Relations
     in Blue-Collar Families', Family Relations,
     33, 503-11
Liem, G.R. and J.H. Liem (1979) 'Social Support and
     Stress: Some General Issues and Their
     Application to the Problem of Unemployment'
     in .L.A Ferman and J.P. Gordus (eds.) Mental
     Health and the Economy, The W.E. Upjohn
     Institute for Employment Research, Kalamazoo,
     MI, pp.347-77
Liem, R. and P. Rayman (1982) 'Health and Social
     Costs of Unemployment: Research and Policy
     Considerations', American Psychologist, 37
     1116-23
Liem, R. and P. Rayman (1984) 'Perspectives on
     Unemployment, Mental Health, and Social
     Policy', International Journal of Mental
     Health, 13, 3-17
Lipsky, B. (1979) The Labour Market Experience of

Workers Displaced and Relocated by Plant Shutdowns: The General Foods Case, Garland Publishing, Inc., New York

Marshall, G. (1984) 'On the Sociology of Women's Unemployment, Its Neglect and Significance', The Sociological Review, 32, 234-59

Morris, L.D. (1983a) 'Redundancy and Patterns of Household Finance', unpublished paper, University College of Swansea, Wales

Morris, L.D. (1983b) 'Renegotiation of the Domestic Division of Labour in the Context of Male Redundancy', unpublished paper, University College of Swansea, Wales

Nowak, T.C. and K.A. Snyder (1983) 'Women's Struggle to Survive a Plant Shutdown', The Journal of Intergroup Relations, XI, 24-44

Nowak, T.C. and K.A. Snyder (1984) 'Job Loss, Marital Happiness and Household Tension: Do Women Fare Better Than Men?', unpublished paper presented at the Society for the Study of Social Problems Annual Meeting, San Antonio, TX

Pearlin, L.I., M.A. Lieberman, E.G. Menaghan, and J.T. Mullan (1981) 'The Stress Process', Journal of Health and Social Behaviour, 22, 337-56

Pearlin, L.I. and C. Schooler (1978) 'The Structure of Coping', Journal of Health and Social Behaviour, 19, 2-21

Perrucci, C.C. (1978) 'Income Attainment Among College Graduates: A Comparison of Employed Women and Men', Sociology and Social Research, 62, 361-86

Perrucci, C.C. (1980) 'Gender and Achievement: The Early Careers of College Graduates', Sociological Focus, 13, 99-111

Perrucci, C.C. and D.B. Targ (1978) 'Early Work Orientation and Later Situational Factors as Elements of Work Commitment Among Married Women College Graduates', The Sociological Quarterly, 19, 266-80

Perrucci, C.C. and D.B. Targ (1985) 'The Effects of a Plant Closing on Marriage and Family Life', unpublished paper presented at the Symposium on Economic Distress and Families: Coping Strategies and Social Policy, University of Dayton, Dayton, OH

Perrucci, C.C., R. Perrucci, D.B. Targ and H.R. Targ (1985) 'The Impact of a Plant Closing on Workers and the Community' in R.L. Simpson and I.H. Simpson (eds.), Research in the

Sociology of Work: A Research Annual. Vol. 3,
JAI Press, Inc., Greenwich, CT, pp.231-260
Radloff, L.S. and R.S. Rae (1981) 'Components of
the Sex Difference in Depression' in R.G.
Simmons (ed.), _Research in Community and
Mental Health: A Research Annual, Vol. 2_, JAI
Press, Inc., Greenwich, CT, pp.111-37
Rayman, P. (1982) 'The World of Not Working: An
Evaluation of Urban Social Service Response
to Unemployment', _Journal of Health and Human
Resources Administration_, 4, 319-33
Rosen, E.I. (1983) 'Laid Off: Displaced Blue Collar
Women in New England', unpublished paper
presented at the Society for the Study of
Social Problems Annual Meeting, Detroit, MI
Rosenman, L.S. (1979) 'Unemployment of Women: A
Social Policy Issue', _Social Work_, 24, 20-25
Schlozman, K.L. (1979) 'Women and Unemployment:
Assessing the Biggest Myths', in J. Freeman
(ed.), _Women: A Feminist Perspective_, Mayfield
Publishing Co., Palo Alto, CA., pp.290-312
Sheppard, H.L. and A.H. Belitsky (1966) _The Job
Hunt: Job-Seeking Behaviour of Unemployed
Workers in a Local Economy_, Johns Hopkins,
Baltimore, MD
Snyder, K.A. and T.C. Nowak (1983) 'Sex Differences
in the Impact of a Plant Shutdown: The Case of
Robertshaw Controls', unpublished paper
presented at the American Sociological
Association Annual Meeting, Detroit, MI
Targ, D.B. (1983) 'Women and the New Unemployment',
Humboldt Journal of Social Relations, 10,
47-60
Warren, R. (written by Anne E. Fisher) (1978)
'Unemployment, Stress, and Helping Networks'
in _Women's Worlds: NIMH Supported Research on
Women_, U.S. Government Printing Office,
Washington, D.C., pp.96-99
Weeks, E.C. and S. Drengacz (1982) 'The Non-Economic
Impact of Community Economic Shock', _Journal
of Health and Human Resources Administration_,
4, 303-18
Wood, S. (1981) 'Redundancy and Female Employment',
Sociological Review, 29, 649-83

APPENDIX

Economic Variables

Length of unemployment
Number of months from layoff to date of study, August 1983

Re-employment status
1 = currently unemployed
2 = re-employed, part-time
3 = re-employed, full-time

Income loss
1983 weekly income as percentage of 1982 weekly income

Perceived economic distress (Pearlin et. al., 1981)
8 item summary score, sum of the items respondent could not afford
higher score = more distress

Cutbacks in consumer expenditures
20 item summary score, sum of the items cut back
higher score = more cutbacks

Increased engagement in money-saving activities
9 item summary score, sum of increased activities
higher score = more increased activities

APPENDIX (Cont'd)

Psychological Variables

Depression   9 item summary scale (9-27), sum of responses
                                3 = very often has symptom
                                2 = somewhat often has symptom
                                1 = not often has symptom
                                high score = high depression

Family and Friends Variable   4 items/change in relationships with four categories of
                                people: spouse, children, other family members, and friends
                                3 = better
                                2 = no change
                                1 = worse

Moderating Factors

Mastery   7 item summary score (7-28)
                                1 = low mastery
                                4 = high mastery
                                high score = high mastery

Social Support   1 - item indicator of amount of love and support from
                                family and friends
                                3 = lots of love and support
                                2 = sympathetic, but not supportive
                                1 = little support or sympathy
                                high score = high support

APPENDIX (Cont'd)

Moderating Factors

Optimism about Economic Future
1 – item indicator
'No matter what I do it will be near impossible to find a job in the months ahead.'
1 = agree
2 = don't know
3 = disagree
high score = high optimism

Demographic Factors

Gender
1 = male
2 = female

Age
in years

Marital Status
1 = single, divorced, widowed
2 = currently married

Educational Attainment
in years

Chapter Nine

WORKERS' STRUGGLES IN STEEL IN FRANCE AND IN THE USA: AUTONOMY AND CONSTRAINT AT LONGWY, LORRAINE AND AT YOUNGSTOWN, OHIO

Olivier Kourchid

The struggles of workers and communities against industrial restructuring in France and in the USA, their attempts and failures, and their political consequences, have rarely been so significant as they were in the steel industry during the 1970s. In this context it is worth recalling Longwy between December 1978 and July 1979, and Youngstown from September 1977 to March 1980, periods of time still fresh in the memories of those in Lorraine and in Ohio. (Youngstown, pop. 150000 in the Mahoning valley and Longwy, pop. 30000, are both located in typical steel valleys born at the beginnings of capitalist industrialization.)

So, why speak again of these struggles and why try not only to compare but also to contrast the two situations? Of course, there were at that time massive lay-offs in both towns; 15000 in Ohio and 4000 in Lorraine. But this is not a sufficient reason per se. The fact that these events were almost simultaneous is perhaps a better reason since it suggests a certain convergence, or more likely a global concentration of industrial policies in steel production and in the world market. But the most solid reason for the present analysis is embodied in the fact that the modes of action and mobilization developed in the struggles at Longwy and Youngstown seem to have been based on institutional foundations which were diametrically opposed. Even if it is possible to expect that from time to time workers may try to join together internationally at rank-and-file level or through union or political structures, differences between their situations need to be considered in advance of their successes[1].

Connecting two opposite contexts like Longwy and Youngstown has a further significance, since we

208

want to be able to specify two national situations
and the social relations which develop within these
contexts during times of crisis. In order to do so,
it seems appropriate to start from the components
of collective action, in other words: workers,
unions, the local state, corporations and the
national state, and to include the historical
intentions which form part of their actions. These
intentions, as we will try to show, are not used to
'compare' Longwy and Youngstown with the same
quantitative yardstick, on a scale along which each
situation can be located as 'more' or 'less' than
the other. The historical intentions and the
meaning of collective actions are, on the contrary,
opposed from a <u>qualitative</u> standpoint. The analysis
of struggles in the steel industry in France and in
the USA reveals in effect opposing tendencies both
in their intentions and in their possibilities of
action. In the former case, they are oriented
towards the <u>political</u> sphere. In the latter,
towards the <u>economic</u> sphere.

An analysis of Longwy and Youngstown, and of
the content and development of the struggles,
allows us more concretely to explain the opposition
between the political and economic sides of action
rather better than do the grievances expressed by
the participants. Therefore, it will be our task to
try to:

1. indentify and explain the variety of forms
    taken by the power of capital and which
    operate through sets of actors or agents
    at a manifest or latent level who, to a
    greater or lesser extent, drive the
    apparatus in a brutal or a procrastinating
    manner,
2. identify and differentiate the modes of
    actions of significant actors, such as
    workers, unions, businesses, churches or
    the state, a task which requires us to
    differentiate, inside national contexts,
    the <u>props</u> for action arising from the
    struggles, or which are imposed on them,
    and which include individualism, collective
    action, individual or collective relations
    with economic management or political
    grievances; and the acceptance or rejection
    of these relations,
3. identify and differentiate the actual
    limits of workers' <u>autonomy</u> which, it
    might be supposed, become extended during

> major conflicts in order to see the way in
> which national contexts of capitalism
> specifically constrain autonomy on typical
> terrains of action,
> 4. take into account - and overcome - what is
> usually implied in comparisons with the
> USA, that is the ideological and practical
> aspects of the dual relationship between
> archaism and futurism, regression and
> progression, old and new.

In effect, successive legislation which has
attenuated the social and organizational gains of
the New Deal has constantly narrowed the framework
within which workers action can develop in the USA,
as the weakness of struggles for employment
security and a general tendency towards de-unioniz-
ation seem to illustrate[2]. But in France could one
not expect that a political situation which
includes the presence of a socialist government
would permit new judicial attitudes which would
counter-balance not only previous repressive
tendencies but would also establish new frameworks
for workers' action by defining new rights and new
duties?
Finally, putting aside hypotheses about
'strategies of capital', we would also like to
include here illustrations of the range of
strategies used by management and workers during
plant closures. The opposition between the types of
action taken at Longwy and at Youngstown reveals
the complementarity of the situations, but also
reflects the stability of some kinds of social
relations which exist even during times of deep
conflict. It also permits an understanding of the
limits which are imposed on direct action and
spontaneity by deep-seated institutional roots.

CHRONOLOGY

It is not necessary to recall in detail here the
chronology of struggles at Longwy from 1977 to
1979. They have been analyzed a number of times
elsewhere (Durand, 1981; Noiriel, 1980), and, in
any case, we will return to them later since they
serve as a counterpoint to the events at
Youngstown. It is however necessary briefly to
present the conflicts in Ohio as they were
experienced by the actors. There were in fact two
periods of intense struggle at Youngstown, the

first from September 1977 until March 1980, which
followed the closure of the Campbell steelworks
belonging to Youngstown Sheet and Tube, and the
second, from December 1979 until July 1980, which
came after a series of closures at two plants
belonging to US Steel and a plant owned by Jones
and Laughlin[3].

Closure of the Campbell plant and local buy-out plans

In 1969 the Lykes corporation, a conglomerate based
in New Orleans had acquired the Youngstown Sheet
and Tube steel company[4]. Lykes, without any notice
to its workers announced that it had decided to
close the Campbell facility on January 1st, 1978.
(On conglomerate diversification, merger and
disinvestment strategies, see Bluestone and
Harrison, 1980. In the case of Campbell, investments
of the order of $10 million per year prior to the
merger fell to around $3 million.) The reasons
Lykes gave for the closure were the classic ones;
the dumping of imports and federal anti-pollution
legislation, arguments which were addressed by the
steelworkers when they collected 100,000 protest
signatures in the area which were sent to
Washington on September 24th., 1977. In October, as
the result of an idea put forward by a local
steelworker, a coalition was formed in the area,
made up of 272 Catholic, Protestant, Orthodox and
Jewish religious leaders. Its aim was to promote a
buy-out of the steel plant and to create a kind of
local workers cooperative designated as the
'Worker-Community Ownership Plan'. This had goals
similar to OPIC (the Ohio Public Interest
Campaign), an organization set up with the
participation of the AFL-CIO, major unions in the
state, minority, senior citizen and religious
groups, to support anti-plant closing bills in the
state legislature and to put local economic
interests before those of multinationals or
'unattached' conglomerates.

The coalition signed a research contract with
the National Center for Economic Alternatives which
produced a feasibility report[5]. The production of
this report was aided by the US Department of
Housing and Urban Development (HUD) for whom the
buy-out project at Campbell provided, given its
size, an excellent show case in the face of the
many plant closures in the area. The Treasury
Under-secretary of State also backed in principle

the proposals put forward in the feasibility study.
These were that the plant would be bought from
Lykes at scrap value with the administration
guaranteeing loans of up to 20% of $550 million.
The plan assumed that a market existed for 1.4
million tons of production a year (which included
200,000 tons which Lykes would continue to buy).
The proposal also assumed increased productivity in
line with previous instances where stockholding
employees had increased output by 30%. An
additional feature of the plan was that it also
contained some 'socialist' and 'statist' elements
since the federal government would have inspection
rights on the management committee, one third of
whose members would be drawn from the community.

However, during this period the elements of a
bitter defeat for the coalition and for the
Youngstown community were put together. On June
21st., 1978, the Secretary of State at the Justice
Department, Griffin Bell, reversed the recommendation
of the Department's anti-trust division by
approving a merger between Lykes who were selling
the Campbell works and another conglomerate,
Ling-Temco-Voight (LTV) which controlled the
Youngstown steel firm, Jones and Laughlin.

The merger of Lykes, the seventh largest
steelmaker in the US and LTV, the eighth largest,
produced an industrial group which was third
largest in the country. This group, which now
formed a new company in Youngstown, Youngstown
Sheet and Tube-Jones and Laughlin, changed the
conditions of sale for Campbell. The coke ovens and
blast furnaces would no longer be for sale, the
order book would no longer be available and Lykes
were no longer prepared to buy 200,000 tons of
steel. More importantly, the plant and machinery
were no longer to be tagged at scrap value but at
an intermediate price somewhere between scrap value
and book value.

The final rescue proposals for the plant were
ready by September 28th., 1978. These took into
account the adverse conditions outlined above, but
it was stubbornly maintained that the project
remained still feasible. According to the report,
the seeking of help from the federal government had
simply become more important and more urgent.
Campbell ought to be made a moral and an economic
example which would involve the creation of a
taskforce comprising representatives from different
federal departments. The report went on to suggest
that the federal government should set aside a $300

million federal loan guarantee reserve while further loans were being raised elsewhere. However, the final blow fell on March 29th., 1979 when the federal Economic Development Agency (EDA) refused to grant the loan and the guarantees because they considered the project not to be viable[6].

Subsequent closures and new local projects: protest and failure

When US Steel decided to close down two units in Youngstown at the end of 1979, 300 union delegates went to Pittsburgh to demand that federal benefits be linked to the lay-offs, and when the Brier Hill plant was closed down in December, a new coalition was formed. In January 1980 steelworkers occupied the regional headquarters of US Steel for six hours - an exceptionally rare event in the United States. The demonstrators left the premises after management promised to discuss the sale of the two plants to the workforce, and workers began to consider the possibility of investing lay-off compensation, retirement benefits and productivity bonuses in the plant, while giving up 20% of their wages.

An Employee Stock Ownership Plan (ESOP) called 'Community Steel' was initiated although it soon almost foundered when the local court authorized US Steel to close the plants[7]. Then, on March 23rd., 1980, the workers suffered a new defeat. Judge Lambros confirmed the right of US Steel to close the two production units. Anti-trust legislation could have compelled US Steel to accept the buy-out proposals, but under capitalism a unit has to be profitable, so the project's survival chances began to look slim. The city of Youngstown agreed to activate an 'eminent domain' clause which would have helped Community Steel acquire the necessary land and investments, but this would also have aided bills at state and local level aimed at imposing penalties on industries leaving the area and establishing various planning requirments - something which cannot yet be accepted in the US economy.

SOCIAL ACTORS IN LONGWY AND YOUNGSTOWN AND THEIR OPPOSING STRATEGIES

Compared to Longwy with its continuous violence over a period of time, the actions and their results at Youngstown were very different, although in the past collective action in both Lorraine and Ohio have been marked by violent struggle. As Bonnet and Humbert (1981) remind us in their book on the 1905-06 strikes in Longwy, the workers during these conflicts never limited themselves to work stoppages alone, but often destroyed machines, stocks and equipment as a way of attacking future production and curbing the activities of employers and scab labour. There have been violent conflicts too in the past in Youngstown, although these have not always been successful. As Ed Mann, a union representative, has recalled 'In 1919 workers burned down steelmills. In 1937 workers died in fights against US Steel. Now it is time to fight back again'. (Progressive Alliance, 1980).

In fact, however, workers in Ohio in 1978 did not seem to be quite so determined to fight back as those at Longwy. Why was this so? It is not enough simply to say that the New Deal had legitimized as well as legalized forms of action such as decentralized bargaining and contracts, grievance procedures and control of union elections. Nor is it sufficient to recall the institutional segmentation between the Northern deindustrialized states and those in the South which are anti-union, or that the recession has of necessity lowered the collective will for direct action. Instead, as a specific hypothesis, it is possible to suggest that in both cases the possibilities for action were located within a succession of frameworks. These are: the <u>battening down of struggles</u> by capital, <u>temporization</u>, <u>individualization</u> and <u>division</u> and, finally, the <u>failure of collective projects</u>. But, in addition to this, the possibilities of action in each case have developed within historical contexts which are radically opposite in terms of their relationship to production. In the first case, in Ohio, workers and their local representatives demanded the taking over of control of failing plants. In Lorraine, on the other hand, collective action was supported to the end by the often violent <u>negation</u> of all earlier dominant strategies whether this emerged from the state or from economic institutions.

Composition of the dominant groups: segmentation and homogenization processes

In the USA as in France steelmaking firms are undergoing a deep economic and institutional transformation, but it would be overly simplistic to see this as a process of restructuration and concentration. In fact, in both countries patterns of concentration and differentiation are simultaneously at work, the different levels of which need to be located. In the USA, as illustrated by Youngstown, it is clear that government intervened in the situation in a relatively indirect fashion, pretending, in a sense, to play the game of capitalist efficiency. Thus, since freedom of interstate commerce is one of the pillars of the constitution, it must find a way to favour concentration while showing explicitly that it respects the anti-trust laws. On the same basis it protects domestic steel from imports through the trigger price mechanism which activates anti-dumping procedures when price levels justify it, and regulates issues such as compliance with anti-pollution legislation or the fiscal arrangements specific to the steel industry.

However, in all of this, the restructuring of steel is primarily linked to the dynamics of conglomeration, which in turn leads to the development of economic monsters whose activities are very diverse and which operate on the basis of inter-subsidiary competition and on purely financial criteria. Takeovers and mergers allow one to 'put one's eggs in different baskets' and to lower market pressures. Conglomeration allows for rapid cash accumulation before investments are sold off or scrapped. As already seen, the closures at Youngstown and the failure of the Worker-Community Buy-out Plan were directly a consequence of the economic and financial strategies of the conglomerates. As these economic institutions become more and more diversified, they take an increasingly dismissive attitude towards steel, an old industry where competition is extremely fierce, and shift their investments instead into, for example, petro-chemicals, property, fertilizers, aviation and oil. These tendencies suggest therefore that the situation in the US is anchored - schematically - on the following key-words: <u>explicit economic stakes</u>, <u>relatively homogeneous decision making</u> and <u>conglomeration and diversification</u>[8]. Without going into the details of French economic history, it is obvious that the steel crisis in France displays quite opposite tendencies at least conceptually. Here the dominant key-words are the <u>continuous manifestation of political stakes</u> which leads to a process of <u>quasi-nationalization</u> (and actual nationalization after 1981), and to <u>a greater</u>

<u>specialization of activities</u>.

To take each of these in turn. <u>Political</u>
<u>stakes</u> can easily be seen in France where the steel
industry has for a long time been a concern of the
state. As Padioleau (1981) notes, 'the rationality
which prevails in the steel industry is political'[9].
The system therefore operates in both an ideological
and an economic direction. The state had instituted
an industrial policy based on growth which had
begun to suffer a number of severe reversals
towards the end of the 1970s. Despite this and
despite technological changes and debates about
issues such as the siting of steelworks at
deep-water sites, policy towards steel has
straddled the major shifts in French political life
- from planning, to dirigism, to liberalism, all of
them sustained by a quasi-corporatist state and a
consensus on steel of the kind indicated by
Padioleau. In this context, major restructuring
took place only at the end of the 1970s, after the
problems of the industry had been put off again and
again.

Turning now to the role of <u>differentiated</u>
<u>decision-making centres</u>, one can see that the
international dimensions of the steel crisis
require the participation of steel producers in
organizations like OECD in which both Japan and the
USA are also members. Differentiation, however, is
even more notable at the European level where the
role of the European Economic Community and the
European Coal and Steel Community (ECSC) are even
more marked. In fact these institutions have
produced restructuring plans one after another -
the Simmonet plan at the end of 1976 and the
Davignon plan (1977)[10]. In addition steel industrialists in Europe have also created their own defence
associations such as the <u>Groupement Economique</u>
<u>International</u> 'Denelux' created in 1976 and which
drew together business associations in the industry
from Germany, the Netherlands and Luxemburg. This
organization later became 'Eurofer', a European
steelmakers association which includes France[11]
(although countries like Germany better placed to
withstand the recession in steel naturally complain
that the financial contributions asked of members
are unequally distributed).

This same pattern of differentiation and
division appears within the decision-making system
inside France. The subsidies given to the steel
industry are generally processed by the FDES (Fonds
de Développment Economique et Social - the Social

and Economic Development Fund) with the agreement
of the Ministry of Finance - although it is the
Industry Ministry which exerts its authority over
steel decisions. The agreements between the state
and the steel industry define the various methods
of subsidy and deal with related matters particularly
in the area of employment protection. In the area
of forecasting the Commissariat au Plan - the
Planning Commission in France - has created a steel
committee although its reports seem to bear little
relation to reality. As Freyssenet (1979) has
commented 'no report from the Steel Committee in
preparation of a plan has ever been so sketchy, so
vague and so purposeless as the one issued for the
seventh plan' (for 1976-80). In effect the
forecasts assumed a two to three per cent growth
per year while in reality there was a decrease of
17% on the 1976 figures.

Finally, however, the strategies of the
decision making groups have produced a paradoxical
telescoping of events. Eventually, the 1977 Steel
Planning Report predicted a long series of lay-offs
(somewhere around 20,000 jobs). These predictions
were made public after municipal elections which
had shown strong gains for the left. At the same
time the state organized a system of 'surveillance'
for the steel companies. These were not at that
time nationalized although a portion of their stock
had to be lodged at the Caisse des Depots et
Consignations, a national deposit bank. In fact it
was a year later that the government took control
of the steel companies, converting loans from the
state and from public investors into shares in the
new capital stock. In a sense therefore it is only
formally that one cannot speak of real nationalization
until 1981. Before then the companies had a free
hand which they used in different ways. For
example, as Freyssenet points out Usinor simply
'sentenced to death' Longwy in Lorraine and Denain
in the North of France while the other group,
Sacilor-Sollac, acted in a more muted but equally
efficient way.

Nationalization was voted by Parliament at the
end of 1981. As for specialization, it could be
adopted as an economic policy, should companies
like Usinor, with its new president, decide to
invest in special steels as opposed to bulk
steelmaking.

Strategies of the dominant groups at local level
The victims of the steel recession at the community
level, Youngstown or Longwy, must face two kinds of
adversaries: in the former case they are faced by
conglomerates and mergers (Lykes and LTV) which
obey a brutal economic logic and in the latter they
must face a much more complex and diversified set
of bodies which include employers, the State, and
European institutions. In the first case, Youngstown,
the conglomerate suffered heavily from the world
crises in steel, and protested vocally about it,
demanding for example more protectionism, but also
more freedom from the regulations of the Environmental
Protection Agency. The conglomerate also blamed the
unions who were too strong for their taste and who
created social and wage demands which, as it said,
finally hurt the communities. Therefore, it didn't
lack reasons to justify its disinvestment, and
behaved, urbi et orbi, as it were, in the manner
typical of a 'mobile conglomerate'. This was
precisely why there were local and regional
attempts to pass bills punishing such practices,
even if they were relatively mild. (Indeed, there
are in fact only a few examples of implementation,
one of them being in Massachussetts). This does not
mean that there is no link at the economic or
political level between plant management and local
power: businessmen's clubs, and banks confirm the
fact. But generally speaking, decisions on
disinvestment in steel come usually from distant
centres (Pittsburgh, New Orleans, Dallas) and were
implemented with maximum efficiency by managers who
were usually mobile, and unattached to the
community. Moreover, the employer in this case was
not only quite distant but also autonomous with
respect to the social reproduction of the labour
force since housing, social services and health
care were dependent on private institutions, even
in cases where a union contract existed. At the
local level, the characteristics of the Youngstown
community which best explain the types of struggle
undertaken and the ways they are constrained seem
therefore to be embodied in the substantial and
dynamic autonomy of economic institutions, which
have been independent for a long time from the
'social' management of the labour force.
      The decision context in Longwy shows by
contrast a series of specific oppositions. As
suggested above, the 'political' nature of the
steel crisis does not emerge only at the highest
level where political and economic decisions were

made and closely intertwined. It results also from the strong differentiation inside the relevant decision making bodies. If issues flow down in a political form to the local level, it is not only because of the affiliations of the political representatives (Communist or Socialist) and of the unions (CGT and CFDT), it is also because there are explicit political divisions among the various levels of management. For example, the president of the powerful Association of Steel Manufacturers, M. Ferry, thought that the restructuration plan of 1978 was insufficiently protectionist and, in his own words, sufficiently lacking in any 'real political will at the "base" level' (see Noiriel, 1981, 54-82; Durand, 1981, 99-152).

The plan was also challenged by members of the former board of Usinor and the chairman of one of its subsidiaries (Vallourec, which makes tubes and pipes) resigned in protest. When the chairman and executive officer of Usinor decided to continue the construction of a plant at Neuves-Maisons - although Longwy would have been a more rational choice, since basic steel was produced there - several hundred managers and engineers mobilized in the plant, signed motions, and sent an open letter to the Minister of Industry. In May 1979 the director of Usinor-Longwy, who had stood firmly in favour of a new steel mill at Longwy, and had made his position known to a parliamentary commission, was transferred to another location (Noiriel, p. 59:60). There were also protests from the former rightist majority: while the Gaullist RPR (Rassemblement Pour la Republique) which represents some of the interests of the local petite bourgeoisie and the small businessmen's associations, criticized the Metal Manufacturer's Association of Lorraine which was chaired by a parliamentary deputy from the UDF (a party close to Valery Giscard d'Estaing) for the lack of diversification in the Longwy area. The local representatives of the UDF and those of the PR (the Parti Republicain, led by Valery Giscard d'Estaing) as well as the local conservative paper were also very critical. All this bitterness was not forgotten when the political action of the former majority was assessed against the socialist programme in May 1981.

Steel withdraws from the sites
Massive lay-offs such as those at Longwy and Youngstown do not come all of a sudden. Previous

warnings, some of them visible a long time before could have been observed. In the aftermath it was at least possible to discuss specific arrangements according to the level of mobilization in the area. However, in both cases all those concerned stressed that the closure announcements were exceptionally sudden and brutal - so much so that when the Campbell works closed workers spoke of 'Black Monday' a reference to the Wall Street crash.

Of course sudden lay-offs are part of the usual pattern of labour relations in the United States - notice is very often non-existent. Beyond this, managements try and often succeed to establish around the firm a boundary which is resistant to social and economic changes. In France, for example, managers very often refuse to provide basic information on the company to the Comite d'Enterprise as they should. Lay-offs, then, often come as a surprise, although warning signs do exist: hiring stops, temps are fired, short-term contracts are not renewed and above all temporary lay-offs are instituted. This last, which produces decreases in worktime and in wages but not in the number of employees, is an important source of anxiety for workers even if their reactions often have an individualistic character.

In the USA hiring and firing are part of a normal pattern so that the employer is always able to adjust labour force capacities to expected levels of production. In other words it is always possible to optimize productivity within the boundary of the firm. This was the case for example at the Ohio Works of US Steel at Youngstown, where workers won a company productivity competition to produce even better results than more modern plants.

If this type of economic cynicism resides in the USA inside the economic barriers of the firm, coporate cynicism in Longwy was superimposed on a strategy of 'modernisation' of its social and political relations at the local level. Before, workers' housing was totally owned by the employer. Rents were low and the labour force remained stable. More recently the employers' organization, Union Métallurgique Minière (UMM) decided to become financially involved in the provision of low rent public housing (HLM)[12], but above all Usinor also began to sell back individual houses to the workers (Noiriel, 1980, 23). For most of them this represented a way to own finally their own homes and to deepen their roots in a community they did not want to leave. However after the layoffs, this managerial strategy seems particularly appalling since in these conditions buying a house on a mortgage is more than an impossible dream, it is a nightmare. First, if the employers sell off these homes is it not because they are in trouble, and is it not possible that they intend to get rid of steel production in the area altogether? Second, how is it possible for workers to meet their payments on the house, which are usually based on double incomes, if one or the other or both in the household are about to lose their job? Finally if one has to look elsewhere for another job, what will be the re-sale value of the property in a stagnant regional economy?

Last but not least, the community finally learned just before Christmas 1978 that, in spite of several rescue plans and a number of false starts, only lay-offs would salvage the industry:

> Threatened with bankruptcy the two big steel concerns Usinor and Sacilor-Sollac announced as a condition for their survival at the end of 1978 the elimination of 21,750 jobs between April 1979 and December 1980. Never had so many jobs been lost in such a short period. (Durand, 1981, 101)

At the same time workers and activists in Youngstown who had received their first shock just one year before were still waiting for an answer from Washington on their community buy-out and employee ownership plan at the Campbell works.

THE LAY-OFFS ARE ANNOUNCED: DO STRUGGLES PROCEED FROM WORKERS' AUTONOMY OR FROM EARLIER MANAGEMENT STRATEGIES?

The visible starting points for the conflicts were of course the lay-off notifications which came abruptly in Longwy just as they did at Youngstown. In situations of this kind new forms of action and new forms of workers' solidarity have to develop. In other words struggles for employment protection usually have to be innovative. Strikes of the usual kind, even if they were legal, would not be effective since if they took place negotiations would fail. In Lorraine and in Ohio both solidarity and local mobilization occurred, and in both cases modified in particular ways the course and timing of events, since the state and the employers had to take into account resistance which initially they had not expected. Apart from the historical and ideological foundations of these movements, it is also possible to suggest that in spite of the apparent rupture caused by the announcements, there remains a degree of continuity between what happened before and afterwards. It is this continuity which points to some of the limits on the autonomy of workers' actions.

In effect collective mobilization in the face of dramatic job losses can only become <u>resistance</u> when the victims succeed in regrouping their forces within geographical and institutional spaces where dominant groups are for the time being unable to intervene. This <u>displacement</u> (or delocalization of stakes) outside the 'normal' course of the social relations of production - that is to say, in this case the relation to the <u>stoppage</u> of production - enlarges and diversifies the normal paths of social relations, binding together in the same movement, or at least in the same object, areas of behaviour which are usually separated. However, is this enlargement of the paths of action sufficient? Before answering - in a way which allows us to be more precise than simply making references to reform or revolution - let us first point out the elements of the opposition/comparison with which we are concerned.

In Youngstown the announcement of lay-offs followed a decision made by the company. Calculated as this decision was, it did not take into account, by and large, either the national or regional consequences of that decision. Workers' struggles then took the form of an attempt at long-term economic takeover which originated among religious groups and with only infinitesimal levels of violence. They key words characterizing action are <u>legality</u>, <u>economics</u> and '<u>self management</u>'. In Longwy, the lay-offs were announced after a political decision made necessary by long-term economic problems related to a recurrent preoccupation with voting considerations. <u>Here struggles took the form of long-term violence - almost insurrectional at times - and with the involvement of the workers being not only infinitesimal but also largely negative</u> (in the sense, for example, that the counter-proposals put forward by the union hierarchy were not always accepted by the rank-and-file). The key-words here then are <u>illegality</u>, <u>politics</u> and <u>opposition to any involve-</u>

<u>ment with management</u>.

<u>Coalition in Youngstown: religious pluralism and union monopoly</u>

Community and régional defence committees or associations have existed for a long time in Ohio - the Ohio Public Interest Campaign (OPIC) has already been mentioned. However, the first reaction to the lay-offs at the Campbell works in September 1977 came from the Mahoning Valley Ecumenical Coalition which, as we have already seen, financed the first feasibility studies of the plant, and which later cooperated with a regional development agency, the Mahoning Valley Development Committee, in order to promote further studies and to investigate the possibility of federal financial help to encourage economic regeneration.

The success of religious coalitions is frequently found in the United States where social movements, such as the Equal Rights movement or the movement to unionize farmworkers, have often incorporated a religious dimension. (Chaired by the local Roman Catholic bishop with an Episcopalian bishop as vice-president, the coalition in fact reflects a classic division in US society - the labour force is often Catholic, while management and business are Protestant). Coalitions of this sort make possible the grouping together of some segments of the middle class - middle management, small businessmen and small entrepreneurs - in conjunction with the dismissed workers. The 'liberal-democratic' tone of such movements is often sustained by grass-roots criticism of remote and 'unattached' conglomerates and by the attempt to promote local democracy, itself an important value in American ideology. In this particular case the components of the ideology are 'self-help', the utility of planning in the sense of managing employment as well as profit, and a David versus Goliath attitude premised on the notion that 'small is beautiful'.

The religious coalition expressed the motivations behind its struggle in a memorandum dated November, 1977. Naturally enough, it did not point out that closures would decrease church revenues, but stressed the public issue of economic justice arising from the company's refusal to honour their social responsibilities. In consequence, the coalition was in favour of economic alternatives, launching with the steelworkers union a 'Save our

Valley' campaign which collected $4 million. As we know the coalition project failed after the expenditure on studies and other activities of $300,000 because the Carter administration refused to grant the requested loan, but the coalition did reappear at the end of 1979 when the US Steel plants closed. This time, however, it preferred not to go beyond a consulting role, leaving it to the union to attempt an ultimately unsuccessful buy-out plan.

Organizations in Longwy: pluralism at the political, union and local levels

In Longwy, the Catholic Church has also played a progressivist role which cannot be denied. For example , the local diocesan bishop often celebrated mass in the church the tower of which is used as the antenna for the CGT 'Lorraine Coeur-d'Acier' radio station (the studio for which is in the city hall). Furthermore, many of those militant in the CFDT union are committed Christians. However, the comparison does not go beyond this point. In Youngstown, collective action arose out of a local project involving the union and the ecumenical coalition which, while it was strengthened by the feasibility studies, was eventually weakened by government decisions (the refusal to lend money), judicial decisions (the agreement on the Lykes-LTV merger), and by industrial decisions (the refusal to sell the plant). In Longwy, however, the struggle was, as one activist convincingly put it, 'also a means to overcome divisions'. Many splits existed inside the unions, the political parties and the various activist groups and these remained despite many attempts to promote unity[13].

   In this context one can note that the social groups most attached to the interests of the steel industrialists and to some segments of state power had their own defence organizations (eg. one called l'Avenir du Haut Pays - the Future of the High Country - founded by a steel manufacturer, B Labbe. (see Noiriel, 1980, 22)).Also, the UMM (the Mining and Mineral Association) and the Chamber of Steel created, along with retailers, small businessmen and professionals, an 'Action Group to Promote Industrial Dynamics' in order to attract new industries to the area. The real 'engine' behind the mass movements in Longwy was, however, the 'Intersyndicale' - the union coalition which grouped together unions like the CGT (Confédération

Générale du Travail), the CFDT (Confédération Démocratique des Travailleurs) and the Force Ouvrière and middle class organizations such as the CGC (Confédération Générale des Cadres) and the FEN (Fédération de l'Education Nationale). This interunion coalition ramified inside the plants and even in some cases operated at shop level. At the same time the 'Three Borders Struggle Committee' also brought in associations and unions from Belgium and Luxemburg. Strike committees were organized in the plants while executives also formed a defence committee for steel.

The diversity of organizations also went beyond the immediate problems of steel and an indication of the range of such organizations is in order. In June 1979 a Womens' Action Committee was set up which eventually became the CAS (Contraception, Avortement, Sexualité) movement. Teachers organized a 'Comité des Flammes de l'Espoir (Committee of the Flames of Hope) in order to organize demonstrations by school students. Artisans and retailers created an Intertrade and Interdistrict Action Committee (CAII) while young people and students grouped themselves into a 'Comité des Jeunes en Lutte' (The Committee of Youth in Struggle).

Beyond these specific organizations there were also, of course, political organizations. In these the left was dominant since 64% of the population of the cities in the area live in Communist municipalities. At this time the Communist Party had eight 'conseillers généraux' (officers elected at county level) and two 'députés' (elected to the House of Representatives). The Socialist Party, too, had a good electoral base (Noiriel, 1980) although the split inside the Union de la Gauche created persistent divisions which were much resented by the workers.

Out of this extremely differentiated context arose, after December 1978, an uninterrupted series of collective actions and mobilizations which lasted until July 1979. These actions explored practically every opportunity for occupying 'enemy territory'. In this way, struggles generated a new unitary will while unity yielded new forms of struggle. Beyond this, new organizations and new associations mushroomed with action beginning and then renewing itself out of precisely the connection between differentiation and mass unity.

Struggles and forms of action

It seems that the Youngstown situation did not present a variety of possibilities in this way, although it remains as the striking example of mobilization in the United States at the end of the 1970s. Never in the USA had workers' control been attempted in this sort of industrial sector and in companies of this kind of scale. Never also, as we shall see, had certain types of action been attempted in the recent history of the American labour movement. It will be remembered that the first closure at the Campbell works had led to a buy-out plan sustained by a religious coalition. Although it was perfectly legal, or perhaps because of that, this particular project was not massively supported by the workers. According to one of the union leaders of local 1462 (Progressive Alliance, 1980),

> Workers are not aggressive activists. We have been taught for thirty years that movements and collective actions are not pure. One cannot expect radical changes in attitude from one year to another.

The second closure in November 1979 led to similar buy-out projects and attempts at workers' control in which the unions and their members were more deeply involved and which included an occupation. This occupation which took the form of a sit-in at the company's regional headquarters - exceptional though it may have been - in fact points towards both the possibilities and the limitations of this kind of action in the US. It began simply as yet another meeting of local 1330 with about 600 people in attendance who were discussing ways in which US Steel could be persuaded to sell its two plants. House representatives and senators from Ohio, Democratic and Republican, were present, as were the media. Union representatives issued a directive to 'Occupy the US Steel headquarters in Youngstown'. A hundred workers ran into the building, some of them unfolding banners demanding job security. Others sat in the chairman's office, saying that they would not come out until 'we can discuss matters with the director'.

Upper management in Pittsburgh finally gave in and authorized its director to discuss the sale of the two plants. This promise appeared to the union and to its members as a sign of possible victory.

However, there was a lack of unanimous action such that if the local representative of the AFL-CIO joined the sit-in, the regional director of the United Steelworkers became conspicuous by his absence. This was a situation which did not impress members of the local who put their feelings in the following way. 'We know what we could expect from this guy ... it's like those politicians who were at the meeting this morning and who stayed behind this afternoon. In any case, we are the union here at the local, not the international' (ie. the union as a whole).

Occupation is a form of demonstration which comes close to being scandalous in a country where management's business property and prerogatives are sacred. It might then have looked like an uncontrolled initiative, like a 'savage' coup. But it should not. Rather, as one of the union representatives insisted 'there was nothing spontaneous in this occupation. It was a planned demonstration and it worked perfectly'. However, after the buy-out plan failed not everyone was convinced that the occupation had been a success. As S. Lynd, a long-time activist, historian and people's lawyer put it, 'We all agree to say that occupying a company is one of the more efficient forms of struggle ... Our biggest tactical error was not to occupy the place a longer time'[14].

The events at Longwy, as we have said, were made up of a series of constantly renewed modes of action which involved the temporary or permanent occupation of all types of institutional spaces; economic territory (the plants), state territory (police, treasury, prefecture and other administrative buildings) and the national media (the TV towers). Regional and national spaces were also occupied by many marches and demonstrations, in Longwy, of course, in Metz and above all in Paris. Social life was significantly 'occupied' by associations like CAS or by the local radio networks created during the conflict and there were of course constant and bitter clashes with the CRS riot police.

The general meaning of these actions is undoubtedly 'political' in the most basic sense of the word, and, concretely, there is a strong possibility that these much publicised struggles may have tilted the balance towards the left in the 1981 elections. (Mitterand's share of the vote was only 1% better than that of Giscard.) However, if we consider the more specific framework of mobilization, the protection of employment and the defence of the regional economy, the actions addressed themselves to very different objects in the social world. Besides making the struggles known and gathering popular support, the strikes, occupations, marches and demonstrations attempted to strike at the dominant power in the following ways:

1. within economic space action was taken against any form of takeover of the control of production ('anti-gestionnaire'),
2. within political-administrative space action was directed against the state,
3. within the space of local and social demands, action was aimed at class identity.

These directions can be found coexisting in most of the struggles to be found in Lorraine and elsewhere, but some specific examples may be given.

'Actions anti-gestionnaires'[15]

These may appear totally external to the realm of production, certainly as compared with the hopes and intentions of the community at Youngstown, and they may also seem at first sight as quite 'spontaneous' actions. In fact, though, they should be seen in many ways as being directed towards the defence of trade and employment. These actions are basically protectionist; they are intended to defend - at least symbolically - regional and national economies against European integration which appears as a screen behind which hides supranational interests. Thus, it is possible to find, for example, trains carrying imported raw materials being unloaded onto the track. Swedish iron ore, German coke, ingots from different places were spilt in this manner on a dozen occasions in what activists refer to as 'commando-style operations' (opérations coup de poing). In a similar way the pipe bringing gas from Holland was cut and railways and motorways were frequently blocked. At the same time, of course, many initiatives took place within the plants and the mills with a number of strikes and stoppages, at least at the beginning of the struggles (Durand, 1981, 20-22).

If the workers in Youngstown did not want to strike (in any case it would have been illegal), in France strikes were costly to the workers and were rapidly seen to be an insufficient response to restructuration. For this reason workers began to develop actions both <u>inside</u> the plants in the for of occupations and <u>outside</u> in the shape of demonstrations. It was in the <u>'intersyndicale'</u> that unions and militants came together but also where they were brought into competition. The rank-and-file from the CFDT refused to stay on industrial territory and wanted instead to extend its actions outside the firm. On the other hand, the CGT, at least in the beginning, favoured action in the workplace, although it then pushed rapidly for demonstrations in the streets. At this stage CGT activists at the 'base' level also became involved in <u>'opérations coup de poing'</u> - although these sometimes ended up being disavowed by the union hierarchy.

<u>The general dimension of these struggles, though, is that categories usually excluded from particular spaces succeeded in conquering them</u>. Workers opened the doors of the mills to the population, with families and friends, students and journalists coming to visit the workshops. The offices of managment and higher executives were occupied many times and files and documents were taken away for examination. Sometimes desks and furniture were thrown out of windows, an action the workers referred to as 'moving out', since they had been told that if they wanted to find another job they would just have to move out of the area.

Demonstrators neutralised the management process within plants by attacking the industrial bureaucracy; offices and desks were locked and bureaucrats shut up in their offices. Also neutralised were negotiating bodies like the workers' councils in the plant, the offices of the personnel and industrial relations staff and both the regional and the national offices of Usinor and of the Steel Manufacturers Association. Indeed they even found a way of striking at a historical symbol of domination in the steel mills by pulling down the statue of Baron d'Huart, a famous aristocrat and steel magnate. They also 'cleaned' the <u>Association du Haut Pays</u>, another symbol of dominant power in the region.

Anti-state actions

These can be a response to police violence but arose in the first place out of the fact that the workers, as citizens, wanted to occupy those

centres of power and decision making which organise
and manage social and individual life in an
alienating manner. For example, branches of the
Banque de France and of the Crédit Lyonnais bank
were occupied by members of the Force Ouvriere
union as were the income tax offices and the local
branch of the Treasury. A meeting of the
interdistrict Board of Mayors was disturbed and
interrupted so as to prevent the mandatory
submission of income tax forms to meet the legal
deadline. The telephone exchange at Gorcy, the
post-office and unemployment offices at Longwy were
also occupied by CGT and CFDT members, who also
caused havoc at the sous-préfecture at Briey.
Perhaps more significant were the struggles,
attacks and counter-attacks linked to the occupation
of the television relay station. Initiated by the
CFDT this action provoked violent charges from the
police and the CRS especially in the Bois de Châ
which surrounds the relay station. Following this,
and a number of more or less violent demonstrations,
militants and demonstrators attacked the district
court, and the youth wing of the CGT occupied the
office of the president of the county court. The
judicial powers being temporarily paralysed or, at
least, in disarray, the city appeared at times to
be in a quasi-insurrectional situation. At this
point, there was still one thing left to do - to
chop off in a symbolic way the head of the
'aristocratic supreme power'. Pictures of Valéry
Giscard d'Estaing were unhooked from the walls of
the city halls in the area and fell, as it were,
into the same basket as Baron d'Huart's statue.
Workers' and union struggles in Longwy revived, it
is clear, old revolutionary patterns which were
linked to stable forms of relationship between the
central state power and civil society.

Class identity: social, local and cultural expression

People from Longwy, besides wanting to publicise
their struggles, also wanted to have a communication
tool which was in the hands of workers and
strikers. They wanted in other words to have their
own radio and to control their own collective
expression in an autonomous fashion. The temporary
neutralisation of the TV relay station was not
directed only at breaking the monopoly of the
national broadcasting system, it was also aimed at
preventing the jamming of the workers' radio. The

fight over communications and the media set in
train a cycle which strengthened the relationship
between collective defence and working class
identity.

The first attempt to have an autonomous radio
was made by the CFDT who started to broadcast using
a low-powered transmitter with the call-sign SOS
Emploi (SOS Employment).[16] Later, the CGT started a
powerful radio station, LCA ('Lorraine Coeur
d'Acier') with two professional journalists and a
studio in the city hall. It was generally noticed
that these radio stations began to have a
liberating role in relation to many things such as
collective expression, the relationship between the
media and media technique and the relationship
between intellectual and manual workers. Moreover,
the radio had an important organising function in
particular in relation to the 'Paris March'. This
march involved 300,000 people. Despite some police
provocation and a few incidents in which shop
windows were broken and garbage cans set on fire,
and in spite of the fact that the CGT was not
joined by other unions (the CFDT refused to join
regarding it as a cosmetic exercise prior to the
district elections), the march represented a major
movement of crowds into the centre of power - Paris
- and was a major demonstration against 'Parisianism'.

The march, the LCA radio, the numerous
demonstrations and happenings which took place in
the Longwy area represented a radical change in
social relations which shows clearly the constitution
of a collective identity for workers - and at the
local level - which represents a massive social
phenomenon with deep historical roots reaching back
to the utopias of the 19th century revolutions. It
is in this respect, at the level of action, that
the contrast with Youngstown is most marked,
although at the level of intentions the gap is
probably smaller since in both cases the expression
of basic grass-roots 'policies' is present.

After 15 months of uninterrupted broadcasting
and after 10 months of financing at the local level
by the CGT and local militants, Lorraine Coeur
d'Acier was 'dropped' by the Confederation in
Paris, probably under strong pressure from the
Communist Party. Those in charge of the radio in
Longwy resigned in total disgust and the journalists
and broadcasters involved were left unemployed. The
more committed activists were convinced that the
radio had been silenced for not following the
correct 'line', and because of that, LCA died out

for ever. It was as if local freedom was forced to fall silent not only before the state apparatus but also in the face of the union apparatus.

CONCLUSION: OUTCOMES OF THE STRUGGLE, WHAT LIES BEYOND INDIVIDUALISATION AND DIVISION?

Only the short term can be dealt with here although, for sure, Longwy and Youngstown will leave behind landmarks in history. In the short term, however, processes have been at work which have tended to encourage demobilisation. On the one hand, we find patterns of <u>individualisation</u>, a process which is an institutional feature of the American projects, since employees there may become small shareholders responsible for the destiny of the firm. Although in the case of the Ohio closures this is unlikely to attain a concrete realisation because the state and the judicial authorities have purposively temporised too much.

In France, individualisation has a more practical, if brutal, character which takes the form of 'social agreements' (<u>conventions sociales</u>) negotiated with the employers (although they have been signed by only some unions such as the CFDT). These agreements include the right of older workers to take early retirement and for younger workers to leave with a severance bonus amounting to 50,000 Francs - about a year and a half's wages: offers of a tempting if poisoned kind, which have been accepted by thousands of workers and union militants.

At the same time the <u>divisions between rank-and-file and the unions</u> focus on the real possibilities offered by the different plans. At Youngstown the unions promoting Community Steel denounced the technical irrealism proposed by people sympathetic to the movement but based in Philadelphia, hundreds of miles away. As the Cleveland Plain Dealer observed (December 2nd, 1979), 'The plan needed here must come from people from here, from people who know best what they want and what they need'. At Longwy the economic studies department of the CGT - with the agreement of the Confederation in Paris - produced a report on the steel industry, which appeared however to those on the ground to have been 'parachuted' in from above. In this case, as Noiriel (1980, 97) says, 'the framework necessary for discussions at local level and for information on industrial projects is not yet built'.

Whatever the different splits and divisions at the functional or the institutional level, it is possible to ask if the local opposition to restructuration and deindustrialisation has discouraged struggles or reinforced them. In Youngstown counter-proposals undoubtedly mobilized workers and aligned them with fractions of the militant or even of the simply interested middle classes. But here radicalisation did not go very far. With the exception of the occupation of the regional headquarters of US Steel, the coalitions and the Worker-Community Ownership Plans appealed rather to the virtues of productivism and self-help inherited from the original principles of American history. In Longwy, projects and counter-proposals 'belonged' to union organisations or to administrative institutions. Did the rank-and-file believe in them? In fact they knew that only radical struggles would let them obtain individual benefits and some short-term arrangements and that no massive revitalisation would be undertaken by the political powers of the time. Their only hope was that a radicalisation of struggles over employment would encourage a change of majority at the national political level. This was indeed what happened in the presidential elections in May 1981 in the tradition of recurrent shifts which periodically allow adjustment to change in France.

Was there a similar kind of hope when the AFL-CIO decided to organise a giant march on Washington at the end of December 1981 to defend union and social gains against the policies of Ronald Reagan? Perhaps, but it is also worth remembering that what is sometimes regarded as the apathy of the labour movement is due in part to the New Deal legislation and the laws which came after it, like Taft-Hartley. The workers indeed made many gains, especially in relation to organisational rules, but in the end there is a sense in which their armour ended up being too heavy. While legislation and organisation represent strength and protection for unions, they bind their movement too tightly, especially where the rank-and-file is concerned.

The political and economic aspects of these conflicts permitted us to hold in opposition the most salient features of the two countries. We have no reason to make any judgement on Longwy or Youngstown; only in the long term will history show in what sense the economic struggles at Youngstown were political, and what the historical significance of collective action in Longwy will be. In both cases the economic dimensions of counter-proposals and management projects did not seem seriously to convince rank-and-file workers who were much more concerned with the defence of their trade and the preservation of employment in their own area. Doing so, they showed in both countries that they wanted to preserve the history and traditions of their own world while demanding in a utopian way a greater degree of diversification and flexibility from industry. This is something which places into serious question the mentality and understanding of industrial decision makers.

Postscript

The purpose of this paper has been to describe diametrically opposing modes of action which have been found within the dramatic context of massive lay-offs in steel. It is not intended now, five years later to bring the story up to date. What happened has become a part of the history of labour and community movements and indeed has acquired a uniqueness which places them inside the pantheon of cultural and institutional symbols. It is true that since the 1970s major changes have occurred in the political context. In the United States 'hard liberalism' under Ronald Reagan has meant more massive lay-offs, more wage-cuts, reduced levels of union membership, more big mergers and a further restructuration in steel under the threat of bankruptcy. Workers and communities in the steel valleys have continued to fight, providing locally organised assistance to the unemployed, with self-help groups, unemployed committees, and once again religious coalitions (see Deitch and Erickson, this volume). In some cases, such as that of Weirton, ESOP plans have been formulated, while in other cases there have been attempts to develop anti-closing legislation (Rothstein, 1982). With the exception of a few incidents during marches or the famous disruption of religious ceremonies· in the Monongahella Valley in 1984, direct action has stayed within legal limits.

One thing which has become apparent in the USA, not only in steel but in many significant segments of the economy, is that job security should no longer be seen to be the privilege of timorous civil servants or a bargaining issue which can be negotiated in contracts through seniority rights. Job security consciousness has developed strongly not only because lay-offs cost a lot to all concerned - employees, employers, the state and unions - but because the issue can be regarded as an aspect of human dignity and, as such, as a moral issue. This is something which serves to remind us that the 'right to a job' is a principle enshrined in many constitutions, East and West, although it has never become a reality, except under some stringent regimes or during the utopian period following the 1848 revolution in France.

As in the USA the key-word in the fight against disinvestment in steel in France has been diversification. The socialist government would like to be remembered as the true moderniser of the old 'grey belt', for Lorraine and the North of France were areas where former bosses and rightist technocrats remained extremely conservative in terms of regional development. However, the North still has a long way to go, although it has benefited from a number of strong decentralisation programmes not unconnected with the fact that Pierre Mauroy - the former mayor of Lille - was Prime Minister for three years and the area is a long-time socialist base.

In Lorraine, one of the most significant responses of government to the short but violent demonstrations in Spring 1984 has been the appointment of the Lorraine-born former union leader of the CFDT as the prefect in charge of industrial development. New industries and services have begun to invest if only in a small way, although it is a step in the right direction. Still, though, the rank-and-file complain as bitterly at the present time about socialist policy as they did about that of the former rightist team.

Several important steel plants have closed down (like Trith St.-Léger in the North) and promises made by the government about the decentralisation of public offices or the high technology departments of nationalised campanies remain often only words. The new 'Convention Générale de Prévention Sociale' allows for early retirement at 50, although this does not prevent what the workers fear and hate most, the 'mutation', or transfer, from one of the three steel areas, Dunkerque in the North, Lorraine, or Fos in the South, to another. Strongly attached to the region into which their families migrated several generations ago, the workers refer to transfer as 'deportation'. They also resent the fact that training programmes are insufficient and that promotions have now become a dream of the past rather than a stimulating reward.

Finally, and this is one thing which gives life to the comparison between Longwy and Youngstown, workers and activists from both areas have finally met, something which became a reality in 1984 when shop stewards from different plants in Longwy made a study trip to the Pittsburgh area, supported by active local defence groups and workers' study groups. The report of this trip (A.E.R.O.T. - A.P.E.P., 1985) analyzes the different modes of action arising out of the steel crises, with various initiatives, such as ESOPs (Employee Stock Ownership Plans), the Dusquene project, the Tri-state conference, unemployed committees, Carnegie-Mellon training programmes (again, see Deitch and Erickson) being examined from a comparative point of view and on the basis of a clear perspective on what constitutes the 'political'. A trip of this kind stands in diametrical opposition (naturally!) to that made in 1979 by top union leaders from the United Auto Workers, the Machinists' union and the United Steelworkers to Germany, England and Sweden in order to study legislation dealing with economic dislocation (Labor Union Study Tour, 1979). Had these leaders come to Longwy they would have seen quite another aspect of the labour movement, and one not in the least insignificant.

NOTES

1. As I have mentioned elsewhere (Kourchid, 1981) union delegates in the USA have been extremely interested in redundancy and employment legislation in Europe. At higher levels union officials sometimes get involved in economic analysis or even industrial marketing. At the local level, however, the rank-and-file show more interest in 'illegal' collective actions like strikes and sit ins. Many union activists in Youngstown felt that their struggle should have been continued through the kinds of plant occupations seen in Longwy or in the United States during the 1930s.

2. See, for example, Kourchid (1980; 1981).

3. This section draws on Progressive Alliance (1980). The following newspaper sources have also been used: In These Times (Cicero, Illinois), National Catholic Reporter, New York Times, The Phoenix Gazette, The Plain Dealer (Cleveland, Ohio), The Progressive, The Tribune Chronicle, Wall Street Journal, Washington Post, Youngstown Vindicator.

4. At that time Youngstown Sheet and Tube was six times bigger than Lykes.

5. The report (National Center for Economic Alternatives, 1978) had the backing of Bishop Malone, president of the religious coalition, House representative, C.J. Carney, Mayor Richley of Youngstown and F. Leseganich, the director of United Steelworkers district No. 26.

6. Although the administration did reserve $100 million for other cases.

7. One member of the ecumenical coalition observed that 'Each time we go to court for this sort of question we are caught in swamps of legislation built for business in the 1890s. The battlefield now should be on the legislative ground' (Progressive Alliance, 1980).

8. 'Homogenous decision making' does not, of course, exclude the possibility of individual quarrels within the management group.

9. Padioleau from time to time makes use of rather mechanistic analogies. He refers, for example, to the 'ballistic visions' of decisions. One can rightly ask whether the political level is characterised by 'automatic' decision making in the way that business and finance often are.

10. Even if here we are able to identify actors, it does not mean that we can identify their

real power. This is perhaps easier to do at the local level. According to the Communist represent- atives in Longwy, 'It's Davignon which dictates its policy to Usinor' (Durand, 1981, 109. See also Espace et Luttes, 1980).

11. See the last chapters in Freyssenet (1981).

12. The employers' organisation UMM includes industrialists from the large steel companies and fabricated metal industries. Local business also controls the Hospital Association of the Bassin de Longwy, the Real Estate Company for Industrial Development, 'La Familale' a housing company, the Croix Bleue an anti-alcoholic organisation and several other associations including sporting clubs (Noiriel, 1980, 26) - a fairly classic example of industrial involvement and paternalism in mono-indust- rial locations.

13. The end of the 'union de la gauche' in September 1977 produced a great deal of disappoint- ment.

14. Lynd, personal communication, May 5th., 1981. See also Lynd, (1982).

15. When we differentiate collective action through its objects we put to one side the traditional chronology of events. We believe that these actions had a meaning, a sense, over and above the simple counter-response to economic desertion. The term 'antigestionnaire' refers to rank-and-file reactions not to the economic counter-projects put forward by the political or union apparatus.

16. The SOS radio antenna was on top of a slag heap, upon which the CFDT also erected a giant flashing SOS sign. See Charasse (1981) and also the documentary made by M. Serre and A. Poirier. Both the book and the film take the phrase Lorraine Coeur d'Acier (Lorraine, Heart of Steel) as their title.

REFERENCES

A.E.R.O.T.-A.P.E.P. (1985) Enquête sur la situation de sidérurgistes de Pittsburgh dans la période actuelle (1984-85): Licenciements, chômage, formation, reconversion, Longwy

Bluestone, B. and B. Harrison (1980) Capital and Communities: the Causes and Consequences of Private Disinvestment, Progressive Alliance, Washington D.C.

Bonnet, S. and R. Humbert (1981) La Ligne des Hauts-Fourneaux, Denoel, Paris

Charrasse, D. (1981) Lorraine Coeur d'Acier, Maspero, Paris

Durand, C. (1981) Chômage et Violence, Galilee, Paris

Espace et Luttes, (1980) 'Lorraine', (Special Issue), 3-4

Freysennet, M. (1979) Le Sidégrurgie Française, Savelli, Paris

Guienne R. and A. Pierrard (1979) Denain: un crime signé Usinor, Privately Published, Condé-sur-Escaut

Kourchid, O. (1980) Recession et Syndicalisme, Groupe de Sociologie du Travail, Paris

Kourchid, O. (1981) 'L'emploi et la crise aux USA: le déplacement de l'action syndicale', Sociologie du Travail, 23, 192-217

Labour Union Study Tour (1979) Economic Dislocation: Joint Report, UAW-IAM-USWA

Lynd, S. (1982) The Fight against Shutdowns, Youngstown's Steel Mill Closures, Single Kack, San Pedro

National Center for Economic Alternatives, (1978) Youngstown Demonstration Planning Project: Final Report, NCEA, Washington, D.C.

Noiriel, G. (1980) Vivre et Lutter à Longwy, Maspero, Paris

Padioleau, J. (1981) Quand la France S'enferre, PUF, Paris

Progressive Alliance (1980) A religious response to the Mahoning Valley Steel Crisis, Progressive Alliance, Washington, D.C.

Rothstein, L. (1982) La réglementation Americaine face aux fermetures d'usines, en comparaison avec celles de la France, University of Rhode Island and Laboratoire d'Economie et de Sociologie du Travail, Providence and Paris

Rothstein, L. (1984) <u>Myth, Power and the Politics of Plant Closing: a Comparative Perspective</u>, forthcoming
Zarifian, J. (1979) 'Restructurer ou non', <u>Dialectiques</u>, <u>28</u>

Chapter Ten

'SAVE DOROTHY': A POLITICAL RESPONSE TO STRUCTURAL
CHANGE IN THE STEEL INDUSTRY

Cynthia Deitch and Robert Erickson

1. INTRODUCTION

In October 1984, the US Steel Corporation announced
plans to demolish the blast furnace and basic
oxygen shop of its Duquesne works, which had
recently employed about 3,000 workers, and had been
shut down since the previous June. Scheduled for
demolition was 'Dorothy 6', the most modern blast
furnace in the Pittsburgh region, and the largest
of US Steel's Mon Valley facilities.[1] In response,
unemployed steelworkers, labour and community
activists succeeded in stopping demolition three
times. The groups mobilized to save Dorothy 6 also
succeeded in creating a new political structure
with the power to legally seize the mill from US
Steel, and transfer it, or other closed industrial
facilities, to the workers, or to another party
willing to resume operation and employ the workers.
Despite some dramatic initial achievements, the
effort to reopen the mill ultimately failed. In
this chapter we examine the mobilization process
and the successes and limitations of the strategies
developed. We are interested in analysing how
labour protest and political response is structured
by new strategies of capital accumulation and
disinvestment. The steel industry in the Pittsburgh
area provides an ideal setting for studying the
emergence of new forms of political response to
plant closings. The material we present on the
mobilization of local groups is based upon
observation and participation in the events and
organizations discussed, discussions and interviews
with participants, and review of relevant documents
and media accounts for the time period covered.
Our study of Duquesne may contribute to the work
of researchers in the · United States and Europe

241

concerned with the social and political dimensions of deindustrialization (Bluestone and Harrison, 1982; Summers, 1984).

In recent years the world steel industry has undergone rather fundamental restructuring of production and markets. The restructuring has been due, at least in part, to new technologies, to the development of steel industries in lower wage countries, and to the reduction in world demand for steel in recent years of economic recession and stagnation. Steel-producing regions throughout Western Europe and North America have experienced plant closings; and the workers displaced have not been readily reabsorbed into the local economies, which are in transition or decline. Despite these similarities, labour and community response is constrained by and directed toward rather different national political and economic conditions. In Western Europe, steel industries tend to be nationalized or highly state subsidized; major reductions in capacity and decisions to close specific plants result from national policies and international (European Economic Community) agreements. As in the French case discussed by Kourchid (this volume) worker protest has been directed at state policy. In contrast, in the United States, the Federal government has played almost no role in the industry restructuring; individual steel companies have pursued diverse and changing investment and market strategies. The traditional form of labour protest, the strike, is of little use against plants that are closed or by workers who are unemployed.

Despite the widespread incidence of plant closings and manufacturing job loss in the United States in recent years - US Steel Corporation alone has closed over 150 plants and idled over 100,000 workers (Cuff, 1985) - protest and political mobilization by labour and community groups in steel and other manufacturing communities have been relatively rare. Two theoretical perspectives which we find fruitful for analysing the difficulty in mobilizing and sustaining a rank and file response to unemployment are the resource mobilization framework from the social movements literature, and a structural analysis of class conflict. These two perspectives guide our analysis of the political mobilization at Duquesne. Basic elements of each framework are summarized below. The resource mobilization perspective considers 'the confines

within which a movement's strategy develops, the
resources it can realistically mobilize, the limits
on the use of those resources, and the environment
that moulds the possibilites for effective action'
(Freeman, 1979, p. 168). This framework is most
appropriate for analysing movements which require
third party support and resources not controlled by
the group experiencing deprivation (Piven and
Cloward, 1977; Tilly, 1978; Jenkins, 1983), as was
the case in Duquesne. All resources mobilized,
internal and external, have constraints upon their
use that mould strategic options open to a group.
Internal constraints on solidarity, according to
Tilly (1978, 1979) are a function of the strength
of shared identity, and the density of social
networks and interpersonal links among members of
the group. There may be costs, reprisals or other
disincentives for participation. Movement success
or failure is also influenced by links with and
responses by external parties, especially government,
media and other social groups (Zald and McCarthy,
1979; Fireman and Gamson, 1979). Mass media
resources may be critical for reaching constituents,
and for gaining support of groups which may in turn
pressure elites and provide or withhold needed
resources (Molotch, 1979).

Because the case we are examining involves
labour and working class communities confronting
one of the largest multinational corporations in
the world, it is relevant to link the resource
mobilization perspective to a class conflict
analysis. Erik Wright (1978) provides a framework
for doing so. For Wright, class capacities are 'the
social relations within a class which to a greater
or lesser extent unite the agents of that class',
and constitute the potential basis for the
realization of class interests. Working class
capacity includes structural and organizational
capacities. Structural capacities are links within
the working class rooted in (a) the development of
capitalist organization of production (such as job
hierarchies which weaken class solidarity) and (b)
community organization, outside of production (such
as home-ownership and suburbanization which may
weaken class ties). Organizational capacities,
represented primarily by trade unions, are
consciously directed toward the realization of
class interests. The state may serve to facilitate
or demobilize class capacities. Capital's class
capacity in a given conflict is also determined by
its structural and organizational capacities, and

its ability to use the state. Like the resource mobilization framework, Wright's analysis points to social structural constraints, rather than false consciousness or apathy, to explain the failure of people with common interests to act collectively on those interests at a given juncture.

Three main sections of the paper follow. Part 2 covers background material on the decline of the steel industry in Pittsburgh and the depoliticization of labour in the period since the last national steel strike in 1959. From the class capacity perspective, the background section is important for understanding the weakening of working class capacity over time and in relation to capital through changes in the industry, community, and the union. From the resource mobilization perspective, the background sections on the steel industry, the union and the impact of unemployment, illuminate obstacles to mobilization and constraints on rank and file participation that any movement to organize unemployed steelworkers would face. This section provides the context in which the movement emerged. In Part 3, US Steel's actions at Duquesne are placed within the context of corporate disinvestment policies and the restructuring of the steel industry. Our thesis is that the possibilities for effective action by labour are limited by the new accumulation strategies of capital in the steel industry, and that these strategies vary from case to case. Part 4 presents the descriptive material on the mobilization process in the Duquesne case.

2.   BACKGROUND: THE DECLINE OF STEEL IN PITTSBURGH

Recent literature on deindustrialization has tended to emphasize common features across various industries. The case of steel in Pittsburgh fits many of the general trends, but there are also important industry specific differences. Bluestone and Harrison define deindustrialization as disinvestment in the productive capacity of American manufacturing (Bluestone and Harrison, 1982). In the steel industry, this took the form of lack of modernization, leading to a decline in competitiveness on the world market, and ultimately a decline in jobs. By the 1960s, technology in the steel industry had changed. The basic oxygen furnace had replaced open hearths, and continuous casters were replacing ingot moulds and rolling mills. Modern mills were computerizing their operations in the

1970s. No mills in the United States met new world
technology standards in the 1970s. By the late
1970s, low-wage developing countries such as South
Korea and Brazil had more technologically advanced,
capital intensive steel industries than did the US
(Crandall, 1981; Adams and Mueller, 1983; Erickson,
1983). Whereas much of the deindustrialization
literature attributes loss of manufacturing jobs in
the US to the movement of more labour intensive
production processes to lower wage countries, and
to the technological displacement of manufacturing
workers in capital intensive industries within the
US (Summers, 1984), this has not been the case in
steel.

Deindustrialization in steel involved a shift
in corporate investments out of steel (and out of
Pittsburgh), into more profitable activities in
real estate, banking, chemicals and oil, for
example. Although the American steel industry has
been one of the most profitable steel industries in
the world, steel has at best a 8-9 per cent profit
rate; other investment opportunities may yield
stockholders more than twice that return. In
Western Europe and Japan, steel profits are
generally lower, but retaining a steel industry is
a national priority and therefore subsidized
(Metzger, 1982). Major Pittsburgh based steel
producers such as US Steel, Jones and Laughlin
(later LTV), National Steel, and Allegheny Ludlum
(later Allegheny International), aggressively
pursued strategies of moving capital investments
out of steel production. When the American steel
industry had record profits in 1981, five of the
seven largest steel companies further decreased
capital expenditures in steel the following year,
led by US Steel's purchase of Marathon Oil
(Metzger, 1984).[2] After the purchase of Marathon
Oil in 1982, steel was reduced to only 32 per cent
of US Steel's corporate revenues in 1984, compared
to 73 per cent in 1979. A top US Steel executive
was quoted as saying 'We no longer want to be the
No. 1 producer, we want to be the No. 1 profitable
steel company' (Business Week, 1985).[3] In order to
maintain the cash flow from older facilities, some
investments in modernization were made, but on a
piece-meal basis. For example, US Steel's Duquesne
works received a new, much more efficient blast
furnace in 1964 (Dorothy 6), and a basic oxygen
shop; but US Steel did not invest in a continuous
caster for producing semifinished steel slabs at
Duquesne or any of its Mon Valley mills. LTV'S

Aliquippa works has the most computer controlled operations of any mill in the Pittsburgh region - six; whereas modern Japanese mills have over 200 (Office of Technology Assessment, 1981; Erickson, 1983). Thus, partial modernization maintained short term revenues, but did not make facilities competitive in the world market.

Despite capital disinvestment, manufacturing employment in steel declined very slowly in the Pittsburgh area and in most of the United States, in the 1960s and 1970s. Steel industry employment in the Pittsburgh area declined by only 17 per cent in the 20 year period from 1959 to 1979, an average of less than one per cent per year (Bureau of Labor Statistics, 1985). Relative labour intensity of production slowed the decline in employment. For example, US Steel continued to use open hearths at its Homestead mill in the Pittsburgh area until that section of the mill was closed in 1981. Open hearths require five times more labour-hours than basic oxygen furnaces. In mills throughout the Pittsburgh area, large maintenance staffs were employed to repair old equipment. In the long run, however, the failure to modernize resulted in the permanent loss of tens of thousands of jobs in Pittsburgh area mills. The American Iron and Steel Institute estimated that for every one job lost to modernization, four were eliminated by facilities closing (American Iron and Steel Institute, 1980; Metzger, 1984).

Along with relatively stable employment, wages remained high in the 1960s and 1970s, despite the declining competitiveness of the industry. Nationally, steelworkers' wages rose from 135 per cent of the average industrial wage in 1964, to 164 per cent in 1981 (Kuttner, 1985, p. 172). By 1981 the wage and benefit package was worth over $25 per hour. Before the demand for concessions in 1982, high labour costs were <u>not</u> one of the industry's public complaints (Metzger, 1984). A recent study by Robert Lawrence of the Brookings Institution (who is not at all known for defending unions or high wages) made the case that high wages in the steel industry were the <u>result</u> of short term revenue maximization, and not the cause of the industry's decline (Lawrence and Lawrence, 1985). The consequences of the long period of disinvestment, in conjunction with severe recession, produced a year of record losses, record low capacity utilization (down to 34 per cent), and record low employment (down by 50 per cent from 1981) for the

steel industry in 1982 (Metzger, 1984). Steel
companies demanded wage and benefit concessions,
and closed divisions, parts of facilities, or
entire plants. The economy-wide recession and
global patterns.of reduced demand for steel marked
a point of no return for steel employment,
particularly in the Pittsburgh area. Twenty-four
thousand Pittsburgh area steel jobs were lost in
1982 alone, and 53.8 thousand (or a 54 per cent
reduction) for the 1979-85 period as a whole
(Bureau of Labor Statistics, 1985). Unemployment
remained high, and steel and other manufacturing
employment in the Pittsburgh area continued to
decline despite the national economic recovery of
1983-5.

Demobilization of Labour
As described by a number of writers (Bowles and
Gintis, 1982; Gordon, Edwards and Reich, 1982;
Aronowitz, 1983), the post-war accommodation
between labour and capital within monopoly sector
manufacturing industries in the United States
reflected the gains won by the US working class in
the 1930s, including limited welfare state
programmes, the unionization of basic industry, and
the acceptance of labour's role within the
Democratic Party's New Deal coalition. After the
1930s, the rights of workers to unionize were
legally protected but also regulated, as secondary
boycotts were outlawed, radicals and leftists
purged from union leadership positions, strike and
bargaining power effectively restricted to a narrow
range of wage, benefit and work rule issues. In
major industries, the permanent role of unions was
accommodated, labour peace and cooperation established
by means of multi-year contracts with no-strike
clauses for the contract duration. Pattern
bargaining was established whereby industry-wide
agreements granted workers real wage gains tied to
productivity gains. Over time, rank and file
activity within unions declined, as did the
proportion of the labour force in unions, the
number of jobs in the highly unionized sectors, and
the unions' political role within electoral and
(Democratic) party politics. Some aspects of rank
and file depoliticization were specific to the
United Steelworkers of America (USWA). Union
members do not ratify their contract - only local
presidents vote.[4] After the 116 day steel strike in
1959, the industry had no strikes for 25 years. The

Experimental Negotiating Agreement (ENA) from 1973-80 outlawed strikes at a contract's end, in exchange for regular wage increases. Under the ENA, real wages as well as cost of living increases for steelworkers increased their gains from 1972 to 1982 above those of auto or coal, thus making USWA members 'the highest paid industrial workers in the world' (USWA, 1983; Metzger, 1984). Membership grew primarily through mergers with smaller unions and competition with unions in other industries; by the 1980s less than one third of the total USWA membership was in basic steel (Metzger 1984; Nyden, 1984; Kuttner, 1985).

The USWA became an increasingly top-down bureaucracy. Individual advancement was gained through personal loyalty. Rank and file participation was frequently discouraged (Kuttner, 1985). In the Pittsburgh area, local union meetings were generally poorly attended. Rank and file activisim was mostly focused internally in conflicts with the USWA International,[5] rather than outward at corporate policies. The real wage gains made it difficult for union dissidents who wanted to maintain the right to strike to gain a large rank and file following. Rank and file links across locals in the Pittsburgh area, even among activists and even within the same company, were very limited. Rising affluence from middle income wages enabled many steelworkers in the Pittsburgh area to own their own homes, and over the post-war decades, increasingly to buy homes in the suburbs and communities surrounding the towns in which the mills were located. People who worked together no longer lived in the same immediate community, or near their union hall, as they had in earlier periods (Carnegie-Mellon, 1983). After lay offs, workers were physically dispersed. The workers and the milltown residents were both economically dependent upon the steel industry, but were not the same community.

The Impact of Unemployment

We suggest that the experience of unemployment, rather than serving as an impetus to protest and political action by the rank and file, tended to reinforce previous divisions and add new obstacles to mobilization. Available survey data suggests such divisions. In October 1982, a random sample telephone survey of 351 unemployed steelworkers from US Steel's Dequesne and Homestead mills, was

conducted in conjunction with the Mon Valley
Unemployed Committee's campaign to stop mortgage
foreclosures (Action Housing, 1983).[6] These data
show that the first wave of lay offs in 1982 had
hit younger workers with less seniority first - 85
per cent of this first group was under age 40, and
74 per cent had been in the mill for less than ten
years. Although the average length of unemployment
at the time of the interview was 11 months, only 5
per cent had had any full-time work since they left
the mill. Over half still reported hopes of being
called back. Most (58 per cent) owned their own
home, 92 per cent had lived in the Pittsburgh area
all of their lives, but only 23 per cent of the
Homestead and 28 per cent of the Duquesne workers
lived in the municipality in which they had worked.
The study concluded, from personal finance data,
that two-thirds of the mortgagees were at risk of
losing their homes in the near future, and 75 per
cent of the renters were at risk of eviction. All
but 10 per cent were still receiving unemployment
benefits at the time of the interview, but another
70 per cent expected benefits to run out within
another three months.

The gradual process of lay-offs divided groups
of workers by age, seniority, plant and division.
Almost all of those laid off in 1982, had never
participated in a strike, since the last strike was
in 1959. Because the mills and the decent paying
jobs had been there as long as they (the younger
workers) could remember, and because steelworkers
were accustomed to cycles of lay-offs and recalls,
for the first few years of large scale job loss in
the area's steel industry, many people still
believed steel would always come back. There were
enough cases of some people in the mill   still
working, and some people called back for short
stints to hold onto the belief. The hope of being
called back may have made workers reluctant to
engage in actions that would allow the company to
permanently discharge them, or that might lose them
their pension and severance payments if they were
dismissed for cause. Unemployment and other
benefits meant that it might be a year or more
after they left the mill, that workers faced the
greatest economic hardship. From a resource
mobilization perspective we may view hopes of
recall and various unemployment compensation and
severence pay benefits as disincentives to
participation in protest. Divisions by plant, shop,
age, seniority, residential patterns and immediate

personal financial problems, along with traditional
race, sex and ethnicity divisions weakened
solidarity based on shared identity as workers. The
bureaucratization of union activities, and the
accustomed lack of participation of rank and file
workers in the union or local politics, were
organizational constraints on mobilization.

Grass-roots Response

Despite these obstacles, grass-roots organizing and
protest in response to unemployment did develop in
the Pittsburgh area in the 1980s (Deitch, 1984).
Clergy and labour members of the Denominational
Ministry Strategy-Network to Save the Mon-Ohio
Valley (DMS) demonstrated at churches and homes of
corporate executives, and waged publicity campaigns
against the largest bank in the region for
investing abroad rather than in local industry.
Several Lutheran Ministers associated with DMS
attracted considerable national media attention in
1984-5 when they were jailed as a result of
conflicts with church authorities over their
involvement with DMS. Pursuing a different set of
strategies, groups such as the Mon Valley
Unemployed Committee, the Rainbow Kitchen and
Unemployed Center in Homestead, and smaller
unemployed committees, organized protests and
mobilized resources for the extension of social
welfare services and benefits. Activities included
food distribution and counselling services, and
winning demands for mortgage relief, protection
against utility shut off, extension of unemployment
compensation, and access to medical care for the
unemployed. These groups and actions were not
limited to steelworkers, although steelworkers were
active in starting the organizations. A third
category of unemployed organizing focused on
efforts to stop plant closings, save jobs and
reopen closed facilities. The mobilization to save
Dorothy 6 was initiated by the Tri-State Conference
on Steel (Tri-State), a Pittsburgh area organization
which formed in 1979-80 in support of the effort to
stop steel mill closings in Youngstown, Ohio. It
drew upon the experiences of Youngstown (Lynd,
1982; Kourchid, this volume), to develop a strategy
for rebuilding the region's steel industry with
increased worker and community control and public
financing. Tri-State explicitly challenged the
right of US Steel and other multinational
corporations to make economic decisions for the

workers and communities of the Pittsburgh region
(Tri-State Conference on Steel, 1984). Tri-State
gained the attention and occasional assistance of a
number of academics, researchers and journalists
around the country in 1982-4. Locally, however,
Tri-State's proposals were ignored or rejected by
the USWA International and public officials before
the campaign to save Dorothy 6.

At different times the groups mentioned above
have overlapped in activities and participants. The
unemployed steelworkers active in these groups were
frequently rank and file union activists, who had
often opposed the policies of the USWA International
leadership. The USWA's initial hostility to the
various unemployed organizing efforts at times
included redbaiting, threats of physical harassment
and warnings to local union officials not to work
with Tri-State, for example. Relations with the
USWA International changed substantially after the
death of USWA President Lloyd McBride. Lynn
Williams won the union-wide successor election, but
lost heavily in the basic steel locals in the
Pittsburgh area. After his election, Williams and
the USWA staff reached out to some of the union
dissidents who had opposed his election, and
increased support for unemployed organizing
efforts, but continued to oppose the DMS. Although
active participation by rank and file unemployed
workers was not widespread, the broader social
movement environment described above was significant
for several reasons. New organizations formed, led
by rank and file union activists, but outside the
USWA structure, and not limited to steelworkers.
Some cooperation with the USWA was established.
Contacts and networks including media·representatives,
clergy, public officials and community groups had
been formed. Thus some of the resource mobilization
necessary for the Duquesne campaign had already
begun. Before turning to the actual mobilization to
save Dorothy 6, we examine the corporate disinvestment
strategy local groups faced at Duquesne.

3.   CORPORATE DISINVESTMENT STRATEGIES

Steel mill closings in recent years reflect diverse
and changing restructuring and disinvestment
patterns, and therefore present different strategic
options to rank and file workers, the union and
local communities. One example is National Steel
which substantially shifted investments out of

steel. To free capital and to avoid substantial shutdown costs and pension obligations, National Steel initiated and facilitated the sale of its Weirton (West Virginia) steel mill to employees. A contrasting case is the Wheeling-Pittsburgh steel corporation which borrowed heavily to remain in steel, eventually entered legal bankruptcy proceedings to avoid liquidation by creditors, and had the bankruptcy court void the union contract. The last action resulted in a strike in the summer of 1985, a response by labour which only makes sense when a company wants to resume production. Workers at Duquesne were confronting, in US Steel, a corporation pursuing a much more complex and flexible disinvestment strategy.

US Steel had closed many of its steel divisions, substantially reduced its steel-making capacity, made major non-steel investments with additional diversification indicated, but at the same time sought to regain its former dominance in the American steel market (<u>Business Week</u>, 1985; Cuff, 1985).[7] US Steel had already incurred shutdown costs at Duquesne. The decision to demolish a relatively modern efficient blast furnace, and the refusal to consider a sale to new owners, must be analyzed in the context of broader corporate strategies. Three aspects of US Steel's corporate strategy relevant for Duquesne are noted below. First, failure to modernize its mills enabled US Steel to reduce the fixed interest charges of its steel division below the costs of those steel companies that invested capital in modernization. Steel companies that invested in new technology, such as continuous casters and computerized operations, pay high fixed capital charges on such investments. Unless the companies operate these facilities at full capacity, they can not cover the interest charges. In a depressed steel market, few steel companies can operate at or near full capacity. The lack of high fixed interest charges allowed US Steel to operate over the short run with lower costs, even though US Steel facilities were less modern. Second, US Steel successfully increased its market share over competitors in 1985 by lowering steel prices on some products. For years US Steel had set the price for the rest of the industry; now market analysts find a price collapse in the industry, with fierce competition replacing the old oligopoly (Cuff, 1985). The combination of short run cost advantages from lack of modernization plus the cash flow from non-steel investments, particularly Marathon Oil, gave US Steel considerable advantage in the price competition over smaller companies such as Cyclops, Lukens, Sharon, and Armco which could be squeezed out of the market; and over the large steel producers who remained primarily in steel such as Wheeling-Pittsburgh (which entered bankruptcy), Bethlehem, or Inland. Third, rather than tie up capital in basic steel production, which is extremely capital intensive, US Steel shifted toward concentrating capital and production in finishing and marketing steel, with plans to import semifinished steel. Very low prices may be obtained on the world market for semifinished steel from Brazil and South Korea. These countries need to export steel because of the high fixed interest costs on their new steel mills, and to pay the interest costs on their foreign debt. Shipments of semifinished steel are not counted in the import control program.

By 1985 US Steel was quite clearly pursuing a strategy of both reducing basic steel producing capacity within the United States and improving its market position in steel - potentially driving smaller competitors out of the finishing and marketing end of the business. Policies toward specific plants are better understood when viewed in this light. In 1983, US Steel unsuccessfully attempted to negotiate an agreement to import semifinished steel from British Steel's Ravenscraig plant in Scotland, for finishing at US Steel's Fairless works, on the Atlantic coast near Philadelphia. After this failed, US Steel continued to look for a similar arrangement with a foreign supplier (Cuff, 1985). A more modern facility for basic steel production at Duquesne was to be demolished, while US Steel continued to produce semifinished steel with open hearth furnaces at its much less modern Fairless works.

In a very different vein, in 1984, in Johnstown (Pennsylvania), US Steel absorbed the pension and severance pay costs of eliminating 1200 jobs, and then was willing to sell a machine shop and foundry to a buyer arranged by local business leaders, who restarted production at lower wages and without the previous union (Metzger, 1985). The Johnstown plant represented a part of the market which US Steel had abandoned.[8] In contrast to Johnstown, for two years prior to closing Duquesne, US Steel ignored and refused requests by the local union president to negotiate some form of Employee

Stock Ownership Plan (ESOP). Only the blast furnace and basic oxygen shop were slated for demolition at Duquesne; the rest of the mill was declared temporarily closed on the grounds that US Steel might open the other sections at some later date. This effectively broke the production process at a point where it was not complete - at ingot moulds rather than semifinished slabs. US Steel publicly and privately indicated that it would not sell or lease the rest of the Duquesne facilities if the hot end were sold and restarted. In discussions concerning Duquesne, US Steel representatives at times vowed to destroy Dorothy 6 at all costs, threatened to undercut the price of steel produced by Duquesne if it resumed operation, and informed potential investors of US Steel's intention to drive Duquesne out of business if it opened (Feigen, 1985).

The proposal by workers and community groups to restart basic steel production at Duquesne, and sell cost and quality competitive semifinished steel to US Steel or its competitors, thus appears to have challenged several aspects of US Steel's strategy. First, a successful reopened Duquesne mill would allow basic steel production to remain not only in Pittsburgh, but in the US northeast, and perhaps make it more difficult to import steel slabs. Second, according to the market feasibility studies, Duquesne could provide steel slabs to Sharon, Cyclops, Armco, and Lukens steel, and help these steel companies remain in business (Feigen, 1985; Locker, 1985; Tumazos, 1985). These are the companies some steel analysts suggest US Steel may wish to drive out of business. Third, a successful reopened Duquesne would show that the company had lied to the workers and communities when it claimed that Duquesne and other Mon Valley facilities were closed because they could not be operated profitably. This might increase pressure on US Steel to sell other closed facilities.

A significant effect of the diverse and changing corporate strategies associated with the restructuring of the steel industry has been to weaken the USWA's power to negotiate high wages for its workers. The long established pattern of industry-wide wage bargaining with the union ended in 1985. Union locals have found themselves bidding down wages to keep jobs. Workers and the union frequently face a great deal of pressure from local officials and local media to agree to wage and benefit concessions to keep more marginal facilities and more marginal companies from closing altogether. Other companies then demand similar concessions. Compared to 1959, when workers waged a 116 day national steel strike, major steel producers in the 1980s were much less constrained by investments in fixed capital, by a need to maintain production in marginal facilities, or by union pressure.

4. THE CAMPAIGN TO SAVE DOROTHY 6

Established forms of labour response to capital in the post war period - collective bargaining and the strike - are of very limited utility in the face of the process of disinvestment, and the flexible, multinational strategies of steel corporations described above. The depoliticization of labour discussed earlier, left local unions and communities with few weapons, institutional mechanisms, established union or political leadership for fighting plant closing, and little recent experience with mass mobilization of rank and file workers. The campaign to save the Duquesne mill, by necessity (and reluctantly on the part of many participants), experimented with new forms of confronting capital, new legal weapons, a new political structure, new sources of leadership, and new bases for rank and file participation; and in the process made new demands upon capital and upon government.

As discussed earlier, some of the resources necessary for effective mobilization were already at least partially in place. Previous examples existed of rank-and-file protest at steel mill closings in Youngstown (Lynd 1982; Kourchid, this volume), and of an economically viable worker buy-out at Weirton (Prude, 1984; Lund, 1985).[9] Established institutions in the Pittsburgh area, including unions, churches, and public agencies and local government bodies were under some pressure to show they were doing something to help the unemployed. Without Dorothy 6 to supply semifinished slabs needed for rolling and pipe production at US Steel's nearby Homestead and National works, the future of these and other mills in the area was clearly in jeopardy. Union and political leaders who had previously not paid much attention to Tri-State's proposals were now willing to meet with local groups and listen to possible alternatives. The coalition and campaign to save Dorothy 6 developed a strategy around three objectives. These

were (1) to prevent the demolition of the mill; (2)
to establish a mechanism to take the mill from US
Steel and transfer it to new owners - be it the
workers, a public authority, or a third party; and
(3) to secure the financing necessary to restart
the mill and equip it to operate competitively.
Unless all three objectives were met, the mill
could not reopen and jobs would not be saved. At
the start of the campaign, the Tri-State Conference
on Steel was probably the only part of the
coalition which fully articulated all three
objectives as the strategy. Over a few months time,
critics, opponents, neutral observers, as well as
participants came to describe the effort in terms
of the three objectives. In the section which
follows, we discuss the mobilization of resources
and support, from rank and file workers and from
other parties, associated with each objective.

Objective 1: Preventing Demolition

In response to the announced demolition of Dorothy
6, Tri-State called a meeting which was attended by
a USWA Vice President, two US Congressional
representatives, several Pennsylvania state legislators, numerous local government officials,
members of the clergy, as well as Tri-State and the
Duquesne union local (Local 1256) leaders.
Tri-State proposed a modest agenda - that the
demolition of the mill be delayed until a
feasibility study could be commissioned to
determine whether the mill could operate profitably.
As a result of the meeting, and a bus tour of the
closed Duquesne works, the support of the USWA
International and the County Commissioners was won.
The USWA President and the County Commissioners
officially requested US Steel to delay demolition.
The County committed $50,000 toward the $150,000
feasibility study. The USWA provided most of the
other money, with sizable contributions from the
City of Pittsburgh and a local electrical utility
company. The December 10th deadline was extended,
and a reprieve granted until February 2nd. Winning
the support of the top leadership of the USWA and
of the County Commissioners was an important step,
for stopping the demolition, for funding the
feasibility study, and for mobilizing further
support. Without the USWA International's participation, other unions were reluctant to participate;
and without the County Commissioners, other
officials would have been more hesitant.

Winterization

For certain activities, rank and file participation
was critical. For three days beginning on December
19th, one dozen laid off Duquesne workers entered
the closed mill to winterize the blast furnace,
with their own unpaid time, and tools, and with
borrowed money. If this was not done, pipes could
freeze and cause permanent damage to the furnace,
or entail costly repairs, making the effort to save
the mill fruitless. In response to pressure from
the county officials, US Steel agreed to permit
Local 1256 members to enter the mill and pump 550
gallons of anti-freeze into the furnace. But US
Steel required Local 1256 to pay $16,000 in
insurance premiums, before allowing anyone into the
mill. The workers had to provide the tools and
materials, and had to estimate the amount of labour
and anti-freeze needed. They received a loan of
$20,000 from the USWA International to cover the
insurance and materials. Local 1256 had to raise
money to repay the loan, and began to do so by
appealing to business and local organizations, and
by selling bumper stickers, tee-shirts, sweatshirts,
and mugs with the slogan 'Save Dorothy, she can
work'.

Winterization was a critical and dramatic
moment in the strategy to save the mill from
physical damage and demolition. It drew specifically
upon the unique skills and expertise of the
laid-off steelworkers. It was a small scale
demonstration of worker self-management in operation
- no supervisors or bosses planned the job. It drew
on steelworkers' pride in their trade, and in
knowing their mill and their jobs better than the
bosses did, and in a long tested ability to keep
neglected equipment operating in less than optimal
conditions - skills that the industry had depended
upon for years, but are not very marketable in a
declining economy. The winterization effort
received favourable media attention - here were
unemployed men (all were men), donating their
labour and their skill, in the depth of winter, to
save the furnace where they had been employed for
years. When the workers were interviewed by local
newspapers, they did not express a great deal of
optimism that the mill would reopen; they simply
told reporters that this was the last shot, and
they had to try and do what they could (Post-Gazette
Dec. 20th, 1984). They reminded people that
steelworkers at Dorothy 6, earlier that year, won
the company-wide ironmaster award emblazoned on

many Local 1256 union jackets, and on a banner
displayed at rallies and union meetings, for
outstanding production records.

February 2nd deadline

The coalition prepared for the next (February 2nd)
deadline by mobilizing popular support and media
coverage for the campaign. A rally across from the
plant gates on January 18th, featured Jesse
Jackson, a former (1984) presidential candidate,
and probably the most prominent black national
political figure at that moment. At the rally,
Jackson pledged to join the resistance, imploring
everyone concerned to be arrested at the plant
gates if US Steel moved to demolish the mill, and
called Pittsburgh 'the Selma' of a new movement,
making reference to the early events of the US
civil rights movement in the 1960s. To the
amazement of the coalition members, the President
of the USWA, and the Mayor of Pittsburgh both
contacted Tri-State's office and asked to be
permitted to speak at the rally - a turning point
in comparison with previous relations between union
or political officials and unemployed organizing
efforts. The rally also marked one of the first
times links were made with leaders of the local
black community. The presence of Jackson attracted
extensive local and national media coverage and
broadened local support.

Some of the local media coverage criticized
the rally and the coalition for raising false and
unrealistic hopes among the unemployed, a theme
periodically repeated by local observers. Media
criticism, however, was frequently tempered with
praise for Tri-State and the coalition for
'constructive' and 'positive' forms of protest, in
contrast to the DMS clergy and local labour leaders
who were frequently in the news·during that period
for using confrontational tactics in disruptions at
church functions.[10] As in the development of many
social movements, the emergence of what are viewed
as unacceptable forms of protest, broadens the
spectrum of what is acceptable and pressurizes
public officials and other elites to respond to
more 'constructive' groups.

On January 28th, some 750-800 people,
according to press estimates, crowded into a church
bingo hall in Duquesne to hear the results of the
first feasibility study. The study concluded that a
market did exist for Duquesne's product (semifinished

steel slabs). It suggested that the mill potentially could operate profitably, compete with imported steel, and employ 500-900 workers without reducing wages - by cutting other costs and reorganizing work. The consultants also concluded that more time was needed for additional more detailed market, engineering, and financing studies. In response to the rallying of public support, the media attention, and the results of the feasibility study, US Steel agreed to delay demolition until the corporation's own staff reviewed the study.

Active members of the coalition were confident that the study would find the mill worth saving. Locker-Abrecht, the New York consulting firm doing the feasibility study was clearly sympathetic with the cause. Much more problematic for the coalition were the potential costs, including repair and new equipment[11] and whether a strong enough case could be made for the mill's profitability to secure financing. Because the consultants did not have access to the Duquesne facility itself or to necessary data known by the corporation, the extensive cooperation and support of an engineer and former Duquesne mill superintendent (in other words, the former boss at the mill) was critical, as were interviews with experienced rank and file workers. A well respected Pittsburgh engineering and design firm participated in the initial study, adding to its public acceptability (Locker, 1985).

The Vigil
After the second extension was granted, the next immediate concern of the Local 1256 workers was that the corporation might remove valuable equipment, and potentially add millions of dollars to the restart costs. The local union established a vigil at the mill gate, 24 hours a day, seven days a week, quartered in a trailer personally donated by the local union president. Volunteers from among the laid off workers reported any suspicious activity to the local union officers, who then dealt with the corporation. When US Steel moved trucks into the mill in February, several dozen former workers were called out immediately, along with television crews. The workers prevented the trucks from leaving the mill, and searched each truck to make sure that only scrap materials were removed. On other occasions, workers entered the mill, sneaking past security, to make certain nothing had been damaged. After several confrontations

at the gate, a procedure was negotiated whereby a corporate vice president would inform the local union leadership of any activity planned, such as removing scrap or non-essential material. US Steel retained ownership of the mill, but the corporation's activities within the mill and uses of the property were controlled, to an extent, by the former workers, who had to be accounted to for routine activities, and who won the right to watch over and record company movements.

The vigil trailer became a symbol of workers' response to the declining steel industry. Numerous national media representatives visited the vigil trailer and talked with the unemployed workers. National political leaders visited and used the trailer with the mill in the background as a backdrop for statements to the media on the problems of the structurally unemployed. Such visitors included one of Pennsylvania's Republican US Senators and his probable Democratic opponent a Congressional delegation from other states, and the national president of the AFL-CIO. National media coverage and national political support were resources effectively mobilized by providing a local colour-human interest appeal to the media, and a platform for the politicians. On a day to day basis, however, staffing the vigil was often uneventful, and enthusiasm and participation were difficult to sustain as the months went by.

Preparation for Plant Gate Resistance

As the third deadline approached, a marketing feasibility study commissioned by the USWA International was released (Tumazos, 1985). Once again, until the last minute, US Steel disputed and tried to discredit the findings of the feasibility studies, and turned down requests for further delay, even from Pennsylvania's two Republican US Senators. The coalition again worked to rally public support and media attention before the deadline. High school bands, fire trucks, floats, marching groups and delegations from various unions were recruited to march in a parade in Duquesne ending with a rally at the vigil trailer. The coalition once again promised to bring out hundreds of unemployed steelworkers and supporters to stop demolition at the plant gates; and US Steel once again agreed to delay - with no specific deadline this time.

The Duquesne coalition and supporters had

succeeded in getting US Steel to delay demolition on three separate occasions. For each deadline, the coalition promised to bring out hundreds of unemployed steelworkers and supporters to resist demolition at the plant gates. With the possible exception of a few individuals who talked about arming themselves to fight the bulldozers, the grass-roots organizers understood from the beginning that any confrontation at the plant gates would be symbolic and moral, and could only win by dramatizing the situation, raising the social costs for US Steel, and gaining additional popular and politician support. In the history of labour movements, workers have on occasion occupied factories, forced production to halt, and sometimes damaged property and machinery to make their demands heard. In this case, the company had already stopped production and had no desire to resume it; the company intended to permanently dismantle equipment, while the workers wanted to prevent any harm to the facilities. Therefore, the coalition's strategy was to use the promise of mass mobilization of unemployed workers to avoid actual confrontation, and not to provoke it. This strategy was successful. A variety of public officials and the USWA top leadership used their influence to persuade US Steel to grant a reprieve each time. The promised gate action helped mobilize the officials.

This success had its costs as well. Each deadline ultimately passed without any dramatic event to capture media and public attention. The large numbers of rank and file unemployed steelworkers and their families who had pledged to participate <u>if and when necessary</u>, never found it necessary to personally take a stand, and there were no other activities that drew this level of participation. The coalition's ability to bring people out at this level was never actually tested, and as one result, the psychological, publicity, and solidarity benefits such an action brings a movement were never realized. There is an interesting parallel to be made to the 25 years of no strikes in the steel industry, in which the union's confidence in its mobilizing power eroded, as did rank and file solidarity, while the bargaining power of leadership was highly successful. On the other hand, the possibility of plant gate resistance, as a last resort, retained a level of dramatic tension and attention which helped other aspects of the effort. Non-violent resistance was planned. In the period after the February deadline, activists in peace organizations familiar with techniques of non-violent civil disobedience conducted training sessions at the Local 1256 union hall. The CBS national weekly news programme Sixty Minutes visited one of the training sessions and expressed interest in covering a plant gate confrontation. Organizers expected that US Steel would view the prospect of a physical confrontation with workers who were non-violently defending their mill in a disciplined and well publicized manner, as a public relations disaster to be avoided. Furthermore, to demolish Dorothy 6, US Steel would have had to force local law enforcement and elected officials to take very unpopular stands. This could jeopardize the corporation's long-term working relationships with these public officials. Along with rank and file workers, a number of Catholic priests, other clergy, local mayors, state legislators, and union officials had promised to be arrested if necessary. Democratic Congressman Bob Edgar of Philadelphia, an announced candidate for the US Senate, and former Democratic Presidential candidate and black leader Jesse Jackson were among the public figures who indicated readiness to stand with the workers at the Duquesne plant gates. Virtually no major politician, Democrat or Republican, local, state or national, publicly indicated a willingness to side with US Steel in a confrontation.

After the third deadline, US Steel agreed not to act until all of the union's feasibility studies were complete, and county officials had time to review them. The first objective, stopping demolition, succeeded through the effective mobilization of rank and file unemployed workers, union leaders, clergy and community groups, political figures and public officials, outside experts, and the media. Time, however, worked against sustained mobilization. Once the threat of demolition was no longer as imminent, the media focused less attention on the 'Save Dorothy 6' campaign. The consultants were free to take time completing the studies and finding investors. The politicians turned their attention to other issues. The USWA International turned its attention to the Wheeling-Pittsburgh strike which began in July. Local 1256 had difficulty finding funds to keep the union hall open, since none of its members had been employed steelworkers for over a year. Rank and file unemployed steelworkers were running out of benefits and in need of other jobs.

The winterization, vigil, and plant gate preparation drew upon strengths of shared identity as former Duquesne steelworkers. The first two also utilized knowledge and experience workers had from their years on the job. Rank and file participation in rallies, parades, door to door canvassing, and selling 'Dorothy 6' tee-shirts, though limited, tended to draw upon workers' community and family networks outside the union. All of these activities, however, involved fairly small numbers of workers. As unemployment benefits and personal resources were exhausted, unemployed workers had to find other means of earning a living, and could not be expected to wait for the plant to reopen, or to spend their time in volunteer activity for the Dorothy 6 campaign.

Leaders of the coalition, especially those who were steelworkers themselves, never saw the success of the effort depending primarily on the mobilization of large numbers of unemployed workers. From the beginning, the effort was in large part based upon, and increasingly became dependent upon, other elements of the coalition, such as Tri-State members and paid staff, union officials, clergy, and local politicians. Individuals in each of these categories generally had some source of personal income, and frequently could combine aspects of coalition work with paid employment roles. Incentives for participation often came from long-term commitments to social change. In some cases leadership in the coalition could potentially enhance personal opportunities, within union or local politics for example. Given their social location within the community, the various participants provided the coalition with access to constituencies and networks, institutional resources, professional skills, public legitimacy and credibility, and a range of political organizing experiences critical to the objectives pursued. Concrete institutional resources, such as money, meeting space, staff time, and office services were in varying degrees provided by churches, the USWA International, and community organizations.

Objective 2: The Steel Valley Authority
Creating an institutional structure with the power to take the mill from US Steel, if the corporation refused to sell, was an integral part of the strategy. Tri-State introduced this idea to the

coalition at the beginning of the campaign to save Duquesne, and it gradually gained broader support and credibility, especially after US Steel had indicated its unwillingness to sell on a number of occasions. Existing governmental bodies had the legal power to try to acquire the property through eminent domain, but it is unlikely that many elected officials would choose to do so, given US Steel's considerable economic and political power in Pittsburgh.

Eminent domain is a legal term for the right of governmental bodies to take over private property for public use upon just compensation to the owner, and often has been used in the US for highways and railroads. The Pennsylvania Municipal Authorities Act of 1945 permits eminent domain to be exercised by any municipality, through the creation of a municipal authority. There are legal precedents for interpreting such laws to include machinery and equipment as well as the land and buildings. The municipal authority could, therefore, seize a closed plant to prevent it from being abandoned or sold for scrap in order to save jobs and preserve the tax base, and could then run the plant, apply for loans, and eventually issue municipal bonds to finance operation; or broker the plant to a private buyer who would keep it operating; or sell the plant or part interest in it to the employees under an ESOP arrangement . Through the efforts of Tri-State, the possible use of eminent domain gained limited local attention (but was not implemented) in 1982 and 1983 when a Nabisco baking plant threatened to close in the City of Pittsburgh, when a large steel mill closed in Midland (Pennsylvania), and when Mesta Machine, a steel making machinery manufacturer in West Homestead closed (Deitch, 1984).

The Steel Valley Authority (SVA) strategy targeted about ten local milltown municipalities (including several with major electrical or rail machinery rather than steel plants) to join the authority and appoint representatives. Legally, the procedure was for a municipality to give notice·of intent to create the authority, hold a public hearing at least 30 days later, adopt a resolution, and file articles of incorporation with the state. Between January and October of 1985, ten municipalities did so, including the City of Pittsburgh. Opposition to the SVA was generally expressed as fear that a municipality would lose autonomy over the use of eminent domain within its boundaries, that it would lose tax revenues if the plant could not be sold, or that it would be financially liable for costs it could not meet. Ideologically, the basic idea that some form of public ownership of the means of production might be a desirable alternative to current capital strategy (though not posed in these words), was generally not questioned at the public hearings and town meetings, nor in the local media.[12]

Officials in the city of Duquesne, where the mill was located, did not initially support the request for delaying the demolition, and were extremely reluctant to support the authority, but did not totally oppose it. US Steel promised to build an industrial park (facilities for businesses to lease space) on the site, and to find tenants, which would bring in tax revenue and jobs. If the 100 acres on which the Dorothy 6 blast furnace stood were not levelled, US Steel proposed to leave the site vacant. In response, the coalition made arguments that almost half of the existing industrial park space in the county was vacant; that US Steel was building an industrial park just across the river in McKeesport; and that reopening the hot end of the mill would produce greater tax revenues and more jobs. Although the city of Duquesne suffered significant revenue loss by the closing of the mill, and had high levels of unemployment among its residents, few Duquesne residents who were not old enough to retire, were among those laid off from the mill in their town, and relatively few of the laid off workers hoping to return, lived right in Duquesne. In August and September of 1985, unemployed steelworkers and supporters who were Duquesne residents participated in a door to door campaign for support for the SVA, and for saving Dorothy 6.

By September 1985, nine municipalities had appointed their representatives, three each, to the SVA. The representatives included Tri-State members, union officials from steel and electrical unions, rank and file workers from several other unions, and community activists from unemployed organizations. The predominantly working class, pro-union composition of the appointed directors of the new industrial authority, contrasts with other Pennsylvania public authorities, in which represent- atives associated with corporate and political elites tend to predominate. Thus Tri-State and the coalition appear to have succeeded in the second objective, creating a new political structure, a

part of the state apparatus, through which
representatives of labour can potentially act
against US Steel, American Standard, Westinghouse,
or other corporations. This power has not been
tested.

An additional aspect of the SVA strategy was
legislation to substantially strengthen the
Municipal Authorities Act, by stipulating for
example, that for a six to nine month time period
after the legal process is initiated, equipment may
not be removed or dismantled. A bill was drafted
with the help of a lawyer active in Tri-State and
introduced by a member of the Pennsylvania
Legislature who had worked with the coalition. This
elected official reported (to the coalition) what
he considered an unprecedented lobbying effort by
US Steel in opposition to the bill, directed at
both state representatives and local chambers of
commerce.

The creation of the SVA required mobilization
of outside support from public officials, and this
effort was successful. In the milltown municipalities,
public offices are generally not paying positions.
These small town politicians often had personal
ties through jobs, relatives, friends, or neighbours,
with unemployed steelworkers. At the county and
state, as well as municipal level, the politicians
know that many of the voters in their districts are
union people, or unemployed. In their official
capacities, local public officials faced an eroded
property and wage tax base due to plant closings.
As discussed earlier, most of the milltowns had
been economically dependent upon one main industrial
employer. Many of the municipalities were close to
bankruptcy; some had actually laid off the police
force, turned off street lights, and failed to meet
payrolls. Since most of the local politicians were
Democrats, they were also influenced by higher
level politicians in their party, such as state
legislators. Thus we may explain the support for
the SVA mobilized from public officials, by the
interpersonal and political networks they occupied,
and structural constraints on the institutions they
represented. The City of Duquesne officials,
however, illustrate how some of these same
structural constraints may make public officials
vulnerable to counter pressures from opposing
interests, such as US Steel.

Objective 3: Financing

At a press conference in January 1986, USWA and coalition leaders officially ended the struggle to save Dorothy 6, after consultants had concluded that there was no hope of attracting the capital necessary to reopen the mill. The effort to secure financing reveals some of the limitations and contradictions of the strategy developed at Duquesne, both from a resource mobilization and a class analysis perspective. The obstacles encountered at Duquesne may be relevant to other discussions of worker or public buy-outs as a local strategy to save manufacturing jobs. An examination of the financing objective is key to an understanding of broader national economic and political implications of the Duquesne campaign.

The Steel Valley Authority, once created, could not use the power of eminent domain until it had the resources to pay US Steel for the property. This could have been as little as $10 million for the land and scrap value of the machinery, an amount potentially raised through various existing government programmes. The estimated $200 million (later raised to $300 million) for restart, a continuous caster, and three years working capital was the major obstacle. Clearly, unemployed workers, local clergy, and other allies of the coalition did not have access to the amount of capital needed. Resources of such magnitude are not contributed out of support or sympathy to a cause, or in order to avoid a local civil disturbance. State and local level public officials supportive of the coalition did not have ready access to such funds. As the social movement literature suggests, when such resources are mobilized, there are constraints upon their use which may limit and channel the movement's direction and results.

In the late 1970s, the Youngstown coalition (unsuccessfully) sought large federal loans and loan guarantees under the more liberal Carter administration to save closing steel facilities (see Kourchid, this volume). Such federal funding programmes were no longer even a possibility under the Reagan administration. For the employee buy-out at Weirton, National Steel, the previous corporate owner, became a major creditor, and a member of the Rockefeller family (then Governor of West Virginia) helped locate lenders. These were not options for Duquesne. That the Duquesne mill had been closed for so long, added to the estimated start-up costs - a factor not encountered in most other worker

buy-out plans. Weirton Steel and other recent
worker buy-outs have been based on an ESOP
arrangement which provides investors with certain
tax benefits and a source of capital. For workers,
owning stock potentially may be used to have some
voice in investment and production decisions,
depending upon how the ESOP structured; but usually
this is not the case.[13] Leaders of Local 1256
assumed that some form of ESOP would most likely be
included in their financing arrangements. The
coalition sponsored a conference on employee
ownership in July 1985, to acquaint Local 1256
members with some of the problems experienced by
other worker buy-out efforts. National experts on
worker buy-outs were ready to consult and assist.
There was no lack of expertise. The problem was the
amount of capital needed for Duquesne, which meant
that outside investors would have major shares, and
most likely, major influence on the terms of an
ESOP or other arrangement and that investment
capital would ultimately decide whether to reopen
the plant.

The USWA contracted the New York investment
banking firm of Lazard Frères & Co. to arrange a
financial plan, and to work with the other
consultants who were completing cost and engineering
studies. After several months delay, the various
consultants concluded that the coalition should
raise $50-100 million in public funds before
private capital might be attracted. The coalition
and the USWA then worked with local public
officials to propose a combined federal, state, and
local financial package. A substantial public
subsidy might offset some of the risks and attract
otherwise reluctant private capital. As discussed
earlier, low profits in the steel industry have
made it difficult to obtain investments in steel in
recent years. And as discussed, US Steel had
indicated it would seek to drive Duquesne out of
business, if reopened. The role of public funding
was to ensure and increase private profit. Because
private investment in steel is hard to find, public
funding, employee stock ownership, and concessions
from labour (in wage, benefits, or union power) are
subsidies and enticements that may be offered to
private capital. Under these conditions, private
capital would also have considerable power to
dictate the terms of any agreement between capital
and labour, and between capital and the state.

That Lazard Frères, an internationally
respected investment banking firm, took on the

Duquesne project, and on a contingency fee contract, shows that splits among elites - in this case among fractions of capital - can provide a movement with support from groups with very different class interests. Within the US, Lazard Frères appears to represent the more nationally oriented sector of capital. Felix Rohatyn, a major partner of the firm, was instrumental in designing the New York City 'default' plan, and is an advocate of what is sometimes termed a corporatist industrial policy (Bluestone and Harrison, 1982).[14] Rohatyn has criticized US Steel for pursuing investment strategies detrimental to the national economic interests and the social stability of the United States. He has argued in favour of federal policy aimed at maintaining industrial production in the United States (Rohatyn, 1982, 1984). The history of the New York City Default and the Weirton Steel ESOP, however, suggests that financing arranged by Lazard Frères might entail greater wage concessions from workers, and less worker participation in decision making, than the Duquesne groups would want to accept.[15] Ironically, Staughton Lynd and others associated with Tri-State had published articles criticizing Lazard Frères' role in Weirton, and Rohatyn's industrial policy proposals (Lynd, 1983, 1985). Thus the resources and intervention of powerful external elites had been mobilized, and some participants in the coalition were well aware of the potential constraints this entailed.

Lizard Frères' conclusion that the private capital needed could not be attracted was based on developments not foreseen by the initial study a year earlier. Additional market and engineering studies found a demand for variable size slabs in the market Duquesne would supply. This demand could not be met without a modern double strand continuous caster. Purchase and installation of such a caster would raise the restart cost to over $300 million, and would raise estimated production costs per ton. A number of potential customers were near bankruptcy by 1986, making problematic the long-term purchase agreements investors would require. The market price for steel slabs had continued to drop over the year. Voluntary steel import restraints negotiated by the Reagan administration were not effective, given the high value of the dollar and the need of Brazil and South Korea to push exports. The fierce price competition and price cutting by US Steel and foreign producers in 1985 resulted in a situation where all producers were selling semi-finished slabs at a loss, Duquesne could not promise to restart, refurbish, and operate profitably, and thus could not attract $200-300 dollars in private investment.

It should be noted that Lazard Frères's final study (Lazard Frères, 1986) confirmed the initial assessment (Locker, 1985) that low cost slabs potentially could be produced at Duquesne (or a similar facility), and that there could be an increased demand for domestic slabs in the near future. The Duquesne coalition, however, was too local and too weak to effect the national level industrial, financing, and trade policy changes necessary to make Duquesne successful. Substantial wage concessions by labour - even a one-third reduction - could not have made the difference, nor could available public funding. Continued effort by the coalition, in our judgement, could not have overcome the obstacles to attracting private capital at this juncture.

5.   CONCLUSION

The first two objectives of the Duquesne effort - stopping demolition and creating the Steel Valley Authority - are examples of successful mobilization. Participation of the rank and file workers, and the resources unique to that group, were effectively mobilized when needed. Although constraints on rank and file participation persisted due to conditions of unemployment and the legacy of depoliticization, the movement was able to overcome these constraints by pursuing a strategy that did not depend primarily on the unemployed workers; and by broadening the base of the coalition and recruiting members of other groups who shared an interest in saving the mill. The possibility of confrontation and mass protest was effectively used to pressurize elites who desired to avoid potential confrontations and threats to political stability. Comparisons with the more confrontational tactics of the DMS group, to which union and public officials found it more difficult to respond, worked in the coalition's favour. Finally, grass-roots initiatives, rank and file participation, and the mobilization of outside support functioned to push the union leadership into a more active stance toward the steel corporations and the politicians, which in turn strengthened the organizational capacity of labour.

The coalition was quite successful in gaining resources from more powerful and strategically placed groups such as the media, consultants for the feasibility studies, and public officials. Piven and Cloward (1977) suggest that conditions of economic crisis and dislocation may leave established political elites without clear policies, and may disrupt traditional alignments among elites. Under these conditions, elected officials are more likely to respond to the pressure, demands and initiatives of protest movements, and to break traditional patterns of government accommodation with private elites. In this environment, groups outside established institutional channels may gain increased access to policy making. On a local and limited scale, the success of the Steel Valley Authority initiative in particular, as well as other support for the Dorothy 6 campaign, reflects this dynamic.

The third objective, financing, was not achieved. Given the very large amounts of capital required and the absence of adequate public funding alternatives, the Duquesne effort, in order to achieve its objectives, turned to sectors of capital to rescue labour from the strategies of US Steel. From a resource mobilization perspective, the movement to save the Duquesne mill mobilized resources well beyond its control, including the intervention of elites who by virtue of their substantial resources and power were in a position to limit and channel movement demands, and to an extent, determined the results of the effort. The financing objective also illustrates the limited power of sympathetic local political elites - even when mobilized by popular pressure - to respond to corporate disinvestment policies. From a class analysis perspective investment bankers and private capital determined the fate of the struggle, demonstrating the reduced capacity of the working class and its allies to effectively respond to the new strategies of capital, or to effect the level of state intervention necessary.

Our main thesis, stated in the introduction, is that the possibilities for effective action by labour in the current economic context are limited by the new accumulation strategies of capital, and that the market and investment strategies of capital vary from case to case. We have suggested that it is important to consider industry - specific patterns of deindustrialization. National variations in the restructuring of the steel industry and in the role of the state affects labour's response. In the United States, where the federal government plays little role in the restructuring of the industry, and where reduction in steel capacity is shaped by competition rather than coordination within the industry, different companies pursue different market and investment strategies. The past pattern of coordination among the major American steel companies in setting prices and negotiating with labour has been replaced by increased competition. In this context, it is difficult for local labour and community groups and for unions to chart a response to plant closings.

The new strategies of capital reflect global changes in the steel industry. Compared to an earlier period, and due to the pattern of disinvestment from steel, corporations such as US Steel are much less constrained by investments in fixed capital. Therefore corporations can close facilities or parts of plants and shift production elsewhere, or reduce capacity in one part of the process and import certain products rather than produce them. As investments are shifted out of steel, capital is not restricted to a specific location or industry. In contrast, labour has greater sunk costs, and is more restricted by roots in a specific community and dependence on specific occupational skills with limited market flexibility. We have argued that in this changed economic context, old forms of protest and response by organized labour are not adequate, and often are not even possible - as in the case of plants that have already closed and workers who have permanently lost their jobs. In this context local efforts such as the Duquesne campaign, whether or not they are successful, are significant as sources of organiz-ational tactical and strategic innovation in forms of protest and political response.

The spread of innovation is already evident in two other cases in the Pittsburgh area. When LTV, the second largest steel producer in the US, closed its remaining steel production divisions in Aliquippa (in the next county), clergy, labour, and local politicians there immediately demanded a feasibility study to see if the workers could profitably operate the mill; rank and file workers organized an unemployed committee and sought the assistance of Tri-State and the Duquesne coalition. State legislators financed the study rather

readily. LTV announced that it would cooperate (at
some level) rather than replay US Steel's scenario
at Duquesne. At Aliquippa, the USWA demanded and
won the largely unprecedented right to examine
financial, production and other company records for
the closing plant in order to evaluate the
possibility of reopening under other ownership.
When American Standard announced its plan to move
to Canada two Pittsburgh area rail equipment
plants, a group of rank and file union members
(United Electrical Workers) from the two plants
were joined by state and local politicians, the
USWA and other unions, clergy and community groups
in a campaign to save the plants through the Steel
Valley Authority's use of eminent domain.

Whether the specific efforts mentioned above
are successful remains problematic. The flexibility
of multinational capital substantially reduces a
corporation's stake in any particular production
facility or location, and increases its capacity to
wait out the workers. Although Duquesne will not
reopen, the process of political mobilization has
already expanded the structural and organizational
capacities of the working class, and the repertoire
of protest forms and collective political experience
upon which other struggles may draw. For the first
time in recent history, Pittsburgh area politicians,
clergy, union officials, rank and file workers, and
local community groups are challenging the total
prerogative of individual corporations to own the
means of production, make investment decisions, and
organize production. We are not claiming that these
groups all see themselves as explicitly challenging
capitalism. Rather, the various activities of local
groups protesting against unemployment have
achieved what may be termed a successful intervention
into the dominant discourse on economic development
in the region. That alone is a significant
achievement.

273

NOTES

1. US Steel is the largest steel company in the United States and the largest steel employer in the Pittsburgh area, with six large steel producing facilities located in towns along the Monongehela (Mon) River. Dorothy 6 was the sixth blast furnace at US Steel's Duquesne works to be named for the wife of an early mill superintendent.

2. The major steel producers which did keep more of their assets in steel, invested more in modernization, and are not bankrupt - Republic (now part of LTV), Bethlehem, and Inland - do not have facilities in the Pittsburgh area.

3. The quote is attributed to William R. Roesch, who died in 1983.

4. As of 1986, contracts will be ratified by the membership.

5. The union hierarchy is called 'the international' because it represents USWA locals in the US and Canada.

6. This is one of the only statistical portraits of unemployed steelworkers in the Pittsburgh area based on a scientific sample. The Homestead mill, which had employed about 8,000 in 1979, was down to less than 800 in 1985 with further reductions announced. The Duquesne mill employed about 3,800 in 1979, and was completely shut down in 1984.

7. Our discussion of US Steel is based in part upon off-the-record comments made by industry analysts consulting for the USWA on the Duquesne feasibility studies. Cuff's <u>New York Times</u> article interviews some of the same individuals and presents some of the same analyses of specific companies.

8. US Steel's policies toward mills in other regions of the US are even more complex and diverse than those we have described, which underscores our point that the diverse, changing and sometimes seemingly inconsistent investment policies have made it difficult for labour to develop a coherent response.

9. The articles by Prude and Lynd provide a critical view of the Wierton buy-out.

10. An example is the headline 'Tri-State Conference "Quietly" Working for Jobs', in the McKeesport, Pa. <u>Daily News</u>, Jan 7th, 1985.

11. Subsequent market studies concluded that installation of a continuous caster was essential to produce for the market identified.

12. For examples of local media coverage see the McKeesport (Pa.) Daily News Jan. 3rd, 1985; May 8-10th,1985; Pittsburgh Post Gazette May 10th, 1985; Pittsburgh Press May 31st, June 3rd, June 11th, 1985.

13. Although employees may formally own the company or significant shares under an ESOP, these shares are usually held in trust by a bank, at least initially, which may give the bank considerable power. For discussions of ESOPs and labour, see Lynd, Ellerman, Rothschild-Whitt and other articles in the Spring, 1985 issue of Labor Research Review; also Whyte and Blasi, 1984.

14. Another prominent member of the Lazard Frères firm is Ian McGregor, who worked for the Thatcher government at British Steel and then at the British Coal Board.

15. The specific individual at Lazard Frères who managed the Duquesne study, had arranged the finance package for Weirton Steel, and was director of the New York Municipal Assistance Corporation. In both situations, large wage concessions were negotiated with the unions involved and obtained from the workers as part of the financial arrangement.

REFERENCES

Action-Housing Inc. (1983) <u>The Impact of</u>
    <u>Unemployment on Mortgage Delinquency and</u>
    <u>Foreclosure in Allegheny County</u>, Action-
    Housing, Pittsburgh
Adams, W. and H. Mueller (1982) 'The Steel
    Industry', in W. Adams (ed.), <u>The</u>
    <u>Structure of American Industry</u>, Macmillan,
    New York, pp. 73-135
American Iron and Steel Institute (1980) <u>Steel at</u>
    <u>the Crossroads: The American Steel Industry in</u>
    <u>the 1980's</u>, American Iron and Steel Institute,
    Washington DC
Bluestone, B. and B. Harrison (1982) <u>The</u>
    <u>Deindustrialization of America</u>, Basic Books,
    New York
Bowles, S. and H. Gintis (1982) 'The Crisis of
    Liberal Democratic Capitalism: The Case of the
    United States', <u>Politics and Society</u> 11, 51-93
<u>Business Week</u> (1985) 'The Toughest Job in
    Business: How They're Remaking U.S. Steel',
    <u>Business Week</u>, Feb. 25th, pp. 50-6
Carnegie-Mellon University (1983) <u>Milltowns in the</u>
    <u>Pittsburgh Region: Conditions and Prospects</u>,
    final report by the Dept. of Engineering and
    Public Policy, School of Urban and Public
    Affairs, and Dept. of Social Science,
    Pittsburgh
Crandall, R.W. (1981) <u>The U.S. Steel Industry in</u>
    <u>Recurrent Crisis: Policy Options in a</u>
    <u>Competitive World</u>, The Brookings Institution,
    Washington DC
Cuff, D.F. (1985) 'Steel's Fierce Domestic Battle'
    <u>New York Times</u>, Sept. 16th
<u>Daily News</u>, McKeesport Pennsylvania (1985) Jan.
    3rd, Jan. 7th, May 8-10
Deitch, C. (1984) 'Collective Action and Unemploy-
    ment: Response to Job Loss by Workers and
    Community Groups', <u>International Journal of</u>
    <u>Mental Health</u>, 13 139-53
Ellerman, D. (1985) "ESOPs and Co-ops: Worker
    Capitalism and Worker Democracy, <u>Labor</u>
    <u>Research Review</u>, 1, No. 6, 55-69
Erickson, R. (1983) '<u>The Tri-State Programme for</u>
    <u>Revitalizing and Restructuring the Pittsburgh</u>
    <u>Steel Industry</u>', Tri-State Conference on
    Steel, Homestead, Pennsylvania
Feigen, E. (1985) Presentation at the Duquesne
    ESOP Conference, July 10th.
Fireman, B. and W.A. Gamson (1970) 'Utilitarian

Logic in the Resource Mobilization Perspective', in M. Zald and J. McCarthy (eds.), The Dynamics of Social Movements, Winthrop Publishers, Cambridge Massachusetts, pp. 8-44

Freeman, J. (1979) 'Resource Mobilization and Strategy: A Model for Analyzing Social Movement Organization Actions', in M. Zald and J. McCarthy (eds), The Dynamics of Social Movements, Winthrop Publishers, Cambridge, Massachusetts, pp. 167-89

Gordon, D.M., R. Edwards and M. Reich (1982) Segmented Work, Divided Workers, Cambridge University Press, Cambridge

Jenkins, J.C. (1983) 'Resource Mobilization Theory and the Study of Social Movements', Annual Review of Sociology, 9, 527-53

Kuttner, R. (1985) 'A Troubled Union and its New Leader', Dissent, 32, 167-75

Lawrence, C. and R. Lawrence (1985) 'Manufacturing Wage Dispersion: An End Game Interpretation', Brookings Institution Papers

Lazard Frères & Co. (1986) Dorothy 6: Financial Feasibility of Reopening the Duquesne Works, report to the United Steel Workers of America, Pittsburgh

Locker, M. (1985) Feasibility Study of the Duquesne Works Blast and Oxygen Furnaces for the United Steel Workers of America, preliminary report by Locker-Abrecht Associates, Pittsburgh

Lynd, S. (1982) The Fight Against Shutdowns: Youngstown's Steel Mill Closings, Singlejack Books, San Pedro, California

Lynd, S. (1983) 'The View for Steel Country', Democracy, 1

Lynd, S. (1985) 'Why We Opposed the Buy-Out at Weirton Steel', Labor Research Review, 1, No. 6, 41-53

Lynd, S. (1985) Presentation at the Duquesne ESOP Conference, July 20th

Metzger, J. (1982) 'Public Policy and Steel', Dissent, 29, 325-28

Metzger, J. (1984) 'The Humbling of the Steelworkers', Socialist Review, No. 75-6, pp. 41-71

Metzger, J. (1985) 'Johnstown, Pa.: Ordeal of a Union Town', Dissent, 32, 160-3

Molotch, H. (1979) 'Media and Movements', in M. Zald and J. McCarthy (eds.), The Dynamics of Social Movements, Winthrop

Publishers, Cambridge, Massachusetts, pp. 71-93

Nyden, P. (1984) Steelworkers Rank and File: The Political Economy of the Union Reform Movement, Praeger, New York

Office of Technology Assessment, Congress of the United States (1981) U.S. Industrial Competitiveness: A Comparison of Steel, Electronics, and Automobiles, Government Printing Office, Washington DC

Pittsburgh Post-Gazette (1984) Dec. 10th; (1985) May 5th.

Pittsburgh Press (1985) May 31st, June 3rd, June 11th.

Piven, F.F. and R.A. Cloward (1977) Poor People's Movements, Pantheon, New York

Prude, J. (1984) 'Esop's Fable', Socialist Review, No. 78

Rohatyn, F. (1982) 'A State of Banks', New York Review of Books, 29, Nov. 4, pp. 3+

Rohatyn, F. (1982) 'Alternatives to Reaganomics', New York Times Magazine, Dec. 5th. pp. 72+

Rohatyn, F. (1984) 'American Roulette', New York Review of Books, 32, Mar. 29th, pp. 11-15

Rohatyn, F. (1984) 'The Debtor Economy: A Proposal', New York Review of Books, 31, Nov. 8th, pp. 16-21

Rothschild-Whitt, J. (1985) 'Who Will Benefit from ESOPs?' Labor Research Review, 1, No. 6, 71-80

Summers, G.F. (1984) 'Preface to Deindustrialization: Restructuring the Economy', a special issue of The Annals, No. 475, pp. 9-14

Tilly, C. (1978) From Mobilization to Revolution, Addison-Wesley, Reading Massachusetts

Tilly, C. (1979) 'Repertoires of Contention in America and Britain, 1750-1830' in M. Zald and J. McCarthy (eds.), The Dynamics of Social Movements, Winthrop Publishers, Cambridge Massachusetts, pp. 126-55

Tri-State Conference on Steel (1984) 'Rebuild Steel!', Homestead, Pennsylvania

Tumazos, R.T. (1985) 'Study on the Demand and Supply of Semifinished Steel Products in the United States', report to Lazard Frères & Co., and Russell, Rea & Zappala, Inc., prepared in conjunction with the feasibility study to reactivate the Duquesne Works, Pittsburgh

United Steel Workers of America (1983) 'Basic Steel Agreement'

'Save Dorothy'

US Dept. of Labor, Bureau of Labor Statistics
     (1985) States and Metropolitan Areas Data,
     Government Printing Office, Washington DC
Whyte, W.F. and J. Blasi (1984) 'Employee Owner-
     ship and the Future of Unions', The Annals,
     No. 473, pp. 128-40
Wright, E.O. (1978) Class, Crisis and the State,
     New Left Books, London
Zald, M.N. and J.D. McCarthy (1979) 'Introduction'
     in M. Zald and J. McCarthy (eds.), The
     Dynamics of Social Movements, Winthrop
     Publishers, Cambridge Massachusetts, pp. 1-7

Chapter Eleven

UNEMPLOYMENT AFTER REDUNDANCY AND POLITICAL
ATTITUDES: SOME EMPIRICAL EVIDENCE

Iain Noble

There are few reasons to doubt that relatively high
levels of unemployment (say above five per cent and
approaching ten per cent of the labour force) will
persist at least until the end of the decade in the
UK. Even if the gross rate of unemployment starts
to fall we will still be faced with two major
problems. Firstly, among the unemployed there has
been a growth in the number of long-term
unemployed, for whom the effects of unemployment
are the most distressing and who have the lowest
chances of securing re-employment. Even if the
long-promised revival of the economy materialises
it is probable that they will be the last to be
taken up. Many of the unemployed are likely to stay
so for the next five years or longer and they will
leave unemployment only to enter a spurious,
pauperised, 'early retirement'. Secondly, as is
well known, the number of unemployed - whether
taken from the statistics of those registering in
order to claim benefit or estimated from social
surveys - understates severely the number of
involuntary workless. The young on their schemes
and programmes, married women withdrawing from paid
employment to unpaid work in the household, older
workers over 55 recognising their de facto
exclusion from the labour force by a 'voluntary'
withdrawal, generally without the compensatory
benefits awarded to those excluded on the grounds
of age. The current recession has not simply
generated mass unemployment, it has persuaded many
to write off paid employment as a feasible option
altogether.
    The importance of establishing the possible
effects of unemployment on political attitudes
following redundancy cannot be stressed too highly,
yet it would seem that social scientists, both

280

currently and in previous periods of mass unemployment, have for some reason been unwilling to take up the challenge. At the time of writing there remains a dearth of reliable evidence concerning unemployment and politics in general and, in particular, on whether or not being unemployed will affect an individual's politics. This is curious for at least two reasons. The first is that unemployment is thoroughly researched in many other respects. The summary provided by Warr (1983) for social psychology alone, the two recent British cohort studies (Daniel, 1981 and Wood, 1982) and hosts of other studies, make this clear. We are still a long way from being able to answer certain questions concerning the effects of unemployment, partly because identifying the unemployed is difficult, partly because certain questions require long-term panel studies to answer, and much evidence produced is of a piecemeal variety which does not lead to definitive statements. Nevertheless, it is clear that researching unemployment with survey techniques is far from impossible. Secondly, this topic seems to be precisely the sort of thing that sociologists ought to be interested in. Our discipline (this seems less contentious than science) can be traced directly to a point of origin in the fears or hopes aroused in the liberal intelligentsia by the conditions of the working class under industrialisation. We may have abandoned by and large the fears of De Toqueville and Comte or the hopes of Marx and Engels in favour of the weary resignation of Weber, but industrial societies are still societies where a high value is placed on work defined as paid employment, and it is still an intrinsic assumption of sociology that social experience determines consciousness rather than vice-versa. At a time when, in many parts of Britain, the conventional social ice-breaker "And what do you do?" has been replaced by the enquiry "Are you in work?", this silence is perplexing. In this respect, we are, as in so many others, repeating what has gone before. The sociographers of Marienthal (Jahoda et. al., 1972) were uninterested in the problem, Bakke (1933) makes a few references to the politics of his informants but little else. The sparseness and inadequate reliability of available English language material (with the exception of Schlozman and Verba, 1979) can be seen in the review of previous studies in Fraser et. al. (1985).

In 1980 the Department of Sociological Studies

at the University of Sheffield[1] was approached by
the management of a private sector steel firm in
the city. In the summer of the previous year this
firm had made just over 600 employees redundant on
the closure of its Forgings Division; these were
with few exceptions 'voluntary' redundancies and
took place at a time when Sheffield's unemployment
rate was, as it had been for three decades, below
the national average. The reason for the firm's
approach was never made clear, and they withdrew
from the project on learning of the cost and time
factors involved in any survey of their former
employees. Before their withdrawal, however, the
firm agreed to supply us with the names and
addresses of redundant workers. The redundancies
arose when, following the takeover of the firm by a
large multi-national in 1978, the new management
concluded that its Forgings Division was unable to
survive in a shrinking market with enhanced
capacity on the part of its main competitors
(another private firm and a part of the public
sector British Steel Corporation, both producing in
Sheffield and subsequently merged under rationalisation plans with substantial job loss). The
Division was closed as a whole and, although part
of the workforce were either re-deployed within the
firm or taken on by one of its competitors, the
majority of those working in the Division were made
redundant during or shortly after the summer of
1979.

There were several 'contexts' which shaped the
research and which derived from local factors.
Sheffield had been for some years an area that
combined working class affluence with a continuing
commitment to traditional working class institutions
and aspirations. Although unemployment had risen to
high levels during the 1930s, this was limited to a
few years and was a new experience for many of the
local workforce. In the post-war period unemployment
was consistently lower than the national average
and markedly lower than in other areas of South
Yorkshire, such as Rotherham (Walker, 1981). To
some extent this prosperity has been based directly
on the special steels industry and associated
engineering industries. Special steels managed to
resist the early waves of 'deindustrialisation'
much better than bulk steel production and was
brought down as an industry rather by the effects
of the general recession. In particular, the
special steels industry has been dependent on motor
manufacturing industry for the sale of a large

number of its products. The collapse of demand from
this sector as the recession got into its stride
was the first major problem, soon to be exacerbated
by 'import dumping' as other producers sought to
dispose of surpluses generated by their own slumps
in demand. From the late 1970s, then, Sheffield
began to experience a rapid increase in the number
of redundancies, especially in engineering steels:
the number of notified redundancies in 1979 was
6354, the next year this rose to 11,515 and the
year after 15,441. In all three years the
proportion of these redundancies in either metal
manufacture or engineering never fell below
two-thirds. We thus had good reason to suspect that
those made redundant were entering a period of
economic insecurity, and an economic insecurity
that would be for the large majority a novel
experience. The majority of our sample had been
employed by the firm for over ten years prior to
redundancy, nearly half (46%) for 20 years or more.
In part this reflected a similar tendency in the
steel industry as a whole, as well as in the
particular firm studied, towards long periods of
service with the same firm. It also resulted from
the well-kown skewedness of post-redundancy samples
towards the upper end of the age scale. Despite
this age skew, which meant that over half of the
sample were over 55, and a severe sex bias (only
13% of the sample were women, while 29% of the
Sheffield labour force in 1981 were women), we were
in other respects lucky in the sample. The closure
of a whole division, rather than certain parts of
it, meant a reasonably good spread across the
occupational structure. Roughly one-third of the
sample were skilled manual workers in a number of
engineering trades, another third were semi-skilled
and unskilled manual workers, while the remaining
third of non-manual workers were in roughly equal
proportion routine clerical and managerial,
technical and administrative staffs.

    Another of the special contexts of the
research was so important it came to provide one of
the main themes of the interview schedule. Although
now part of a major multi-national company, the
firm concerned had only recently been absorbed into
the organisation. Its origin lay in the great wave
of industrialisation in Sheffield that followed
upon the foundation there (by Bessemer himself) of
large-scale steel production in the mid-nineteenth
century. The founder of this firm was, like
Bessemer, an entrepreneurial scientist rather than

a straightforward businessman. A member of a minor local gentry family, he became involved in commerce to exploit his own discoveries and inventions, particularly in the area of alloy steels. This and his own inclinations lay behind an essential paternalism that was characteristic of many an enterprise of that day. What interested us was that not only did this paternalism have the reputation of surviving beyond its 'natural' environment - 19th century industrialisation - up to the present day, but that its counterpart - a 'deferential' workforce - was thought by many to have survived as well. There had been, in the post-war period, precisely one strike at this firm, which was highly unionised, large-scale and in heavy manufacturing: three characteristics generally associated with relatively high rates of industrial dispute. The employees of the firm had a local reputation for what some may call 'moderation' or 'realism' but which was regarded by many union activists in the steel industry in Sheffield as an overly friendly attitude to management. These suspicions were confirmed for many during the national steel strike of 1980 when the employees of this firm continued to work (largely because there were few members of the Iron and Steel Trades Confederation (ISTC), the largest British steel union, employed there), becoming the target of mass picketing and the media event of the month.

As has been pointed out on several occasions (eg Lockwood, 1966 and Martin and Fryer, 1975) much discussion about the beliefs of 'deferential traditionalist' workers has been essentially speculative. However, anecdotal evidence from management, employees and union full-timers (as well as the behaviour of the other employees in 1980) appeared to confirm the popular image of the firm as one where it had been possible to create within a plant management-employee relations which cut across the normal partisan alignments to such a degree as to encourage employees to risk insult and injury to cross a picket line. This was all the more interesting because recent sociological research (Newby, 1979; Lane and Roberts, 1971; Martin and Fryer, 1973) has taken the position - either directly or by implication - that 'deference' is extracted by the paternalist employer by means of his or her labour market position. This is characteristically one of greater than average strength either through control (or dominance) of the local labour market, through being the largest

employer in a relatively isolated area or because
of control of factors external to the labour market
that can affect severely the autonomy of action of
employees (eg farmers' ownership of the tied
housing relied on by agricultural workers). Such
conditions do not exist in Sheffield, a city of
just under half a million with a diverse industrial
base and a housing stock generally either
owner-occupied or public rented.

We were thus led to concentrate our attention
on three major concerns. First, we had an interest
in political and social attitudes, especially on
matters of industrial relations such as strikes,
unions and management prerogatives, but not to the
exclusion of more general ideas of social
consciousness. This was initially an interest in
whether or not we could isolate 'deference' among
our sample as a valid measure, but we were also
concerned with the possible roots and determinants
of deference. Next, we were concerned with the
economic insecurity of our informants: at a crude
level, which were most likely to be unemployed and
for how long, which were liable to find unemployment
most distressing in financial and personal terms,
in terms of factors such as age, sex and
occupational class. Finally, we were interested in
the connections between the two. We knew several
things already: political and social attitudes vary
by occupational class and other factors; earlier
post-redundancy studies and local labour market
studies have shown clearly that the likelihood of
re-employment and the length of time before
re-employment vary considerably with age, skill
group and original industry; social psychologists
in particular have found unemployment to be an
extremely powerful factor in affecting the
individual's level of well-being, his or her
chances of suffering from such things as depression
and anxiety as well as other symptoms of
psychological distress and disorder (Warr, 1983).
Once we controlled for the effects of the
background variables on political and social
attitudes, we reasoned it should then be possible
to test for the effect of economic insecurity of
itself on social and political attitudes. We
proposed to define economic insecurity in three
main ways: being unemployed at time of interview,
having a period of unemployment between redundancy
and interview greater than six months in length, or
being unemployed for a higher proportion than
average in total over the three years after

redundancy.

When the data were analysed, however, this triple definition, as well as the concentration on unemployment per se, were seen to be mistaken. For the first we found that nearly all those unemployed at time of interview had been so for over six months, nearly 90% of them for a year or more, while they were also the group with the highest amount of time since redundancy in unemployment. Secondly, we found that the incidence of labour force withdrawal was more common than simple unemployment. That is, particularly among older workers and women, informants were often more likely to have become economically inactive (neither employed nor seeking a job) than unemployed. Nevertheless, we persisted with our attempts to measure the effects of unemployment on political and social attitudes, not least because we became aware at the same time of a crucial characteristic of unemployment as distinct from non-employment.

We distinguish unemployment from non-employment partly because we wish to correct other studies that, looking solely at unemployment (that is being registered with a government employment agency, or claiming Unemployment Benefit or describing individuals as 'actively seeking work') fail to show the extent to which members of some social groups are forced out of the labour market altogether after redundancy. The employment histories gathered from our informants recorded all employment statuses in the three years after redundancy rather than just jobs and spells of unemployment. It is also clear, however, that although unemployment is for many the tip of the iceberg (the time spent unemployed being a fraction of that spent workless) there is something special about unemployment as a state, particularly with regard to the effects on individual psyches. Unemployment is distinguished from other forms of non-employment, such as retirement, household work or sickness and injury by being stigmatised. More importantly it is stigmatised in the minds of the unemployed themselves rather than in the attitudes of others. One of the most powerful factors behind withdrawal from the labour market is the desire to avoid this self-stigmatisation. Mass unemployment not only reduces the employed workforce, it also encourages (with sticks rather than carrots) those with possible escape routes to take them so reducing the size of the labour force. Those who are unable or unwilling to escape are obliged to bear the burden. We have discussed in detail elsewhere (Walker, 1982 and Walker, Noble and Westergaard, 1985) this process of labour market exclusion and the associated creation of structured dependency and age poverty. Further evidence of this process can be found in studies of unemployment and ill-health (eg Fagin and Little, 1984 and Bytheway, this volume). Such studies have shown that one of the major difficulties in establishing a causal link between the two lies in the possibility that many people may accept a 'sickness role' with relief, and even seek one out, precisely to release themselves from the intolerable obligations imposed on them by internalised work commitment values while they define themselves as unemployed (see Bartley, this volume).

Therefore we concluded that: although we had overestimated the extent to which unemployment (as distinct from non-employment) would affect our sample, we were right in identifying unemployment as something that would be deeply disturbing to those who suffered it. Of those in our sample who were unemployed at any time during the time between redundancy and interview, over half (52%) described unemployment as the worst thing they had ever experienced. One illustration of the difference between unemployment and non-employment can be seen in Table 11.1. Here are shown the employment rates immediately after redundancy for certain groups, the first column gives the proportion of the group registering as unemployed, the second column the total proportion without work, and the third column the difference between these which gives the proportion becoming economically inactive by withdrawing from the labour force.

It is interesting to note that employment prospects increased markedly for all groups over the next few months so that after six months higher proportions were employed in all categories. These extra employed were drawn, however, almost exclusively from the unemployed rather than other non-working groups, and there was little or no improvement in employment prospects after this time in terms of proportion of a group employed except for the youngest. We can see clearly from this table that women and older men were forced out of the labour market, as were routine clerical workers and those lacking formal skill training, while the most at risk from unemployment were middle-aged males. These impressions are confirmed by the

Table 11.1: Immediate Post-Redundancy Employment Rates

	% Unemployed	% Non-employed	% Non Labour Force	(N)
Males				
Under 40	29	34	5	(63)
40-55	52	56	4	(64)
55 or over	42	84	42	(179)
Total	42	67	25	(306)
Females				
Under 40	32	58	26	(19)
Over 40	32	72	40	(25)
Total	32	64	32	(44)
Skilled manual	45	59	14	(106)
Semi- and unskilled	51	81	30	(126)
Routine non-manual	30	66	36	(45)
Other non-manual	29	60	31	(73)
All	41	68	26	(350)

Table 11.2: Labour Market Experience Since Redundancy

Average number of months:	Working	Unemployed	Non-working
Males			
Under 40	30	7	8
40-55	22	11	16
55 or over	9	10	29
Total	16	10	22
Females			
Under 40	19	5	20
40 or over	17	5	20
Total	18	5	20
Skilled manual	22	8	16
Semi/unskilled	11	13	27
Routine non-manual	14	6	24
Other non-manual	16	5	22
Total	16	9	22

summary data in Table 11.2, which gives average
number of months in various employment statuses
during the period between redundancy and interview.
Clearly, again older men were the group with the
worst employment prospects: those over 55 averaged
only 9 months in employment after redundancy
compared with 30 months for those under 40, and 22
months for those between 40 and 55. Similarly,
women under 40 fared much worse than men under 40,
while skilled manual workers had twice as much time
in work as semi-skilled. Further evidence to
support the view that non-employment of any kind,
and unemployment in particular, are liable to lead
to a severely reduced income can be found in Table
11.3. Studies of unemployed working class men
suggest that two-thirds of them have a household
income that is below half of their previous income
(Warr and Jackson, 1983). The data for household
income we have (using exhaustive questions
developed originally for the British Government's
General Household Survey) show that the non-employed
as a group are considerably worse off than the
employed, even when the effect is diminished by
having dependents in the household, while the
unemployed are the worst off. All our unemployed
informants reported having to cut down on essential
expenditure and the necessity of drawing out
savings to meet expenses that formerly would have
been paid from income. The longer someone was
unemployed, the lower their income as savings
became exhausted by both necessity and the
requirements of Social Security regulations.

Another well attested effect of unemployment
is shown in Table 11.4 Negative Affect is a scale
devised by Bradburn (Bradburn, 1969) which asks if
informants have suffered any of five common
symptoms of psychological distress during the few
weeks prior to interview. An individual received a
score of 1 for each symptom reported; these are
then summed for the scale. The mean level was
markedly higher for the unemployed than for any
other group, the odds of someone who was unemployed
reporting three or more of these symptoms were 17
times the odds of someone who was employed.

The data shown in Tables 11.3 and 11.4,
showing the lowered financial position of the
unemployed and their lower levels of well-being,
are undoubtedly connected. Financial anxieties are
high on the list of worries for the unemployed
(Warr, 1983), while they are also a strong
predictor of people's overall distress score

(Payne, Warr and Hartley, 1983). We can also see that the nonworking other than the unemployed had noticeably lower levels of negative affect despite levels of income only slightly above. The difference between the unemployed and the non-working is almost certainly due to two factors: the unemployed are notably more likely than other groups to feel threatened, in particular to feel anxious and insecure about what may happen in the future, and they also consider themselves to have lost a socially valuable place and acquired one which is stigmatised.

Table 11.3: Average Weekly Income of Informant and Spouse: All Sources (post tax)

Household Type	Working	Employment Status Unemployed	Retired	Other
2 people under 60	142.80	–	–	47.20
2 people (either = 60+)	101.00	50.80	71.90	50.70
Small family (two adults, 1 or 2 children)	116.80	74.00	–	–
Large family (3 or more children)	115.80	81.10	–	–
Large adult	120.90	61.20	86.50	69.30
Total	121.40	56.30	74.10	60.40

Note: Informant = Male Head of Household

Table 11.4: Mean Level of Negative Affect ('Feeling Bad')

		N
Working	0.8	(150)
Unemployed	2.4	(72)
Retired	1.0	(78)
Other non-working	1.9	(50)

It is clear that paid employment was differentially distributed amongst our sample after redundancy. The non-working were divided into two distinct groups: those who withdrew from the labour market (in most cases before official retirement age), and those who continued to seek work. This latter group had markedly lower levels of income and well-being compared to other groups, the latter being directly due to their status as unemployed. To test the effect of post-redundancy experience on political attitudes we used three main variables, one independent, Per Cent Time Unemployed (PTU) and two dependent variables, 'Deference' and 'Solidarity'. Per Cent Time Unemployed was the proportion of the time between redundancy and interview that the informant was either registered as unemployed or reported seeking work (but excludes cases where informants - usually over 60 - registered as unemployed but told us this was merely to collect benefit and they did not regard themselves as genuinely unemployed). At the interview we collected a history of employment statuses between redundancy and interview using as a model the employment status history question used by the PSI/MSC Cohort Study (Daniel, 1981). Informants were asked how long they had been in their current employment status (to the nearest month), then what their previous status had been and the number of months in that and so on back to the time they were made redundant. The number of unemployed months were summed and divided by the total time between redundancy and interview (average 38 months). Finally the item was categorised into five groups: those with no unemployment since redundancy; those with up to 33% of their time since redundancy unemployed; those with between 33% and 66%; those with between 66% and 99% and those who had been unemployed for the full time between redundancy and interview.

The two attitude scales 'Deference' and 'Solidarity', were created by summation of scores to individual opinion items. Although the two scales were derived by different methods, the method of scoring was the same for both. Informants were given a number of opinion items (just over 40) at various points of the interview and asked to respond on the conventional five-point Likert scale (Strongly Agree to Strongly Disagree), and received a score for the item from 0 to 4 depending on their answer and whether the item was negatively coded. Where the item was positively coded Strongly Disagree scored 0 and Strongly Agree scored 4, where the item was negatively coded the scoring was reversed so that the higher the level of disagreement the higher the score. The item scores were then summed and divided by the number of items making up the scale (6 for 'Deference', 10 for 'Solidarity'). The items for the scales were selected in two different ways. For 'Deference' we relied considerably on earlier discussion of what industrial deference 'ought' to imply, especially Lockwood's discussion (Lockwood, 1966). We included in our questions both items used by earlier researchers on class-consciousness and ones of our own devising. The key elements we tried to encapsulate in these items were: a sense of the legitimate nature of management powers; the obligation on the worker to comply with management orders; a reliance on the ability and good intentions of management; a recognition of their rights to autonomous desision making, and both the necessity of high rewards for managers and the moral legitimacy of such differentials. From the pool of items we were able to create a scale of only limited reliability with six items, listed in Appendix 1, removing or adding items both reduced reliability (as measured by Cronbach's alpha) even further. The 'Solidarity' scale was devised after an exploratory factor analysis of over 30 items relating to class structure, industrial relations and class consciousness. Some of these items were taken from previous research on this matter, some of these were again devised by us either as improved wordings or to cover matters we considered should be included. Although factor analysis was used in the construction of the scale to identify items, this is still a summated, not factor-weighted scale. The final ten items are also shown in Appendix 1. Further factor analysis of the ten items generated a two factor solution with the first factor explaining over 60% of the variance. This second scale was more reliable than the first as well as having equal numbers of positively and negatively coded items.

We carried out a number of Analyses of Variance for both scales using a number of factors known to be associated with differences in political attitudes. These analyses were carried out using factors both singly and in a variety of combinations to test for interactions. It was clear that the proportion of time since redundancy spent unemployed was not associated directly with any difference in levels of deference or solidarity. Neither was there any association through interaction with other variables when analyses were carried out with them. Deference was seen to be linked with age and age alone, and even age explained only a small proportion of the variance as shown by beta-squared. Interestingly, length of service had no effect on deference even when age was controlled for by confining analysis to those over 55. From this it would seem unlikely that our subject firm's industrial peace was due to the presence or promotion of deferential attitudes among the employees, either through socialisation of new recruits into workforce norms or values radically different to those elsewhere in industry or through the creation of economic dependence. The explanation is more likely to be found in the institutional arrangements in the enterprise, whereby all negotiations were between management and two shop stewards representing all workplace unions, rather than with the combined committee for the enterprise representing more than a dozen separate unions.

As for levels of solidarity, occupational class was found to be the main explanatory variable with the most significant differences between manual and non-manual workers. Those who believe that younger workers have noticeably different attitudes from older workers, that class is withering away because of such factors as increased education, will find some confirming evidence (younger workers were significantly less deferential) and some disconfirming evidence (age made little difference to the level of solidarity). The experience of a relatively higher level of unemployment or non-employment over the three years after redundancy did not have a radicalising effect, neither was it associated with higher levels of less radical solidaristic orientations. Other analyses, however, show the persistence of differences in political outlook associated (in particular) with status/class division between manual and non-manual occupations as well as contradictory outlooks (Westergaard, Noble and Walker, 1986).

This article has reported on scaled variables because such scales are intrinsically more resistant to errors and bias from several sources than individual opinion items. Additionally, we have not shown analyses for these scales by the proportion of time spent out of work altogether, rather than just unemployed. Taking the latter point first, substituting per cent non-employed for per cent unemployed failed to show a significant effect. For the former point, when we ignored the methodologically well-founded strictures against the analysis of individual items (MacKennell,

1978), and looked at individual items by employment status, per cent unemployed and per cent non-working, the picture was the same as in the analysis of scaled variables. With a few exceptions employment status was not associated with significant response differences across a wide range of social and political issues. The few exceptions were that unemployed informants were slightly more likely to have favourable opinions about the unemployed and reject suggestions that unemployment or poverty were primarily the fault of the unemployed or poor themselves. Variation was much more likely to be associated with differences in factors such as age, occupational class and sex. The only opinion item where major differences were associated with variation in employment status is shown in Table 11.5 and here the effect was of non-employment, not unemployment.

Table 11.5: Odds of Agreeing with 'The main reason for unemployment at the minute is that there are too many immigrants in the country'

Age:	Agree	Disagree	Odds of Agreeing
Over 40	117	134	0.873
Under 40	15	76	0.197

Odds ratio: Over 40: Under 40: 4.43

Employment Status:	Agree	Disagree	Odds of Agreeing
Working	38	112	0.322
Non-working	94	91	1.032

Odds ratio: Non-working:working: 3.21

Occupational Class:	Agree	Disagree	Odds of Agreeing
Manual	90	113	0.796
Non-manual	42	90	0.467

Odds ratio: Manual:Non-manual: 1.7

What then are we to make of these results? The first comment must be to repeat earlier warnings concerning the sample, even though our informants, previously securely employed affluent workers pitchforked into the recession, can be regarded as a 'critical case'. This group of mainly male informants was drawn from those employed in one division of a private sector large-scale manufacturing firm which had a reputation for paternalism and deference. Some data gave us cause to doubt the special nature of the firm having much effect on employee attitudes but, even so, we cannot generalise from this group. Further research is needed using bigger and more heterogeneous samples. A second note of caution also concerns sampling: a wide range of political opinion questions were put to our informants but it is always possible that key variables reflecting shifts in attitude that did take place were omitted. Further research is also needed whereby such issues can be identified; this would require more extensive and exploratory interviews over periods of time than we were able to carry out, constrained by budget and timetable.

But if we accept the results as valid, what explanations can there be? Such answers as can be given must be speculative. One major candidate for prime explanation is the nature of unemployment itself where unemployment is defined as the absence of desired paid employment. We have already drawn attention to the general psychological effects of unemployment: depression, anxiety about personal finance, fear of the future and a loss of self-respect. In addition, the unemployed are liable to become personally isolated - going out much less and seeing fewer people - to have a much lower level of activity and to feel powerless to affect events around them. This <u>atomisation</u> would seem a powerful barrier to active political modes of thought and goes a long way to explaining why political movements do not develop among the unemployed. It does not, however, seem to offer an explanation of why political attitudes among the unemployed do not differ.

A person's politics at any one time are the product of a lengthy socialisation process and can not be disturbed overnight, not even by events as traumatic as redundancy and unemployment. In the same way that individual party identification can be essentially expressive, for most people political attitudes are important in that they express for the holder an important aspect of what he or she believe themselves to be socially. If this is the case then we might expect unemployment to rigidify rather than dissolve existing political attitudes. For unemployment is seen, by all but the fortunate few, as an essentially threatening experience. In addition, as we have seen, the individual is threatened in terms of social identity in a quite substantial way. Other research (Morris, 1985) on the aftermath of redundancy gives us evidence that gender roles within the household, far from breaking down under the impact of unemployment, are in fact reinforced. Morris's enthnographic evidence is supported by the more extensive quantitative analysis reported in Laite and Noble (1986). Although there may be minor redistributions of domestic labour tasks during a husband's unemployment, which may persist after he returns to work, they are essentially minor and variation in other factors (such as whether or not there are children in the household) is more likely to be associated with variation in male domestic working. Morris's crucial point is that while there may be changes in behaviour during male unemployment, attitudes about domestic work and the 'correct' division of labour are maintained by the social networks of both husband and wife. Political attitudes may be affected in a similar way as the unemployed person holds fast to what they can in a dangerous world, striving to maintain his or her self-identity under attack. Most importantly it is dangerous, if not impossible, to discuss changes in political attitudes without discussing the alternatives that are on offer, the politics that are articulated by parties and trade unions, the real political conjuncture in which our informants found themselves. This, it is suggested, was far more important to and influential upon our informants than their employment status.

A perennial and somewhat misguided criticism of Marxism has been to ask why immiseration of itself does not produce revolutionary consciousness. The answer is that unemployment and recession do not produce a revolutionary socialist vanguard simply because Marxism has little or no appeal·to 'the working class' (itself a figment of Marxist imagination) no matter what the state of the economy. Whether in slump or boom, it is simply not credible. Where 'Marxist' parties are successful in industrialised countries it tends to be in direct proportion to their abandonment of Marxism. This political failure of Marxism to take advantage of supposedly favourable conditions is compounded by the inability to explain the failure other than through ideological discourse of the most contorted kind. Both failures stem from the inadequacies of Marxist theories of action and in particular from the idea of a universal transcendent intrinsic proletarian class interest (Lockwood, 1981). A much more interesting question, however, is why a reformist social-democratic movement such as the British Labour Party, historically associated with full employment, with policies designed to create employment (aka 'Keynesianism') and strongest in those areas of the country and in those social groups most at risk from unemployment, has not gained but <u>lost</u> support during an era of mass unemployment. To give a brief answer to this let us refer to the one political shift we are sure has taken place among our informants. The large majority, nearly 80%, of our informants described themselves as 'usual' Labour voters up until 1979. However, over a third (34%) of these usual Labour voters either deserted at 1979 or told us their intention was not to vote Labour at the next election (our interviews were carried out in late 1982 and the first two months of 1983), not far different from voting shifts that actually did take place locally at the two most recent General Elections. Examining the data, these shifts appear unconnected with employment changes over the past three years, although younger skilled workers, who were less likely than others to be workless, were slightly more likely to defect. Rather housing tenure and social class, with owner-occupiers and non-manual workers most likely to change, are implicated (for further analysis see Noble, 1986). It seems likely, however, that one of the major reasons for defecting was doubts about the specific policies to which the Labour Party was, or appeared to be, committed.

We found, as did others (eg Himmelweit <u>et</u>. <u>al</u>., 1985) that while many informants saw unemployment as the most important political issue, thought that the government was doing too little to reduce it and thought that numbers unemployed could be reduced by appropriate policies they had little confidence in either the Labour Party itself (because of its factionalism)' or in its specific policies against unemployment. The Party was perceived as caring but not credible. We put a number of proposed policies for dealing with unemployment to our informants and asked them to score them in terms of effectiveness on a five-point scale. Significant differences (Scheffe test, .001 level) existed between Labour loyalists and Labour defectors on three of these policies with defectors assigning a lower score to all three for their effectiveness in reducing unemployment. The three policies were: nationalising North Sea oil; leaving the EEC and giving employees a much greater say in the running of companies. In addition, loyalists and defectors were separated on a number of political attitudes with trade unions noticeably prominent among them and defectors much more hostile to matters such as secondary picketing. It would seem that Labour's perceived move to the left was a major reason why it was unable, in 1983, to take advantage of public concern on unemployment and one of the main reasons why unemployment, either directly experienced or as a social issue, did not appear to have led to many political upheavals.

Finally, what about a change that did appear to have taken place, that being unemployed makes one more likely to be prejudiced against immigrants? There is other evidence of both an anecdotal, and a more reliable kind, that makes such a change all too probable; British race relations, and those of other countries in Europe, do appear to have worsened markedly under the impact of recession. The reasons for this seem to be connected with non-employment, that is exclusion from paid employment generally, rather than the specific state of unemployment. Those excluded have been so on the basis of criteria (age, skill, etc.) that they would probably accept themselves as valid bases for discrimination. It is plausible to suggest that in order to reduce the pressure on themselves they seek for a group they feel can be defined, by generally accepted criteria, as more deserving of exclusion. There can be no doubt that racialism and xenophobia are deeply rooted in British working class culture. It is probable that such values are latent among many, especially older manual workers, and are brought to the surface by the experience of economic insecurity. Inequality, arising from the two class structures (the division between capital and labour and the occupational hierarchy) as well as from gender and age stratification, is resisted through claims made on a perceived status system founded on citizenship. To confirm this, however, we need research not simply on what changes occur as a result of unemployment, but how such processes are structured: both require that we research the employed and the other non-working at the same time as and on a comparable basis to the unemployed. In a short space we have elaborated a considerable research agenda but then we have time. After all one of the results of the failure of unemployment to change people's politics may be that the unemployed will be with us for quite a while yet.

NOTE

1. The After Redundancy Study was carried out in the Department of Sociological Studies, University of Sheffield. The project was directed by John Westergaard and Alan Walker, Research Officer was Iain Noble. We carried out 370 structured interviews (average length two hours twelve minutes) between October 1982 and March 1983 with former employees of a private sector steel company in Sheffield. We wish to acknowledge the assistance of the Social Science Research Council in carrying out the research.

REFERENCES

Bakke, E.W., (1933) The Unemployed Man, Nisbet
    and Co., London
Bradburn, N.M. (1969) The Structure of Psycho-
    logical Well-Being, Aldine, Chicago
Bulmer, M. (1975) Working Class Images of Society,
    RKP/SSRC, London
Crick, B. (ed.) (1981) Unemployment, Methuen,
    London
Daniel, W.W. (1981) The Unemployed Flow, PSI,
    London
Fagin, L. and M. Little, (1984) The Forsaken
    Families, Penguin, Harmondsworth
Fraser, C., C. Marsh, and R. Jobling, (1985),
    'Political Responses to Unemployment', in B.
    Roberts, R. Finnegan, and D. Gallie, D.
    (eds.) New Approaches to Economic Life
    Manchester University Press, Manchester, pp.
    351-64
Fryer, D., and P. Ullah, (eds.) (1986) The
    Experience of Unemployment, Open University
    Press, Milton Keynes
Himmelweit, H., P. Humphreys, and M. Jaeger,
    (1985) How Voters Decide, Open University
    Press, Milton Keynes
Jahoda, M., P. Lazarsfeld and H. Zeisel (1972)
    Marienthal: The Sociography of an Unemployed
    Community, Tavistock, London
Laite, A.J. and I.A. Noble, (1986) 'Caring and
    Sharing: Factors affecting the Domestic
    Division of Labour' in D. Fryer, and P. Ullah
    The Experience of Unemployment, Open
    University Press, Milton Keynes
Lane, T. and K. Roberts, (1971) Strike at
    Pilkington's, Fontana, London
Lockwood, D. (1966) 'Sources of Variation in
    Working Class Images of Society',
    Sociological Review, 14,
Lockwood, D. (1981) 'The Weakest Link in the
    Chain? Some Comments on the Marxist Theory
    of Action', Research in the Sociology of
    Work, 1, 435-81
McKennell, A. C., (1977), 'Attitude Scale
    Construction', in C.A. O'Muircheartaigh, and
    C. Payne, (1977) The Analysis of Survey Data,
    Wiley, New York
Martin, R. and Fryer, R.H. (1973) Redundancy and
    Paternalist Capitalism, Allen and Unwin,
    London
Martin, R. and Fryer, R.H. (1975) 'The Deferential

Worker', in M. Bulmer, Working Class Images of Society, RKP/SSRC, London

Morris, L.D. (1985) 'Re-negotiation of the Domestic Division of Labour in the Context of Male Redundancy', in B. Roberts, R. Finnegan, and D. Gallie, New Approaches to Economic Life, Manchester University Press, Manchester

Newby, H. (1977) The Deferential Worker, Penguin, Harmondsworth

Noble, I. (1985) 'Voting with their Feet: an Analysis of Some Labour Defectors', After Redundancy Working Paper No. 5. Department of Sociological Studies, University of Sheffield

O'Muircheartaigh, C.A. and C. Payne, (eds.) (1977) The Analysis of Survey Data, Wiley, London

Payne, R. et. al. (1983) 'Social class and the experience of unemployment', SAPU Memo No. 549, MRC/ESRC Social and Applied Psychology Unit, University of Sheffield

Roberts, B., R. Finnegan, and D. Gallie (1985), New Approaches to Economic Life, Manchester University Press, Manchester

Rose, D. (ed.) (1986) Social Stratification and Economic Decline, Hutchinson, London

Verba, S. and K.L. Schlozman, (1979) Injury to Insult, Harvard University Press, Boston

Walker, A. (1981) 'South Yorkshire: the Economic and Social impact of Unemployment', in B. Crick, Unemployment, Methuen, London

Walker, A. (1982) 'The social consequences of early retirement', Political Quarterly, 53, 61-72

Walker, A, I. Noble, and J. Westergaard (1985) 'From Secure Employment to Labour Market Insecurity', in B. Roberts, R. Finnegan, and D. Gallie, New Approaches to Economic Life, Manchester University Press, Manchester

Warr, P. (1983) 'Economic Recession and Mental Health', SAPU Memo No. 609, MRC/ESRC Social and Applied Psychology Unit, University of Sheffield

Warr, P. and P.R. Jackson, (1983) 'Men Without Jobs: Some Correlates of Age and Length of Unemployment', SAPU Memo No. 593 MRC/ESRC Social and Applied Psychology Unit, University of Sheffield

Westergaard, J, I. Noble, and A. Walker, (1986) 'After Redundancy: Economic Experience and

Political Outlook among Former Steelworkers' in D. Rose, <u>Social Stratification and Economic Decline</u>, Hutchinson, London

Wood, D. (1982) <u>DHSS Cohort Study of Unemployed Men</u>, <u>Working Paper No. 1</u>, D.H.S.S. London

APPENDIX I

'Deference' Items

1. Most managers have the welfare of their workers at heart. (+)

2. Obedience to management and a respect for their authority are the most important characteristics of a good worker. (+)

3. If someone is in a position of authority in a firm, it's usually because of their ability. (+)

4. You've got to pay top managers a lot more than others, it's the only way to get the right people. (+)

5. When I was at .... I had a great deal of respect for top management there. (+)

6. People in top management should not be paid as much as they are, they don't deserve to be paid a lot more than other people. (-)

'Solidarity' Items

1. Working class people have got to stand together and stick up for one another. (+)

2. Given half a chance most managements will try and put one over on their workforce. (+)

3. A union member should be prepared to strike in support of other workers even when they don't work in the same place. (+)

4. If it wasn't for unions bosses could do what they wanted to with their workforce and most of them would. (+)

5. Trade unions don't have enough power, it's time they started to take a tougher line against employers and the government. (+)

6. Unions should not be allowed to stop people working when they want to. (-)

7. There should be a law to stop people joining pickets outside places where they don't work themselves. (-)

8. Unions only get in the way of good relations in industry. (-)

9. Most major conflicts in industry are caused by agitators or extemists. (-)

10. If you go on strike it should only be about matters that affect you directly in your own workplace. (-)

(+) Positively coded for scale.
(-) Negatively coded for scale.

Chapter Twelve

REDUNDANCY AND HEALTH[1]

Mel Bartley

The Iroquois, according to Sterling and Eyer
(1981), 'believed that disease could be prevented
or cured by encouraging fierce warriors to be
dependent, by helping members of the community to
act out their fantasies and by providing lonely
people with friends'. These authors go on to
discuss comprehensively the - still controversial -
question of the 'biological bases of stress related
mortality'. Their work is based on a very old
tradition in both medicine and sociology, which
sees social solidarity as related to health by way
of the 'bodily humours'. The modern version of this
humoural theory concentrates upon the responses of
the endocrine and immune systems to social
situations. It is a considerable task to relate
often very tiny physiological changes to elusive
changes in mood. Very serious problems of
measurement arise, and for this reason, research
stands in need of firm guiding theory. Only a
well-directed gaze will be able to discriminate
signal from noise.

STRESS THEORY: THE NEW HUMOURALISM

In the attempt to stimulate a longer-term interest
among non-medical sociologists in the relationship
between economic activity and health, it is
necessary briefly to outline current thinking on
the mechanisms and effects of stress. The body
possesses a self-regulating or homeostatic mechanism
which, so to speak, keeps it 'ticking over' and
ensures that changes in the internal or external
environments (caused, say, by eating or by
temperature changes) are adjusted for without
conscious effort. This balance is partly brought

about by 'local' controls, quite independent of consciousness - for example, after eating, blood sugar rises and a homeostatic feedback mechanism causes insulin to be released into the bloodstream. Failure of this mechanism is described as diabetes and regarded as a disease. Not only are these processes independent of thought, they are presently regarded as uncontrollable by conscious effort. However, some mechanisms can be set off by conscious anticipation: by thinking about food we set up secretions in the stomach if it is empty (which cause it to rumble hungrily), by fearing an event we raise our heart-rate and blood pressure, without any event having occurred.

The ability of anticipation to prepare the body physically for, say, a meal, or the necessity to take swift action is itself an important part of homeostasis. But this body-mind interface is also the mechanism which, according to stress theory, makes certain social situations harmful to health. This is because the brain and central nervous system (CNS) have the ability to override local homeostatic mechanisms and maintain, say, a high blood pressure in a situation of long-term anxiety, even when this may not be adaptive for the individual, who cannot actually do anything about it.[2]

St -George (1984) points out that arousal may produce long-term effects when it is combined with a long-term inability to resolve the source of arousal by physical action (fight or flight), or by successful 'coping' responses which change conscious response to the threatening situation. Short-term physiological responses to stress include the release of free fatty acids and cholesterol in to the blood, raised heart rate, and raised blood pressure. These responses are designed to provide energy for violent action, rather than to be maintained on a chronic basis, when they may result in harm to the cardiovascular system. In St -George's words:

> If the environmental demands cannot be removed or adequately controlled, and if attentiveness must be retained, the CNS mechanisms tend to keep the body in a state of perpetual arousal, continually mobilising energy and maintaining an increased level of cardiovascular activity. (St -George, 1984)

Work in this area continues to be controversial,

and research results are often inconsistent. As Sterling and Eyer point out:

> Hormones cause particular metabolic and physiological responses which may be associated with a _variety_ of emotions and behaviours depending on the context. The context is simply too rich and our measurements of hormonal patterns under different circumstances too impoverished to adopt ... a narrow focus.

Stress theory has made a major contribution to research on the effects of redundancy on health. Up to the present, the results are widely regarded as inconclusive. This may be because, against all common sense and against the convictions of many who have experienced redundancy, the event has in fact little or no significance for health over and above some passing emotional reaction. Or it may be that researchers have not so much a problem of method as a problem of theory. This essay will plead for the latter interpretation, and attempt to justify that plea by reviewing existing studies. The 'problems of theory' proposed here must be addressed by promoting a far wider debate on redundancy and health, and attempting to catch the interest of sociologists outside the medical field. This paper sets out to address the literature on the health effects of redundancy with three specific questions in mind: 1. What evidence do they provide that redundancy affects health? 2. How has this evidence been affected by the academic traditions of social and psychiatric epidemiology? 3. How might epidemiological accounts of the health effect of redundancy be complemented by recent advances in the sociological study of the labour process and labour markets?

The present paper will address only the question of the effect of redundancy, layoff, and plant closures on the subsequent health of redundant workers. That is, it will not attempt to deal directly with the broader issues of the effect of _unemployment_ or _recession_ on health. Although there is obvious overlap between these areas of inquiry, the investigation of the effect of redundancy is not in fact confined to looking at unemployment. Unemployment is only _one_ possible consequence of the loss of a job, and it may be that ways in which redundant workers seek and obtain re-entry to the labour force have health consequences of equal importance to those of being

laid off. Although the broader debate on unemployment
and health is not the subject of this paper (but
see Bartley 1985), it does form the background
against which the research reviewed here must be
set.

UNEMPLOYMENT AND HEALTH: THE POLITICS OF RESEARCH

In the mid-1960s, when Sidney Cobb and S.V. Kasl
were setting up the most important of the
redundancy-and-health studies (Cobb and Kasl 1977),
they needed to emphasise the possibility that
layoff, through creating stress, might precipitate
ill-health. Cobb had spent many years investigating
the effects of life events and stress upon the
development or rheumatoid arthritis, and wished to
continue this line of research. Observing a factory
closure was a way of pursuing these interests. One
method of attracting attention (and funding) into
the area was to publicise the dire financial
results of the closure of the Studebaker plant in
South Bend, Indiana, where Cobb had studied the
health of laid-off workers in the mid-1950s (Kahn
1981). The company had agreed to pay continuing
health insurance coverage for their ex-workers,
until they found new jobs. But, wrote Cobb and his
collaborators in 1966,

> the health insurance claims ... rose so high
> that for a while the corporation was unwilling
> to meet the payments. (Cobb et. al. 1966)

And they went on:

> even we who started this project with the
> expectation of a high level of social stress
> are startled. The extent to which the men are
> showing their disturbance, both at work and at
> home, is striking ... This is a project that
> is designed to carry out some basic research
> in the investigation of a significant social
> problem. (Cobb et. al. 1966)

By using this rhetoric, Cobb and co-workers
based at the University of Michigan engage in the
sort of necessary entrepreneurialism described by
Aronson (1982), which scientists adopt to draw
attention to a field in which they wish to work.
'Redundancy and health' was claimed as a 'social
problem' in order to enable research on stress and

health to be carried forward. The issue was duly adopted by, amongst other institutions, the United Auto Workers, who offered both moral and financial support, and ensured the co-operation of the workforce with the study. By 1974, eight years later, Cobb could still complain that 'longitudinal studies of the effects of social stress are quite rare'. In 1975, Kasl, Gore and Cobb pronounced themselves convinced that:

> studying intensively and longitudinally the effects of one stressful life event, such as job loss, is an exceedingly complex business. Different outcome variables may show strikingly different patterns of changes and all appear to be sensitive to characteristics of the person and of the social situation. (Kasl, Gore and Cobb, 1975).

In 1977 the Michigan study team felt they could state that:

> ... physiological changes suggesting an increased likelihood of coronary disease took place, as did changes in blood sugar, pepsinogen, and uric acid, suggesting increased risk of diabetes, peptic ulcer and gout. There was an increase in arthritis and hypertension. (Cobb and Kasl 1977, p. iii).

Between 1966 and the late 1970s, two factors had acted to change the tone of the debate on unemployment and health in the USA. One was the rising rate of unemployment, and the other was the work of M.H. Brenner (see Brenner 1971, 1973, 1975). In 1976, Brenner presented a report to the US Congress Joint Economic Committee (Brenner 1976), in which he claimed that a one per cent increase in the US unemployment rate, sustained over a period of six years, had been associated with approximately 36,900 additional deaths (see also Draper et. al. 1979). At a time of rising unemployment and deflationary government policies, both in the United States and in Britain, there was no longer any need for academics to convince policy makers and research funding bodies that 'unemployment and health' constituted a 'social problem' of public importance. But what policy makers were now interested in was a more sober and less sensationalist appraisal of Brenner's gloomy prognostications. Could his conclusions, drawn from studies using macro-economic techniques correlating national rates of unemployment and mortality, be borne out by studies of unemployed individuals? Kasl and Cobb's study (which had run out of funds after the end of the fieldwork and had to be written up by the investigators in their own time) seemed well placed to be used as an example.

However, by 1982, the Michigan investigators' papers reflect a great deal more scepticism about the severity of the health effects of redundancy. Kasl concluded in 1982 that:

> Analyses of cardiovascular risk factors (blood pressure, serum cholesterol, cigarette smoking, body weight) did not at any point reveal a level of cardiovascular risk amongst men losing their jobs exceeding the risk among controls ... overall, the findings fail to provide support for the hypotheses derived from the business cycle and mortality analyses ... (Kasl 1982).

Interest in investigating the degree to which, and the mechanism by which, stress associated with social change and life event damages physical health, has now decreased. The question of major interest is whether or not press headlines and pressure group activity around 'Deaths on the Dole' can be justified by epidemiological research.

THE MICHIGAN STUDY

Studies of factory closures form a relatively small proportion of the extensive literature on unemployment and health. Yet, as pointed out by Kasl (1982), they make the major contribution to our knowledge about the effect of unemployment on the health of individuals, as opposed to that of communities. Most closure studies have been primarily oriented towards psychological health and 'illness behaviour' (defined by Mechanic and Volkart (1961) as the 'way in which symptoms are perceived, evaluated and acted upon by a person who recognises some pain, discomfort or other signal organic malfunction'). This is at least partly because (a) change in psychological health often takes place relatively quickly after stressful events; and (b) changes in illness behaviour have implications for demand on health services and thus attract the attention of research funding bodies.

Of the studies of physical health, that of Cobb and Kasl (which is usually referred to as the 'Michigan Study' and has already been mentioned) has been by far the most influential. There appear to be two major findings of persisting relevance:

(i) That the physiological and psychological effects of job-loss on the men they sampled were no more severe than those of <u>anticipation</u> of redundancy

(ii) That the social and economic context of the two factories which closed made a large impact on the health effects of the closures. The differences between redundant rural workers and redundant urban workers were as great as those between those who lost their jobs and those who kept them (Kasl and Cobb, 1982).

Two plants were chosen which were about to close down; 'Baker' (an urban factory producing paint for the automobile industry) and 'Dawson' (a rural plant making lightweight indent fixtures). In accordance with good epidemiological practice, two factories <u>not</u> about to close were used as 'controls'. Both 'cases' (men who underwent redundancy) and 'controls' (men in steady employment) were chosen to be between 35 and 60, married and with considerable seniority in their jobs. Forty-six men were sampled from 'Baker' and 54 from 'Dawson'.

Measures of physical and mental health were compared between the terminees and the continuously employed men, and also between the terminees at various stages of job loss and re-employment. Men who knew that their jobs were to be abolished showed some differences from controls in those physiological functions regarded as related to stress (as discussed earlier) (Cobb 1974). But these differences were already observable during the anticipation phase, and further deterioration directly attributable to unemployment itself was relatively minor. High levels of, for example, blood pressure and serum uric acid, registered for cases at the anticipation phase, returned towards the control group levels at the end of two years, in those men who went more or less straight into steady re-employment, and eventually the cases once again began to look <u>healthier</u> than the control group, as they had at the beginning of the study. However, all the physiological changes recorded

311

were small.

On measures of depression, anxiety and lack of self-esteem, Cobb and Kasl found no significant support for their prediction 'that men becoming re-employed will show a sizeable drop, men remaining unemployed will show some increase, ...' They go on: 'The major conclusion would seem to be that it is not always wise to predict continued response to prolonged stress from the evidence of sensitivity to brief stress' (Cobb and Kasl, 1977, pp. 65-8).

The mortality experience of 208 men from the 'Baker' factory was followed for three years. Eight of these men died, which was no more than expected on the basis of their age. Amongst the 46 'Baker' men more closely studied, however, two committed suicide in the two-year period from three months prior to closure. This is 30 times the number expected on the basis of age-sex-specific US national suicide rates. On the subject of stress-related risk factors for heart disease, Cobb and Kasl concluded (in their 1977 Report): 'To those familiar with factors contributing to the risk of heart disease, this narrative will certainly suggest that the unemployment experience raised the risk' (Cobb and Kasl 1977, p.135). But they were later to revise this opinion, as we have seen.

In a 1982 paper, Kasl and Cobb turned their attention to the effects of urban versus rural location. Only in the urban setting was the length of unemployment correlated with the amount of 'subjective impact', that is, with scores on a scale measuring how the subject rated the impact of his redundancy as compared to other life events, in terms of severity. Being still unemployed at Phase 2 of the follow-up (six weeks after closure) was a far less depressive and anxiety-provoking experience for rural men, but it was also associated with a rise in blood pressure, whereas the urban men experienced falls in blood pressure once they had been laid off, whether or not they regained employment (Kasl and Cobb 1982). This was a severe blow to the original hypothesis of the Michigan study.

OTHER FACTORY CLOSURE STUDIES

There is only one British study of the health consequences of a factory closure. This was an

eight-year follow-up of 80 male and 49 female
workers who were laid off when the Harris meat
products plant closed down in the small market town
of Calne, Wiltshire (Beale and Nethercott, 1985).
Like 'Dawson', Harris was the only industrial
concern of any size in the town. As at 'Baker',
final closure only came after a protracted period
of anticipation and uncertainty among the workers.

One author of the study is a British general
practitioner, in whose practice all the subjects
were registered throughout the period of observation.
All were laid off between June and July 1982 (at a
time of high unemployment, in contrast to the
mid-1960s in Michigan), and had previously been
employed at Harris' for at least two years in a
full-time capacity. A control group of stably
employed persons was recruited from other local
workplaces (77 men and 22 women). Men aged 61 and
over, and women aged 56 and over were excluded on
the grounds that they could be regarded as 'early
retired'.

The eight-year period of the study was divided
up into three sections: year 1-4 when the jobs of
all members of the study group (cases as well as
controls) were secure; year 5 and 6 which were
'anticipation' years for the Harris workers; and
years 7 and 8 which were post-redundancy for the
cases. This design was possible because all data on
the health of this sample was extracted from their
medical records: no interviews or special health
examinations were carried out. In years 5 to 8,
members of the families of those workers made
redundant consulted their doctors 20% more often
than they had in years 1 to 4. There was also a
10.6% increase in the number of episodes of illness
reported by the families of terminees in the
'insecure' and 'redundant' phases of the study
(years 5 to 8) compared to a 9.3% decrease in
episodes amongst controls, although this result was
not statistically significant. Beale and Nethercott
were surprised that the increases in illness and
consultation began at the anticipation phase, thus
confirming the suspicion of Cobb and Kasl that
anticipation is as threatening as job loss itself.

However, although this is a controlled study,
the workers and their families were not interviewed,
nor were detailed health measurements carried out.
The conclusion that Harris families' illnesses were
more severe than those of controls during
anticipation and job-loss is derived from the
finding that these individuals consulted more often

per episode of illness, and were more likely to be referred to hospital. The question of whether these differences in illness behaviour and clinical perception reflect underlying physiological 'reality' can only be answered by further follow-up. Further research on this group's post-redundancy work histories is also promised, which will be an important step.

The only other North American study of the effects of a plant closure on health comes from Canada (Grayson 1985). In December 1981 the multi-national bearing manufacturing concern, SKF, closed down its Canadian factory, making 310 men and women redundant. Grayson is careful to take account of the economic environment in which the closure took place. In the early 1980s, the Canadian economy was in a very different state to that in the USA in the mid 1960s. Like 'Baker' and 'Dawson's' parent companies, SKF carried out the closure in the interests of economic efficiency and rationalisation of their corporate operation. Grayson also selected his sample size (approx 100) and designed his interviewing schedule to allow comparison with Cobb and Kasl's work.

Health was measured in 3 ways: 1. Self-reported health, from 'excellent' to 'poor', 2. number of consultations in the past six months, 3. whether or not the respondent was taking prescribed medication. Unlike Cobb and Kasl, Grayson was unable to take physiological measurements. Physical health (so defined) of the employees who did not find work after redundancy deteriorated over time (1982-1984). Interestingly, however, and relevant to the argument being developed here, those who failed to find work were in poorer health prior to redundancy. Also in contrast to Cobb and Kasl, Grayson found that the levels of self-reported stress (measured in the same way) remained high as long as the redundant workers were unemployed. Even amongst those who found work, stress levels rose again, towards the levels found in the continuously unemployed over the subsequent two years of follow-up. In order to examine the various possible relationships between employment status, health, income, age and skill, Grayson adopted the technique of path analysis. The major finding of the path-analysis procedure was that ill-health preceding closure was the major predictor of both future ill-health and future unemployment, and, thereby, of low income level subsequent to closure. He finds support for the idea

> that in times of high unemployment, the 'misfits' - in this case those with ill-health - are not tolerated by prospective employers,

and furthermore,

> should the labour market open up, it is a moot point as to whether or not it will open first to the healthy and only later to those with ill-health. A further possibility is that the latter will end up with low-paying jobs, as employers will be unwilling to pay top dollar for employees who they may view as potential liabilities.

While disagreeing with Cobb and Kasl that the health effects of unemployment decrease over time, Grayson recognises that 'relations between stress attributed to closure, and ill health appear to dissipate'. That is, those former SKF employees who reported feeling more stressed by closure did not go on to become the most ill at 26 months' follow-up. This, he concludes

> would suggest that after the first few months of unemployment, the causes of increased ill-health among the unemployed may have to be sought in factors other than those associated with stress attributed to closure per se.

This point is further supported by the authors of another redundancy study, that of a shipyard in Denmark in 1976 (Iversen and Klausen 1982). They also found that:

> After plant shutdown the workers will undergo a sorting process on the labour market ... the middle aged worker who loses a job often has to be on the dole for months - even years ... And when he is offered a job he is not in a position where he can raise demands about what kind of work he would like. He has to take what comes ...

Once again, there were 100 workers (men and women). All members of the workforce were studied in this case. The authors had intended to carry out a study of work and health, when the shipyard unexpectedly went out of business. As a result, all workers had received comprehensive health screening 6 months before redundancy. Three follow-up interviews were conducted, but there were insufficient

resources to repeat the medical examinations. And
there was no control group. After three months,
there was a rise in the consumption of medicines.
Those workers who experienced the most unemployment
also 'experienced an increase in emotional
problems'. Fifteen months post-closure, medicine
consumption was still high in comparison to the
levels in the pre-redundancy survey. However, in
those workers whose subsequent careers included
long periods of unemployment, bronchitis and heart
trouble had decreased, although psychological
distress continued to increase. Alcohol consumption
fell and remained low, even at a three-year
follow-up. Iversen and Klausen failed to confirm
Cobb and Kasl's findings of raised blood pressure
at the 'anticipation' phase and at the time of
lay-off. They conclude:

> Instead of using highly standarised interviews
> and questionnaires ... it will be preferable
> to make more qualitative intensive interviews
> which allow the workers to describe their
> complex situation in totality and not
> standardised answers.

The other Scandinavian closure study is only
available in English as a summary. This is the
research reported by Westin and Norum on what
happens 'When the Sardine Factory is Shut Down'
(Westin and Norum 1977). Once again, there were
approximately 100 subjects (actually 95), who
constituted the whole workforce. Interviews and
medical examinations were carried out during the
period of closure and again after 15 months. Unlike
all other closure studies in which health outcomes
have been examined, this one included a majority of
women (21 men, 74 women). Most were long-serving
workers, relatively old, and with little formal
education (similar to the 'Baker' and 'Dawson'
men). Westin and Norum found that levels of health
in these workers were low, and their ability to
remain in the labour force at all depended to a
large extent on the nearness of the factory to
their homes, and the flexibility of working hours.
They comment that the sardine factory operated as a
sort of 'sheltered workshop'.

Only 22 of the workers had found new jobs
fifteen months after closure, and 38 had been
continuously unemployed. Some 27 workers, though
registered at the employment exchange, had made no
active effort to find another job. Adding these to

the one retired worker and 10 who had become 'disabled', the authors conclude that the rate of 'labour market exclusion' (i.e. adding up retirement, long-term disability and the housewife role) resulting from the closure was around 40%.

As local doctors, Westin and Norum were interested (like Beale and Nethercott) in the effect of the closure on the health service. They found that:

> Patients in a social role between employment and social welfare will experience problems with a social welfare legislation (sic) that is based on a traditional model of sickness. Special attention has been paid to the conflicting roles experienced by physicians when asked to give medical certificates concerning occupational disability, when the most important reason for the patient's apparent disability is his loss of a very special employment situation rather than his medical condition as such.

Cobb and Kasl had also expressed concern at the consequences of redundancy for the insurance status of the old men in their study. In European welfare states, the redundant worker can often negotiate some kind of alternative status (such as long-term disability benefit or sickness benefit, or early retirement) which is slightly more in financial terms than basic forms of social assistance, and includes provision for health care. In the USA, however, the situation is more serious. Three years after closure of the plants, only 58% of Cobb and Kasl's redundants had pension coverage for their retirement (as compared with 98% of the control group of men who had retained their jobs). They state.:

> These long-term follow-up studies strongly suggest that the biggest economic impact of the original plant closing may not be due to the immediately ensuing episode of unemployment, but will be a delayed effect at retirment. (Cobb and Kasl 1977, p.24)

More recently, Berki et. al. (1985) have shown that in the Detroit area many workers also lose their health insurance along with their jobs. They point out that: '85% of Americans covered by private health insurance obtain it as a fringe benefit of employment'. Yet they were unable to

317

find studies of unemployment populations which investigate health insurance coverage and access to health care. Their own survey included 1332 unemployed individuals, of whom 51% were found to have no health insurance. They also point out that as their sample was of people in receipt of unemployment compensation, it excluded jobless people who, through chronic unemployment or disability, failed to qualify for such compensation, and is therefore likely to overestimate the degree to which the unemployed have health insurance coverage.

In the USA, as in Britain, rising unemployment has been accompanied by cuts in welfare services, and the combined effects are now beginning to show in official health statistics at the regional level. In a 1983 report entitled <u>The Impact of Unemployment on the Health of Mothers and Children in Michigan</u> for the Subcommittee on Labor Standards of the US Committee on Education and Labor, Walker (1983) points out that in 1981, infant mortality in Michigan increased for the first time in thirty years, from 12.8 per 1000 live births in 1980, to 13.2 per 1000 in 1981. The total number of suscribers to Blue Cross/Blue Shield medical insurance plus their dependents in Michigan dropped by nearly 600,000 between 1979 and October of 1982. Of the 20,000 persons each month who exhaust their unemployment benefits, only between 1 and 2,000 are picked up by AFDC or Medicaid schemes. It will be important, in future studies, to take account of national and regional differences not only in the type and availability of jobs, but also the administration of welfare and social insurance.

THE SOCIAL PROCESS OF REDUNDANCY

The wider debate on the effects of unemployment on health has generated a series of puzzles which the (admittedly small) number of studies of health consequences of redundancy, lay-off and plant closure have not succeeded in answering. Among the more important of these puzzles are the following:

1. Aggregate time-series studies of national trends in unemployment and adult mortality yield inconsistant findings, which seem to depend very much on what years are included in the series (Gravelle, Hutchinson and Stern 1981: Forbes 1984: MacAvinchey

1984).

2. Long-term follow-up of people classified as 'seeking work' at the British 1971 Census (Moser et. al. 1984) show that these people have a raised risk of mortality in the following ten year period, but,

3. Small-scale studies (such as Fagin and Little 1984: Iversen and Klausen 1977) show that for some people, a spell of unemployment may result in a diminution of physical symptoms.

4. The subjective experience of redundancy and unemployment is universally found to be unpleasant (see Warr 1985) and to provoke anxiety, depression, and loss of self-esteem amongst most of those who experience it. Yet, studies of groups of redundant workers have not demonstrated consistently adverse health outcomes, as has been done for other major loss experiences such as bereavement.

Perhaps, in the same way that studies of the health effects of bereavement are situated within an understanding of the psycho-social aspects of family life, studies of the health effects of redundancy should be situated more firmly within an understanding of the labour process and labour markets (for example, as in Scheinstock 1985). Wood and Cohen (1977), Harris, Lee and Morris (1985) and Lee (1985) have argued for a greater degree of concern with the 'social process of redundancy'. Existing research on this process reveals certain common features of plant closures and large-scale redundancies, all of which may have implications for the health of workers involved. These are:

1. Redundancy is often selective, 'a process of invidious selection which leaves some individuals attached to the reduced stock of jobs' (Harris, Lee and Morris 1985)

2. Redundancies may be concentrated amongst certain types of jobs - those which can most easily be 'casualised', and hence may produce changes in the whole local labour market by producing an increased demand for certain sorts of labour.

3. There is often a 'cooling-out' process involved in redundancies, which reconciles redundants-to-be with their fate, for

> example, by stressing the attractions of early retirement, disability benefit, self- employment, etc.

Redundant workers should therefore not all be lumped together for purposes of study (whether this be of their health or any other consequence). To do so is to commit the 'fallacy of misplaced aggregation'.

These aspects of the social process of redundancy may be conceptualised in terms of the 'social overhead costs' of employing workers. Although social overhead is not a Marxist term, the concept can be elaborated with the help of certain ideas drawn from Marxist analysis of the labour process (Blane 1985):

> (a) the 'historical and moral' element in the cost of the worker's means of subsistence (i.e. the degree to which wages and conditions allow more than mere survival), a factor exemplified by Marx's discussion of the role of class struggle in determining the length of the working day,
> (b) the cost of the reproduction of labour power itself, i.e. of producing the next generation of workers, and also of replacing the mental and physical energies (the 'health') of the individual worker day by day,
> (c) the costs of training and socialising the new generation of young workers, ·
> (d) another social overhead cost not considered by Marx at all is the question of the maintenance of older and less fit workers in the labour force, despite their lower levels of productivity (Moylan, Millar and Davis 1984).

The question of who bears these costs may be regarded as 'essentially contestable' in industrial societies. An example of a national industrial system bearing as few of these costs as possible may be taken from the Swiss experience, where unskilled workers from other countries are admitted for short periods only, without their families, with no right to vote or join trade unions, and must return home when not gainfully employed (and permanently once they are too old to work). In this case, the vast majority of the social overhead costs are borne by the country of origin.[3] In various other places, and at other historical periods, these costs have been wholly or partly borne by the extended family, the smallholding, the parish, the Friendly societies, and the state. Under conditions of full employment in a capitalist economy, perhaps we come nearest to seeing the <u>individual</u> as able to carry many of these him or herself. Indeed, this development has been an important source of legitimation for ideas of individual freedom, and of a decreasing perceived need for restrictive institutions such as church and extended family. However, in order for this to appear to happen, I want to argue that certain conditions must exist in the labour market.

Firstly, there must be enough demand for labour to allow workers to leave unbearably stressful jobs, regardless of the 'objective' nature of the stress, and for such voting-with the-feet to motivate employers to improve conditions (the 'Social Medicine' of the 1950s contained a huge literature on prevention of turnover and absenteeism, under conditions of very high demand for labour). Secondly, it must not be possible for the threat of exclusion from the workforce to prevent workers organising, both formally and informally, to soften the impact of a constant pace of work. This allows for the normal and inevitable variation in state of health and mood to be accommodated within a worker's routine, without loss of income. Thirdly, a truly 'full-employment' economy must contain occupational roles for those (all workers at <u>some</u> stage in life) who are no longer, or never have been, in full physical health, who are raising children or caring for other dependants. Fourthly, wage levels must be sufficient to allow the worker to insure in some manner against the contingencies which may force him or her to stop waged work, temporarily or permanently.

If we re-define the question of unemployment and health in terms which reflect a wider definition of health such as the World Health Organisation's ('physical, mental and social well-being') and adopt Townsend's definition of 'subsistence' as a level of material welfare which allows full participation in community life, some of the paradoxes in existing research on unemployment and health may be resolved. Redundancy (now regarded as 'socially produced') may be found to have effects along a <u>continuum</u> of 'health' defined in these terms. We therefore need no longer search

for elusive break-points in misleadingly aggregated
data. The idea that redundancies are normally
carried out in order to reduce the social overhead
costs of employing labour may provide a guide to
ways in which redundant workers may be divided into
those expected to be more and less at risk of
adverse health consequences, in the short or the
long term.

When a tightening labour market begins to
economise on social overhead costs, as in Britain
of the 1980s, we see the labour force becoming
truncated at the ends of the age spectrum. The
costs of socialising and training are 'rationalised
out' when young workers cannot find work, or when
they must stick to the first job they find rather
than develop their skills and interests by a
pattern of frequent job-changing often found in
this age group at times of high employment (Daniel
and Stilgoe 1979). Workers with large families find
it more difficult to remain in jobs (Millar 1982;
Stern 1979; Moylan, Millar and Davis 1984).
Disabled and older workers are 'sorted out' into
early retirement, long-term disability, or the
housewife role (Bartley 1985, Bungener et. al.
1982; Arber, Gilbert and Dale 1985). Whiteside
(1985) has shown how, in the 1930s, even the
wearing of spectacles could be enough to 'lose a
man his place'. Furthermore, there is evidence
(Noble, Walker and Westergaard 1985; Fevre 1985)
that less fit and older workers are rendered more
vulnerable, not only to unemployment, but to the
hazards of 'casualised' employment, just at the
very stage in life where they are physically least
able to withstand them. Health status (mental and
physical) following redundancy is therefore to be
expected to be partially determined by prior health
status. But this does not mean that 'unemployment/
redundancy does not harm health'. On the contrary,
disadvantages in the labour market caused by
pre-existing ill-health may result in a form of
double jeopardy. Those least acceptable to
employers are less likely to be able to regain the
sort of stable employment which is most protective,
but may rather find themselves taking a series of
short-term jobs without the benefit of union or
safety representation. It may be that we do not
need to rely on the existence of 'stress effects'
to account for the consequences of redundancy and
unemployment for physical health. At the very
least, research informed by a stress theory should
be complemented by an approach which is sensitive

to post-redundancy work histories and the hazards these may involve.

Martin and Fryer (1973), in a study of redundancy in the late 1960s, found that:

> ... redundancy proved beneficial for many of the voluntary leavers, stimulating them to move to better paid jobs, and rarely involving any significant period of unemployment ... However, it proved to be a different story for the elderly redundant; for them the redundancy proved to be a major calamity, leading to long periods of unemployment and eventually to jobs with lower status and lower wages (Martin and Fryer 1973, p.151)

And Lee and Harris (1985) propose that,

> Workers extruded into the labour market in the kind of situation seen at Port Talbot [in the early 1980s] are likely to be of less productive value to the enterprise from which they have been expelled than other categories of worker. However, they are also more likely to be those whose labour market chances are relatively low.

A RE-INTERPRETATION OF THE REDUNDANCY STUDIES

Ironically, it is also consistent with this argument that those workplaces which carry a greater proportion of the social overhead costs of employing labour (hence to some greater or lesser extent functioning as 'sheltered workshops' as did the Sardine Factory in Westin and Norum's study) will be those most vulnerable to closure. Cobb and Kasl's middle-aged 'Baker' and 'Dawson' men were mysteriously healthier than those in the 'control' factories not threatened with closure. This paradox now becomes fully explicable. As will be seen below, working conditions, at least at 'Baker' (we do not really know enough about 'Dawson') had been relatively favourable for many years. Another puzzle clarified by a view of redundancy as a process is that of the relative severity, relected in terms of illness behaviour and also physio-logical changes, of the 'anticipation' phases of these closures. Prior to the closure of 'Baker' (and Harris Meats), the management put their workforces 'on trial' for up to two years. At

'Baker', productivity rose dramatically, and so did blood pressure. We do not know about productivity at Harris', but there, as at 'Baker', excess consultations began during this period, not after redundancy. At Iversen and Klausen's shipyard, which closed suddenly, without a 'trial period', there was no rise in blood pressure prior to layoff. Locating the events surrounding a closure or large-scale layoff within its local labour market may also help to explain another paradox in the Michigan study. 'Dawson' men were not as depressed as expected by closure, or by consider- able amounts of subsequent unemployment (Gore 1978). However, the authors comment, in passing, that many of them were 'part time farmers' (Cobb and Kasl 1977, p.3,) and therefore participated in quite a different sort of way in the local labour market.

Fortunately there is a complementary account of the closure of 'Baker', one of the factories in the Michigan Study (Slote 1969), which allows us to attempt a re-analysis of this particular case-study, to see whether attention to the social production of redundancy and social overhead costs of the labour process may throw light upon the health consequences. Published in 1969, eight years before the main report (i.e. Cobb and Kasl 1977), it includes a forward by Cobb. Interestingly Cobb commends an approach which can

> break those people who will be affected by the change into groups and predict which groups will suffer the most. Presently it is my impression that the most vulnerable are those who are on special duty because of disability, those who are in the last ten years of their working lives, and those who have problems of physical or mental health even though they may not be currently working under any job restrictions.

Slote interviewed, not a random sample, but key actors in the drama, from the workforce (both blue and white collar), the management and the union. His account is rich with insight, and often very funny. It also anticipates some of the recent sociological work on the social production of redundancy, and allows these ideas to be applied to the closure at 'Baker'.

First, the extent to which social overhead costs were carried within the labour process in this particular factory is openly commented on by many of the people Slote interviewed. One industrial relations manager, for example, told him:

> That's what this place was for forty years. One big family. We carried everyone. Gold-brickers, goof-offs, crooks. We had picnics, bowling leagues, softball teams, chess teams ... We were hiring Negroes [sic] before it was fashionable ... (Slote 1969, p.7)

Slote quotes other members of the management insisting that this had to end: 'Baker had a tradition of goldbricking that went back forty years ... You can't expect a company to subsidise life tenure for an employee ...'. A laboratory technician admitted,

> None of us worked hard there and that's why they closed up. We didn't deserve that plant. All the goof-offs and the goldbrickers. It was a regular old folks home. (Slote 1969, p. 1-2)

Another striking account of the uneconomic humanitarianism of working life at 'Baker' is provided by a story of one employee who was known to be a heavy drinker, but managed to hold down his job, with some help from his friends:

> Why, I can remember one morning Orvie showed up ... drunk as a skunk ... Orvie drives his car right into the truck-well [loading bay], and opens the door and steps out and falls right on his face. Someone calls out 'Get that man back in his car, he's in no shape to walk' ... Well, someone got Orvie off to a corner where he could lay down and sleep it off ... He was still on a bender from Friday night and he came to the only place that'd take him in - Baker. (Slote 1969, p. 236, my emphasis)

Shortly after closure, this worker committed suicide. This example, and others given by Slote of families cracking under the strain of redundancy, implies that in some cases it is the workplace which carries some of the emotional costs of family life. This finding is consistent with British work by Fagin and Little (1984) and Brown and Harris (1978), for example, which indicates that, whilst social support provided by the family may enable some workers to cope with the stresses of work, in other cases, work-roles may also attenuate the effect of family conflict. Although there is insufficient research at present on the effects of unemployment on family life (as remarked by Gallie 1985), what little we have tends to suggest that existing strain in family relationships may be worsened by the unemployment of the breadwinner(s) (McKee and Bell 1985).

Secondly, Slote's account also makes it clear that 'invidious selection' operated in the case of the 'Baker' closure, but here it was extended to the whole of the workforce. All the men were regarded as of sub-optimal productive value to the enterprise. Not only because they were 'goldbricking', and 'goofing-off', but because the strength of the union forced management to adhere to an elaborate grievance procedure and to observe 'seniority' (see Cornfield, this volume). In the words of an industrial relations manager:

> Seniority makes it impossible for a competent young man to be paid more than an incompetent older man. So you find it cheaper in the end to close down the old plant and terminate it and terminate the incompetent older man. (Slote 1969, p. 139)

And in the words of a company lawyer:

> The Baker people would have brought their bad work habits with them ... Transferred employees ... restrict their production to the level they feel was satisfactory at the old plant ... Do you know who we've got working for us in Ohio (the site of the new plant replacing 'Baker')? Farmers. In a paint plant only the maintenance people and maybe the resin kettle operators are legitimately skilled workers. (Slote 1969, p. 141)

By moving the process to a new location, 'Baker's' corporate management could at one stroke rid itself of unionisation, impose a faster pace of work, and abolish 'excessive' worker autonomy associated with 'skilled' status, which had been extended too far down the labour hierarchy, in their opinion. As lack of autonomy at work and machine pacing of work have been associated in several studies with coronary heart disease, this might suggest that one place we should look for the

health effects of the 'Baker' closure would be to
the health of workers in the new plant (Alfredsson,
Spetz and Theorell, 1985; Timio and Gentili, 1979).

The effects of the removal of such forms of
protection are witnessed by one 61 year old
ex-'Baker' employee's case history. When first told
of the impending closure, he was nonchalant.
However, on applying for other jobs, he was obliged
to take fitness examinations, and was found to be
mildly diabetic and hypertensive, despite a
previously clean health record.

> Times were good, I was in good health; I was
> only 58 ... Well, I'm going to tell you
> something, a man doesn't know how old he is
> till something like this happens ... I guess
> in this world some people can manage and
> others got to be taken care of. I always
> thought I could manage, but I don't think that
> any more. (Slote 1969, p. 191-2)

Thirdly, 'cooling-out' was clearly used by the
management, in an attempt to forestall vandalism
and absenteeism by a vengeful workforce. The
plant's senior shop steward was given unlimited
time for union business. A new plant manager was
appointed, who had risen from the ranks and 'knew
all the men'. However, that neither the 'softness'
of normal working conditions, not that of the
'cooling out process' were entirely a result of
management paternalism is also clear. That senior
shop steward's attitude to the management's
negotiating team who came to begin discussions of
the redundancies with the union, was expressed
thus:

> And then in they came, the management. That
> drunk Green [industrial relations manager];
> Harrah [company lawyer] wearing his suspenders
> and looking like a taxi dancer; and little
> Robertson [plant manager] tiptoeing along in
> the rear, smiling his little weasel smile.
> (Slote 1969, p.89)

The importance of demand for the company's
product, and of the state of the local labour
market is also made visible in Slote's account. As
one manager told him,

> We couldn't afford strikes, slowdowns,
> walkouts. We were always counterpunching to

the big Chrysler and Ford plants ... (Slote 1969, p.47)

What this alternative account of one of the factory closure studies shows, is that it is possible to study the process of redundancy in such a way as to be more specific about what it may be about any given workplace or work process that is protective of mental and physical vulnerability, and in what groups the loss of this protection may have the most severe consequences. The epidemiological study of 'Baker' did not complete this task, but in combination with Slote's sociological account, it points a clear way forward. Unfortunately this classic pilot study has never been followed up.

CONCLUSION

The blindness of orthodox epidemiology to social processes is notorious, and has been much commented on (for example, Scott-Samuel 1981; Cameron and Jones 1982, Jones 1983). The Michigan study was no exception, despite the obvious social sensitivity of its senior investigators. The use of 'age, sex and social class' to define and exhaust criteria of comparability is standard practice, ignoring the many other characteristics which may allow health-relevant distinctions between groups to be better understood. In its epidemiological form, medicine performs important social control functions by individualising social problems (Wright and Treacher 1982). Epidemiology, that branch of medicine which is concerned with the health of human communities (see Smith, 1985), finds progress difficult in the absence of theories about social action, some of which force consideration of conflict into unwelcome prominence. The academic debate on the health effects of redundancy is therefore situated at a crucial point in the development of a discipline.

NOTES

 1. I would like to thank Tricia Carroll and Cathy Hanner for invaluable technical assistance in preparing this paper.

 2. This discussion draws heavily on Sterling and Eyer (1981), whose paper is strongly recommended to anyone interested in a fuller elaboration of these points.

 3. I am indebted to David Blane for pointing this out to me.

REFERENCES

Alfredsson, A., C.L. Spetz, and T. Theorell, (1985)
     'Type of Occupation and Near-future Hospital-
     isation for Myocardial Infarction and Some
     Other Diagnoses' International Journal of
     Epidemiology, 14, 378-88
Arber, S., G.N. Gilbert, and A. Dale, (1985) 'Paid
     Employment and Women's Health: Benefit or
     Source of Role Strain?' Sociology of Health
     and Illness, 7, 375-400
Aronson, N. (1982) 'Science as a Social Problem; a
     Case Study of Entrepreneurial Strategy in
     Science' Social Problems, 29, 467-74
Bartley, M.J. (1985a) 'Health and Unemployment'
     Bulletin of the Society for the Social
     History of Medicine, 36, 56-60
_____ (1985b) 'Unemployment and Health, Selection
     or Causation - A false antithesis?' Paper to
     British Sociological Association Medical
     Group Conference 1985
Beale, N.R., and S. Nethercott, (1985) 'Job Loss
     and Family Morbidity. A Factory Closure Study
     in General Practice' Journal of the Royal
     College of General Practitioners, 35, 510-14
Berki, S.E., L. Wyszewianski, R. Lichtenstein,
     P. Gimotty, J.E. Bowlyow, E. Papke, T.B.
     Smith, S.C. Crane, J. Bromberg, (1985)
     'Health Insurance Coverage of the Unemployed'
     Medical Care, 23, 847-54
Blane, D.B. (1985) 'The Value of Labour Power and
     Workers' Health' Paper presented to British
     Sociological Association Medical Sociology
     Group Annual Conference 1985
Brenner, M.H. (1971) 'Economic Changes and Heart
     Disease Mortality' American Journal of Public
     Health, 61, 606-12
_____ (1973) 'Foetal, Infant and Maternal
     Mortality during Periods of Economic
     Instability' International Journal of Health
     Services, 3, 145-59
_____ (1975) 'Trends in Alchohol Consumption and
     Associated Illnesses - Some Effects of
     Economic Change' American Journal of
     Public Health, 65, 1279-1292
_____ (1976) Estimating the Social Costs
     of National Economic Policy U.S. Government
     Printing Office, Washington, D.C.
Bungener, M., C. Horrelou-Lafarge, and M.V. Louis,
     (1982) Chômage et Sante Economica, Paris
Cameron, D., and I. Jones (1982) 'Theory in

Community Medicine' Community Medicine, 4,
3-11
Cobb, S., G.W. Brooks, S.V. Kasl, and W.E.
Connelly, (1966) 'The Health of People
Changing Jobs: a Description of a Longitudinal
Study' American Journal of Public Health, 56,
1476-81
_____ 'Physiological changes in men whose jobs
were abolished' J. of Psychosomatic Medicine,
18, 245-58
_____ and S.V. Kasl, (1977) Termination: The
Consequences of Job Loss DHEW-NIOSH Public-
ation no 77-224, Cincinatti, National
Institute for Occupational Safety and Health
Daniel, W.W., and E. Stilgoe, (1979) Where Are They
Now? A Follow-up Study of the Unemployed,
Political and Economic Planning, London
Draper, P., J. Dennis, J. Griffiths, T. Partridge,
and J. Popay, (1979) 'Micro-processors,
Macro-economic Policy, and Public Health'
Lancet, i, 373-5
Fagin, L., and M. Little, (1984) The Forsaken
Families, Harmondsworth, Penguin
Fevre, R. (1986) 'Contract Work in the Recession'
in Wood, S. and K. Purcell, (eds) The
Changing Experience of Work: Restructuring
and Recession, Macmillan, London
Finnegan, R., B. Roberts, and D. Gallie, (1985) New
Approaches to Economic Life, Manchester
University Press, Manchester
Forbes, J.F., and A. McGregor, (1984) 'Mortality
and Unemployment in Post-War Scotland'
Journal of Health Economics, 3, 239-57
Gallie, D. (1985) 'Social Change and Economic
Life: the Current State of Research'
Quarterly Journal of Social Affairs, 1,
61-86
Gore, S. (1978) 'The Effect of Social Support in
Moderating the Health Consequences of
Unemployment' Journal of Health and Social
Behaviour, 19, 157-65
Gravelle, H.S.E., J. Hutchinson, and J. Stern,
(1981) 'Mortality and Unemployment: a Critique
of Brenner's Time-Series Analysis' Lancet, ii,
675-79
Grayson, J.P. (1985) 'The Closure of a Factory and
its Impact on Health' International Journal
of Health Services, 15, 69-93
Harris, C.C., R.M. Lee, and L.D. Morris, (1985)
'Redundancy in Steel: Labour Market
Behaviour, Local Social Networks and Domestic

Organisation' in R. Finnegan, B. Roberts, and
D. Gallie New Approaches to Economic Life,
Manchester University Press, Manchester,
pp. 154-66

Iversen, L., and H. Clausen, (1981) The Closing of
the Nordhaven Shipyard: the Consequences for
the Workers in relation to Employment, Economy
and Health, Institute for Social Medicine,
University of Copenhagen Publication No. 13,
Copenhagen

Jones, I. (1983) 'A Model of Occupational Health
for Community Medicine' Radical Community
Medicine, Summer, 28-31

Kahn, R.L. (1981) Work and Health, John Wiley and
Sons, New York

Kasl, S.V., S. Gore, and S. Cobb, (1975) 'The
Experience of Losing a Job: Reported Changes
in Health, Symptoms and Illness Behaviour'
Psychosomatic Medicine, 37, 106-22

Kasl, S.V., and S. Cobb,(1982) 'Variability of
Stress Effects among Men Experiencing Job
Loss' in Goldberger, L. and S. Breznitz, (eds)
Handbook of Stress, Free Press, New York

Kasl, S.V. (1982) 'Strategies of Research on
Economic Instability and Health'
Psychological Medicine, 12, 637-49

Lee, R.M. (1985) 'Redundancy, labour markets and
informal relations' Sociological Review, 33,
469-95

_____ and C.C. Harris, (1985) 'Redundancy Studies:
Port Talbot and the Future' Quarterly Journal
of Social Affairs, 1, 19-27

MacAvinchey, I.D. (1985) 'Unemployment and
mortality: some aspects of the Scottish case'
Scottish Journal of Political Economy, 31,
827-32

McKee, L., and C. Bell, (1985) 'Marital and Family
Relations in Times of Unemployment' in
R. Finnegan, B. Roberts, and D. Gallie New
Approaches to Economic Life, Manchester
University Press, Manchester, pp. 387-99

Martin, R., and R.H. Fryer, (1973) Redundancy and
Paternalist Capitalism - A Study in the
Sociology of Work, London, George Allen and
Unwin.

Mechanic, D., and E. Volkart, (1961) 'Stress,
Illness Behaviour and the Sick Role' American
Sociological Review, 5, 51-8

Millar, J. (1982) The DHSS Cohort Study Working
Paper No 4: Family Men, Department of Health
and Social Security, London

Moser, K.A., A.J. Fox, and D.R. Jones, (1984) 'Unemployment and Mortality in the OPCS Longitudinal Study' Lancet, ii, 1324-9

Moylan, S., J. Millar, and R. Davis, (1984) Report of the DHSS Cohort Study of Unemployed Men, Department of Health and Social Security, London

Noble, I., A. Walker, and J. Westergaard, (1985) 'From Secure Employment to Labour Market Insecurity: the Impact of Redundancy on Older Workers' in R. Finnegan, B. Roberts, and D. Gallie New Approaches to Economic Life, Manchester University Press, Manchester, pp. 319-37

Scheinstock, G. (1985) 'The Discovery of the Individual in Stress Research' in Gerhardt, U. and M.E.J. Wadsworth, (eds) Stress and Stigma, Macmillan, London

Scott-Samuel, A. (1981) 'Towards a Socialist Epidemiology' Radical Community Medicine, 7, 13-17

St-George, D.P. (1984) 'Is Coronary Heart Disease Caused by an Environmentally-Induced Chronic Metabolic Imbalance?' Medical Hypotheses, 12, 637-49

Slote, A. (1969) Termination: The Closing at Baker, Bobbs-Merrill, Indianapolis

Smith, A. (1985) 'The Epidemiological Basis of Community Medicine' in A. Smith, (ed) Recent Advances in Community Medicine, Churchill Livingstone, London

Sterling, P., and J. Eyer, (1981) 'Biological Basis of Stress Related Mortality' Social Science and Medicine, 15E, 3-42

Stern, J. (1979) 'Who Bears the Burden of Unemployment?' in W. Becherman, (ed) Slow Growth in Britain, Clarendon Press, Oxford

Timio, M., S. Gentili, and S. Pede, (1979) 'Free Noradrenaline Excretion Related to Occupational Stress' British Heart Journal, 42, 471-4

Walker, B. (1983) The Impact of Unemployment on the Health of Mothers and Children in Michigan: Recommendations for the Nation, Committee on Education and Labor, US Subcommittee on Labor Standards, Washington, D.C.

Warr, P. (1985) 'Twelve Questions about Unemployment and Health' in R. Finnegan, B. Roberts and D. Gallie New Approaches to Economic Life, Manchester University Press, Manchester, pp. 302-18

Westin, S., and D. Norum, (1977) When the Sardine Factory is Shut Down - A Socio-Medical Survey Concerning Unemployment in a Rural Community Institute for Hygiene and Social Medicine, University of Bergen, Bergen

Whiteside, N. (1985) 'Sickness and Disability among Working People 1920-1939' paper presented to Centre for Economic Policy Research seminar, London, February 1985, reported in Bartley, M. (1985a)

Wood, S., and J. Cohen, (1977/8) 'Approaches to the Study of Redundancy' Industrial Relations Journal, 8, 19-27

Wood, D. (1982) The DHSS Cohort Study of Un-employed Men, Working Paper No. 1 - Men registered as unemployed in 1978, a longi-tudinal study, Department of Health and Social Security, London

Wright, P., and A. Treacher, (1982) The Problem of Medical Knowledge Edinburgh University Press, Edinburgh